TRUST-BASED MARKETING

THE ULTIMATE GUIDE TO CREATING TRUST —IN AN— UNDERSTANDABLY UN-TRUSTING WORLD

Dan S. Kennedy & Matt Zagula

Ep
Entrepreneur
PRESS®

Publisher: Entrepreneur Press
Cover Design: Andrew Welyczko
Production and Composition: Eliot House Productions

This publication is designed to provide accurate and authoritative information in regard to the subject matter covered. It is sold with the understanding that the publisher is not engaged in rendering legal, accounting, or other professional services. If legal advice or other expert assistance is required, the services of a competent professional person should be sought.

Library of Congress Cataloging-in-Publication Data
Kennedy, Dan S., 1954–
No B.S. trust-based marketing: the ultimate guide to creating trust in an understandable un-trusting world/by Dan S. Kennedy and Matt Zagula.
p. cm.
ISBN-10: 1-59918-440-0 (alk. paper)
ISBN-13: 978-1-59918-440-1 (alk. paper)
1. Marketing. 2. Customer relations. 3. Trust. I. Zagula, Matt. II. Title.
HF5415.K4516 2012
658.8—dc23 2012007974

Printed in the United States of America

16 15 14 13 12 10 9 8 7 6 5 4 3 2 1

Contents

PREFACE

What If Everything You Were Taught and Believed About Successfully Connecting with Clients WAS WRONG?

Dan Kennedy

Matt Zagula and I are about to change your life. That's a heady, quickly thought of as an arrogant statement; as hyperbolic over-promise.

But virtually every other approach to advertising, marketing, and selling advanced in thousands of books, seminars, courses, coaching, and systems operate within one frame: making your advertising, marketing, or selling more effective by doing the same things everybody does incrementally better. The sales pro is offered more powerful closing techniques, but he is still asked to close the sale for his product or service at the end of a very familiar series of progressive steps. The business owner is given better price-and-offer strategies to imbed in his marketing, or more clever copy for his advertising, but he is still engaged in marketing and selling his products and services via the same old architecture, such as Attention, Interest, Desire, Action. All this is fine, but it is NOT life altering by any stretch of the imagination.

But what if everything you had been taught, thought, and believed about successfully relating to customers, clients, or patients was wrong—at least for these times? At bare minimum, what if traditional approaches, however well executed, actually acted to make your life more stressful and difficult than need be?

What if attempting to sell products or services was entirely the wrong thing to be doing?

This is our groundbreaking premise: These times mandate selling something other than products and services. You should effectively get out of the business you are in altogether.

What the !?!@#!?—you say—*I bought a book only to discover its nutty authors are telling me to exit my business?*

Almost. We want you to stop selling products and services. Instead, get into the business of selling Trust.

One of the greatest demonstrations of this radical change is historical, not contemporary. It occurred years back, when the Chrysler Corporation was dragged back from the brink of bankrupt extinction by its then CEO, Lee Iacocca. He became a reluctant TV commercial star with somewhat surprising influence. Chrysler was in the news and the public mind as a wounded entity suffering a slow death, and a manufacturer of flawed products, not to be trusted to deliver a good car or to stay in business long enough to service it. Its products were entirely unpersuasive. But Iacocca was a plainspoken, personable, believable father figure. And he did the most amazing thing for "a car guy" at the helm of a car company. He guided and starred in TV ads that *did NOT sell cars.*

Let that sink in.

Instead, he stepped forward and sold his personal guarantee backing a then dramatically generous warranty, and outright dared consumers to set aside what they heard and thought, and on his word, actually compare cars, saying, "IF you can find a better car, buy it." I tell you, as a lifelong ad man, my jaw dropped then, and I still consider it one of the most astounding moments in advertising. In a set of circumstances entirely adverse to trust, Iacocca sold exactly that.

I had an opportunity to meet and do a little work with Lee Iacocca over two days. At first glance, he was not a guy you'd see as an obvious choice for commercial spokesperson. But what was evident to the public was, while not likely to be chosen by Hollywood casting directors, he was authentic. In the time spent with me, it became apparent that the guy I'd watched in those TV commercials was pretty much the same guy I was sitting with in his living room. In person, a bit coarser in speech, of course, more casual in appearance, but still something of the crusty but trustworthy, grandfatherly authority figure. If *he* told you it would rain tomorrow, you got your umbrella.

Lesser men with smaller minds—and testicles—would resort to selling at the cheapest price, giant discounts, and zero-interest financing; to trying to entice people into test drives with lures of free cases of Coca-Cola and free Hawaiian vacations. Dumber marketers would go down with the ship, making the futile argument about the features and benefits of the cars; showing the shiny products, perhaps with glamorous people getting in and out of them. Price and product, product and price.

Somehow Iacocca rejected all that and, instead of selling product or price, sold his promise; sold trust.

I asked him about it. He claimed no genius. He would have preferred not starring in his own commercials. He's a car guy at heart, too, so he said his natural inclination would always be to sell cars. But the situation and time called for differentiation by selling something else entirely.

As we write this, virtually every advertiser, marketer, and seller labors in an understandably un-trusting world, in circumstances entirely adverse to trust. The public has very, very, very scorched fingers and badly-bruised confidence. The temptation to fight to overcome this with stronger product pitches, cheaper prices, or deeply discounted fees, more amazing offers, better salesmanship—and did I mention, cheaper prices—

is enormous. And dangerous. Doing so worsens the fundamental problem of low trust. It can also deprive you of the economic strength needed to effectively market at all. Advice from cowboy philosopher Texas Bix Bender is: When yer in a hole, the first thing ya oughtta do is stop digging. It is our belief that waging this war with souped up but normal weaponry is just continued digging, going deeper into the abyss.

We believe in a new "instead"—in place of better, harder, stronger, faster, more.

We believe in exiting or at least subordinating the selling of products and services and instead entering the business of marketing and selling Trust.

That is such a radical departure, we say that with this book we *are* about to change your life.

—Dan Kennedy

PS: Last year, Matt and I combined were paid millions of dollars by business leaders, entrepreneurs, marketers, sales professionals (mostly seven-figure income sales professionals), and investors who trust our acumen and advice. We are *not* theorists. You can trust our insight and input on this prescribed radical departure, because everything we've put between this book's covers is experience-based, market tested, and results proven. My No B.S. brand stands for that integrity, and has stood for it for more than 25 years, spanning 10 books in this popular series, newsletters, training courses, and advisory materials embraced by more than one million business owners and sales and marketing professionals annually. Brief resumes and a few comments about us follow, as reassurance that you are in good hands with us.

A few comments about Matt Zagula

"I've spent a lot of years in this business . . . now running one of the most productive financial planning practices in Florida . . . no one person has had more impact on my practice, in a very short period of time, than Matt Zagula."

—Bob G., Florida*

"Before Matt, about $4 million in production annually. After Matt, over $12 million, plus additional six-figure fee income I didn't even know was possible. And all that growth happened in 18 months."

—Isaac W., Virginia*

"Constant improvement is what I look for in my practice. On recommendations I trusted, I flew to Pittsburgh, then drove into West Virginia to meet with Matt. I kept reminding myself that they had come to see Matt for good reason—he has to be good, but West Virginia isn't exactly where you'd expect to find a sales, persuasion, and marketing expert. Getting picked up in the white Bentley was a cool surprise, but ultimately, I was blown away by the business tweaks Matt recommended. They produced immediate bottom-line impact, starting with a new million-dollar client the very next week."

—Chris H., North Carolina*

---

* Names withheld at clients' request.

A few comments about Dan Kennedy

"Thanks in large part to your strategies we are successfully selling mattresses priced from $2,400.00 to as much as $20,000.00 (vs. the national average of $600.00), in a store in Pennsylvania with 137 other places to purchase a mattress in our same area. Twenty are within five miles of our store."

—Jeff Giagnocavo, GardnersMattressAndMore.com

"Because of your strategies, my business is up year to year—by 19% this year alone. Since I began using your methods, up 300%."

—Dr. Eric Dohner, M.D., The Skin and Vein Center, New York

"We used seven key strategies of yours to go from startup in 2010 and mid six-figures of income to millions in revenue in 2011."

—Richard Strauch and Lawrence Pew, Pew Law Center PLLC, www.PewLawCenter.com. Phoenix, Arizona

"I've been with you for 23 years and I'm still scratching the surface. Just when I think I must have heard it all, I discover more about 'doing business on my terms.' Then 'selling to the affluent.' There's no end to business improvement with you."

—Dr. Gregg Nielsen, D.C., Waterford Chiropractic

"I have used your strategies to triple the size of my family's insurance agency in 36 months, from $3.4 million to $10.5 million. We are now able to dominate our target markets regardless of the economy or competition."

—Michael McLean, McLean InsuranceLive.com

CHAPTER 1

Trust-Based Marketing as the Path to Wealth

Dan Kennedy

You can get laid with lust. But you get married and stay married with trust.

So a lot depends on your objectives. I've long believed in business that, rather than get customers to make sales, it is smarter to make sales to get customers. The first provides only income. The second provides income *and equity*. If all you're after is a day-to-day income boost for yourself or revenue growth for your company, you'll find plenty of ammunition and firepower in this book to achieve those limited goals. But, even if you don't begin in sync with us, I hope as you proceed you expand your thinking about the impact trust-based marketing can have in building wealth. The majority of businesspeople think only about income every day. The exceptionally smart few who get rich from business, think about both, every day.

You may skip over this chapter if you are *not* interested in getting rich. Chapter 2 begins on page 13.

In my own business, I've very deliberately worked at creating what I call "lifers"—customers who stay engaged with me for decades, continuing to buy whatever I next bring forward, so that the getting of one in the first place is not just consummation of a transaction, but the start of a permanent relationship. Not just the grabbing of some money, but taking title to an oil well. In order to do this in my particular business—essentially the dispensing-of-advice business—I knew I had to earn and keep trust, and I figured out the three key factors in trust-based equity for me: one, being known as a candid, blunt teller of truth, even if unwelcome by many, and never pandering. Thus, the "No B.S." brand I created. Two, establishing certain principles as constants in my writing, speaking—all my works—that were evident and did not change. And three, never abusing my customers for short-term profit. Given these three things, they can trust me not to endorse anyone or anything or sell them anything I don't genuinely believe is honest, beneficial, and the best in its category. For me, this has worked out very nicely. What is now the GKIC business, evolved from my personal business, does in fact have large numbers of

GKIC, formerly Glazer-Kennedy Insider's Circle, is the largest membership society and publishing/training/coaching organization serving independent business owners, entrepreneurs, professionals, and sales professionals focused on direct marketing. It publishes five business newsletters, numerous online courses and home study courses, conducts major international conferences, has local Chapter-groups meeting in many cities, all centered around the works of Dan Kennedy. For information, see page 273.

members who've been with me for 10, 20, 30, even approaching 40 years. Many who've spent six figures during their tenure—people attending a GKIC SuperConference℠ now, who first attended a seminar of mine 20 years ago. And this did translate to equity, as the company has been twice sold, and the two sales combined provided a good share of my wealth. This asset can be built upon and leveraged into ever-growing wealth, or it can be destroyed, depending on the thinking and actions of the people who have stewardship of it.

My favorite company of all is Disney. In its present form, it's hard to imagine that, as Walt put it, it all started with a mouse. And with Walt. In industries that were entirely transactional—amusement parks, films, toys—Walt built trust-based brand equity and relationship equity. Relationship equity is still a major part of Disney's business today, driving premium-priced attractions, time-share real estate (Disney Vacation Club), fraternity (D23), and very frequent repeat purchasing. A series of CEOs that have held stewardship of Walt's legacy have, amazingly, resisted almost all temptations to undermine the trust the company's fans, customers, the public, and even investors have for Disney.

I'm a serious student of Donald Trump. Look carefully behind the Barnum-ism and you'll see that he has done something no other real estate developer and magnate has ever done: built a publicly recognized brand that adds price elasticity to every building and real estate project that bears his name, and, most recently, extends to a successful TV franchise and licensing for a wide range of products, from luxury mattresses to steaks to clothing. Real estate buyers trust Trump to provide "the best." Consumers who aren't about to buy a $3 million penthouse apartment on Park Avenue want to get a small, affordable piece of that, so she buys her husband a Trump necktie at Macy's, he splurges for their stay at a Trump hotel or resort.

These are people who understand the matters of income vs. equity, and of the role of trust in equity.

Income tends to be spent. Equity accumulates and converts to wealth. So everybody needs to be thinking about equity, early, and it is my contention that the only real equity, certainly the best equity, and the source of all equity, is quality relationship with committed, continuing customers. So I would suggest anybody in any business engage in the same thought process I did and ask himself: What are the few, key factors for you, that will make you such a trusted and relied on presence in your customers' lives that they stay with you—and spend with you—for life?

"But MY Business Is Different..."

Do NOT reject the question out of hand, because you think your business does not easily, naturally, automatically lend itself to such a relationship. It may seem obvious now that my business lent itself to this, but no one among my peers thought this way. In fact, many in my field joked about making sales and getting out of town before the posse formed. They were all hit-and-runners. Most still are. Today, they're doing it on the internet, sharing massive email lists, driving to one promotion after another, divvying the money like pirates after a raid on defenseless yachts or freighters, rather than as traveling salesmen and speakers out on the hustings. But the effect is the same: income, no equity. So don't reject the question out of hand. If you own hardware stores or other retail stores or restaurants, why can't you become a trusted and significant part of your customers' lives? To many, Martha Stewart has made herself just that, and she dispenses much the same sort of ideas, information, and inspiration it would be appropriate for a hardware store owner to dispense. If you are a physician, chiropractor, a dentist, look at Dr. Oz. *Whatever* your business, there is a way to be found and figured out, to elevate your status and cement your importance to your clientele.

What Is Long-Term Marriage About?

It's about always being there, that you will have the other person's back. That they know you care about them. That you find ways to stay interesting and relevant over years of familiarity. Most business owners and sales professionals don't really think about long-term marriage with customers. They either take it for granted or give it no importance. They are focused on income, not equity. They don't think in terms of: *what will this relationship have to be like, for this customer to stay married to me for life?* It's actually not all that difficult to figure it out in any given business. It's more that nobody tries.

I routinely buy things from stores or service providers, visit restaurants, etc., where not even a feeble attempt at creating ongoing, lifetime relationship is made. Some of this is sloth and stupidity: *We did well—he'll be back.* In many of these cases, relationship equal to equity could be very deliberately created. Yet no attempt is made.

Trust, Relationship, Equity, and Wealth

There are profound links between trust and relationship, relationship and equity, equity and wealth.

Brand-name, over-the-counter remedies—the brands we grew up with—continue to substantially out-sell generic versions of the exact same formulations and products displayed right next to them on the same shelves, and selling for 20% to 50% less. Why do more people buy Bayer® aspirin than generic aspirin? There's nothing proprietary to it whatsoever. *Because Bayer® is a trusted name.* The 50% price and profit differential, from which much wealth can be derived, has nothing to do with product ingredients, product superiority, distribution, or service, and everything to do with trust.

For most, trust is more complex than just a recognized brand name, and few of us have the resources or patience to wait for generations to harvest our future fortunes from such slowly accumulated trust. We need a more complex approach that can accelerate the achievement of high trust, whether for competitive differentiation or support of premium prices or other motives, and all the components of such an approach are in this book. But, for now, I want to simply demonstrate the bridge from trust to wealth.

A seismic shift begins with a change in the fundamental question of all advertising, marketing, selling, and conduct of business, from: *How can I make a sale today?* or *How can I make some money today?* to: *How can I make sales and money today but also create trust today?*

Let's Go Through a Consulting Session on This

If we were having a consultation, you and I, on this, we would begin very broadly. *What will it take for you to grow wealthy from your business, in a reasonable time frame of your choosing?* This shifts thinking. It switches from the most common *How can I make some (more) money today?* to *How can I conduct my business affairs today and everyday to develop the kind of equity that translates to wealth?* We would then examine all the possible kinds of equity in your particular kind of business. That might include unique intellectual property such as patents, trademarks, and copyrights; real estate paid off with business income (as opposed to renting or leasing space); control of distribution; and on and on. But in most cases, it would become evident that all kinds of equity rise or fall based on equity in relationship with continuing customers. Or that the only equity that can be protected is in relationship with continuing customers. And we would ultimately get to the question: *What will this relationship have to be like, for this customer to stay married to me for life?*

Inevitably, a big part of that answer will be: trust. And that will loop us all the way back to trust-based marketing. If it is true, and I believe it is, that the value of the equity you have via customers is a reflection of the level of trust they have in you, then it becomes blatantly obvious that developing trust must begin at the beginning, and must never be jeopardized or sacrificed for any other objective. This will color every decision you make.

> **The Question**
>
> What will this relationship have to be like for this customer to stay married to me for life?

The questions I've just raised are powerful, if taken seriously. They not only get to equity in customers for life, but to price elasticity, to greater numbers of referrals (thus lowered customer acquisition costs and speed of growth liberated from proportionate capital investment), to stability and sustainability, and more. They translate to more immediate, transactional profit, from which money can be siphoned to create permanent wealth, and to greater overall, total, lifetime customer value, which creates equity that can be sold or mined, also to create permanent wealth.

A Wealth Secret from Warren Buffett

If you've read Michael Gerber's work, beginning with the best-selling book *The E-Myth*, you know his core premise: A business (or sales career) should be constructed and systemized as if it would be franchised à la McDonalds, cloned thousands of times, and successfully operated by people with far less talent or skill than you possess. That's a form of operational equity. Of equal or greater importance is customer relationship equity, which can only come from a business deliberately engineered to have it.

I am not a fan of Warren Buffett as a human being. In his meddling in politics, I consider him a charlatan. But he is widely regarded as one of the world's most successful investors, justifiably, and he doesn't just invest in companies: he buys many in entirety based on their equity. As Gerber suggests by engineering a business for cloning, even if you never intend to actually do so, you could benefit by engineering a business to sell to Buffett, even if such an opportunity would never actually occur. You'd think more marketers would dig into Buffett's investment choices to find marketing secrets, but I haven't yet encountered any of my peers or competitors who've had this blinding flash of the obvious. If you did investigate as I have, you'd discover that about 80% of the companies chosen by Buffett have a very high trust component, some by brand identity, others by direct, and in some cases, personality-driven relationship with their customers. In some, a shift to more trust-based marketing has occurred in companies after Buffett's investment in or acquisition of them, so perhaps he is influencing their leaders with such strategic recommendation.

If Buffett were advising you on how to make your business so valuable that he might want to buy it, he'd have to reveal this secret: that he buys trusted companies—companies that have invested in trust.

Buffett knows that the value of equity a business has via its customers is a reflection of those customers' level of trust in that business or even its leaders. Given that, it becomes obvious that the pathway to wealth is in developing high trust with customers from the very beginning, and that this trust must never be jeopardized or sacrificed for any other objective.

Your Navigational System

Most businesspeople are often tactical, rarely strategic. Even this book is loaded with tactical advice. There's nothing wrong with tactics and tactical application, but too often businesspeople are *randomly* tactical. Random is dangerous. Randomly captaining a cruise-liner over the ocean can get you and a boatload of passengers killed. Randomly flying a plane hither and yon can stick you nose first into the side of a mountain. Randomly wandering a large forest can get you hopelessly lost, eventually turn you into a meal for bears. Having a sound, reliable navigational system that overlays, governs, and even restricts all decisions is the remedy for the hazards implicit in random activity.

The best such navigational premise for those interested in sustainability, stability, security, equity, and wealth is creating and leveraging high trust.

What Do People REALLY Exchange Money For?

Very few people understand money. Few grasp that money moves from one person or place to another for definitive reasons of its own. This is why all manner of centralized government confiscation and redistribution of money fails miserably. Money itself simply refuses to cooperate with ignorance and stupidity. After the hundreds of billions, if not trillions, of dollars extracted from the private sector and poured into the government's "war on poverty"—declared by President Johnson—we have more people living beneath the poverty line than ever before, and in the very recent Obama administration, more people have been added to the food stamps rolls than in any other four year period. After coming to foolish consensus that everybody ought go to college, we permitted government to pour untold sums into subsidizing and financing college educations, resulting in monstrous inflation of tuition and other educational costs, and an entire generation of graduates buried in impossible debt. I could go on. What you want to do is escape all the ignorant and inaccurate thinking about how money functions that lies beneath these epic disasters that, combined, have taken the United States in just 40 years from being the world's biggest lender and creditor, possessing unrivaled economic strength, to being the world's biggest borrower and debtor. You want to align your efforts with the ways that money actually operates, and the only reasons why money ever moves of its free will to somebody and therefore remains with that somebody. I explore all of this in my book *No B.S. Guide to Wealth Attraction in the New Economy*, but here is the specific reality most salient to this book:

Something of value to someone must be exchanged for money. Any money moved by coercion or confiscation without this exchange breaks free, runs away, and goes somewhere else for such exchange.

Marketing and selling is about exchange. At the simplest level, Zig Ziglar described his attitude when selling high-priced sets of cookware in homes as: *I've got their pots and pans out in my car, they've got my money in their checkbook in their kitchen drawer, and I'm here to make the exchange.* Fine as far as it goes. It strengthened my spine when I first heard it. But what if we're interested in relationship, not transaction? In equity, not just income? Exchange then becomes more complex and sophisticated.

Most people think very simplistically about their businesses. They have things to sell and they try to figure out how to sell them. To them, business is about sales problems.

Most marketing people are similarly simplistic and narrow in their thinking. They are trained and conditioned to translate products and services into solutions, or desirable experiences, or pride-of-ownership purchases, and to speak about features and benefits. To them, business is about sales message problems.

All this ignores two important facts. One, as I've been beating up here, there's no stability or equity in making sales. Two, everything said by you, your minions, or in media, about products, services, solutions, etc., is grossly devalued and handicapped if not said by somebody whom the prospect or customer trusts.

If I tell you that the Dow will drop or rise by 2,000 points this year, and that you need to re-arrange all your investments accordingly, so what? But if you follow the famous, outspoken economist Harry Dent, Jr. and believe in him because you read his books, get his newsletter, see him interviewed, accept his premise that "demographics are destiny," and know (some of) his past, key predictions are coming true, and he tells you to get your financial house arranged for a 2,000-point swing, you act. Or if you ardently follow Glenn Beck and see him as a truthful, clairvoyant, trustworthy life guide, you may very well have half your garage full of survival food, the other half full of gold bullion, and be guarding it with your own arsenal of guns. And, as advertisers know, if Beck tells you that you can trust one of his advertisers and urges calling them, huge numbers act.

If I tell you that you look pale and sickly, and tell you that heart surgery might be urgently needed, you may start feeling queasy, sweaty, dizzy, or weak if you are highly suggestible, but you are most likely to just go home and take a nap. But if a heart specialist at the Cleveland Clinic is called in by your regular doc, during your yearly physical, and makes the same pronouncement, they can summon the orderlies and you'll climb on the gurney and yell "Go!" Even if I am a sales wizard, I'll find it damnably difficult to make either of these sales, but Dent and the Cleveland Clinic docs can, rather easily. They have the equity I lack: pre-existing trust.

These examples irrefutably demonstrate how powerful and valuable that trust asset is. It sensibly follows that such an asset will produce or make possible production of wealth as no other asset can. You should therefore direct your efforts at the creation and ownership of that asset, more so than any and all others.

CHAPTER 2

Trust Without Trying Is No Longer Enough

Dan Kennedy

Trust is a significant part of a great many decisions—including selection of providers of goods and services—without conscious, deliberate, and creative effort on anyone's part to create the trust. It *does* just happen.

Much Undeserved Trust Occurs

We trust casually when we have no practical choices. If you board an airplane to fly across country, you are trusting the factory workers who built it, the mechanics who maintain it, the FAA inspectors, the pilots, and the air traffic controllers. There is abundant evidence none are worthy of trust. The news has revealed sleeping air traffic controllers, inebriated pilots, and improperly maintained planes. If you fly commercial often as I used to, you know the #2 excuse given for departure delays—after #1, weather—is "a mechanical" one. Surely it has occurred to you that if there are that many mechanical malfunctions occurring while the planes are being driven about on the ground, there damn sure must be some you aren't being told about at 30,000 feet up. But, really, what choice do you have? If you want to go from L.A. to Des Moines, you gotta roll the dice.

This breeds a lot of unnecessary casual trust, as a matter of habit. Few people, for example, investigate whether their chiropractors or even their heart surgeons or their investment advisors have complaints against them, settled or unresolved litigation, license suspensions, let alone—with surgeons and hospitals—their comparative track records of success and failure with the kind of surgery about to be performed, even though this kind of information is a matter of public record and can be obtained. Few people personally research a prescribed drug before taking it; they trust their doctor's prescription, even though information about a drug's side effects, history, etc. is readily available. Hardly anybody asks to visit the kitchen of the restaurant they bumble into.

A Lot of Lazy Trust Occurs

In my business book *No B.S. Guide to Ruthless Management of People and Profits*, I lay out the strongest possible case for live-accessible and recorded audio and video surveillance of all store, shop, or practice employees' interactions with customers, clients, or patients, and for telephone and in-person "mystery shopping" as enforcement and coaching tools to ensure that sales scripts and policies are adhered to. The business owners who have embraced my advice and reported results to me have, without a single exception, engineered substantial improvements in sales, upsells, customer service, customer satisfaction and retention, and profits (albeit with the inconvenience of having to more frequently fire and replace non-compliant personnel—and outright thieves). Still, most owners will not do this even if it is proven to them to be needed. It's just too much work.

It isn't even accurate to think of this as trust. It's more a knowing, shoulder-shrugging acceptance of mediocrity or worse.

In the same way, people accept a lot rather than take on the responsibility of getting it as it should be.

Still, Most Require Trust To Buy Many Things

All this casual trust occurring should not lull you into a false sense of security. Surprisingly, people who trust irrationally, casually, lazily, still require different levels of trust for different purchases and relationships. Furthermore, is this really what you want to settle for? Hope that you'll be lazily trusted enough to make a sale? You can do a lot better, and see it reflected in many measurable ways, possibly including higher conversion rates, higher transaction sizes, shorter sales cycles, less stressful selling, better retention, increased referrals.

Where Trust Comes From

Throughout this book, we're going to explore many different sources of trust. Not every business can effectively draw on every source, but there's no business in existence that cannot be strengthened by drawing on some of these sources. These sources include:

> **Authority**—doctor, lawyer, accountant, police officer, fireman
>
> **Affinity**—shared background, experience, philosophy, fraternity

Credibility—factual basis for trust
Longevity—years in business, in the community
Celebrity—being known or being known for something
Familiarity—reassuring omnipresence
Frequency—the more often heard and seen, the more easily trusted
Second Party Transferral—earned, engineered, borrowed, rented, purchased endorsement
Place—geographic or target market; being for a certain customer
Demonstration—seeing is believing

One of the most important points driven home with relentless repetition throughout this book is that people trust for the wrong reasons. By understanding how people *actually* come to trust, based on the above sources and others, you will be able to deliberately manufacture maximum trust.

Trust as Supreme Marketing Advantage

Consider the backdrop I've painted as a whole. People have an underlying, ever-present, on-going anxiety and angst about nearly everything—from the news they watch, to the car they drive and the roads they drive on, and the other drivers surrounding them, to the food they eat, to virtually everybody from whom they get advice, services, and products. It's called "*defensive* driving" for good reason. Distrust of elected officials and public institutions has never been higher. As I was writing this, one week's news included: the Penn State sex scandal; the collapse of Herman Cain's campaign to sex scandal; another request by former Presidential contender John Edwards to delay his criminal trial; a recall of 100,000 defective cars by Ford and 50,000 by Mazda; and a news warning about a massive recall of dangerously toxic ground beef. A typical week.

People of my age grew up rarely locking our cars when parked out and about, and never in our own driveways. Many of us left our houses' back doors unlocked. Not now. We feel a level of unease, of threat, outside and even at home. We are an uneasy people, because we know we are trusting people and things unworthy of trust. We are very often disappointed, sometimes harmed, and we expect more of the same. We are not just defensive drivers; we are defensive, period.

The worse this environment gets and the more someone is sensitive to it and affected by it, the bigger an advantage trust is. But few advertisers, marketers, or sales professionals truly focus on this advantage. Instead, they drift to cute or comedic advertising, default to low, lower, or lowest price and discount positioning, or—like someone with a dull knife cutting more furiously—rely on classic product-centric presentations, such as features-to-benefits. This is why this book can be such a powerful tool for you. If you adopt its approach, strategies, and tactics, you'll leave your current cluttered and competitive marketing environment and, via a road less traveled, appear as uniquely attractive to your prospects, customers, and clients. The proof that this is true is that so many people are so desperate to trust, they are bamboozled again and again by obviously untrustworthy people making ridiculous claims, political candidates being at the head of that parade. It is actually quite miraculous that about one-third of the U.S. population votes in presidential and Congressional elections, given how consistently disappointed Democrats and Republicans, liberals and conservatives are with their picks when they get power. But people set that aside and hope that this time, it'll be different. That kind of hope is available, and if you find a way to validate it rather than dash it yet again, you will have transformative power for your business.

How Does Trust Affect Buying Decisions?

Even mundane purchases are affected by trust. My wife and I prefer produce and fruit grown in the United States vs. that much more commonly found in most supermarkets, imported from Mexico, Argentina, and other foreign lands. Consequently, we often drive past three supermarkets to go to one 20 miles farther from our home to shop. I eat a lot of blueberries—I'm diabetic, and they are one of the few sweet-tasting fruits I can eat pounds of without damage. I do not want to eat blueberries brought here from Mexico, and if Carla's away at our other home, and I'm hurried and shopping at a close store that has only imported blueberries, I'll do without. We trust U.S.-grown food and we distrust foreign-grown food. But why? I possess no empirical evidence that the U.S.-grown produce is safer. I've done no research, can't recall seeing any news reports, and know of no information to suggest I have reason to distrust blueberries from Argentina or tomatoes from Mexico. Further, I dine out in restaurants frequently and no doubt consume imported produce and fruit, not to mention pasta sauce made from Mexican tomatoes, and think nothing of it. But when choosing the grocery store to shop at, and choosing the foods I purchase in the store, I check labels for country of origin, and I buy or don't buy based on country of origin.

We are obviously in the minority on this particular point about origin of produce, since more supermarkets stock and sell more imported than homegrown product of this nature. But we are not alone. And local farmers' markets' success attests to that. The point is, if "Who do you trust?" plays a part in many rather mundane, ordinary, day-to-day buying decisions, imagine how significant it may be for somebody contemplating a more significant purchase or investment.

Certainly the more significant a purchase is to a buyer, the more consciously he seeks a trustworthy seller or provider, but you can't ignore the role of trust in just about every act of commerce.

Trust Is Rarely Rational

As I said, my wife and I eat unknown quantities of foreign-grown produce and foreign-farmed seafood and meat in restaurants, but refuse to buy it at the supermarket to eat it at home. Is that rational? Of course not. A big breakthrough in your own approach to trust-based marketing will be forcing yourself away from rational, logical thought about why your customers would or should trust you. Instead, if you can "decode" how they really process you and the ideas, information, and propositions you present, you'll find yourself holding a new key to the vault. Abandoning rational thought for customers' actual thought is not an easy shift. This is the challenge before you!

The Trust Virus

One of the main sources of trust is "pass along." You trust somebody because somebody you trust trusts him. It's second-party, passed-along trust. We, for example, have a "Mr. Fix-It" handyman who takes care of everything from yearly backyard deck cleaning, to putting up shelves, to fixing squeaky hinges, to dryer vent cleaning, and smoke detector battery changing. He has a garage door opener and keys to the house. He comes and goes as he pleases, and usually does work when we're away. He has the combination to my safe, because he installed it. He hands me an unitemized bill once a year and I pay it without question.

How did I come to place such open-ended, unfettered trust in this fellow? On the surface, he might not engender such trust. He drives an old, beat-up van filled with tools, supplies, and parts. He is scruffy. But the guy who trains my racehorses and with whom I am partner in some of the racehorses has employed the handyman for many years and trusts him implicitly, therefore that trust transferred to me. I do not know much about the handyman. I've never done a background check. I don't even have an address for him. Yet he has the keys to my house. Clearly, this is not rational behavior on my part, yet I'm a pretty rational person most of the time, with most of what I do. I've managed to build up successful businesses, create a modest personal fortune and manage it prudently, and earn the trust of a great many people, including private clients running companies as large as $2 billion in revenue. How can I act so irrationally when it comes to the handyman?

Bernie Madoff sits rotting in prison after a two-decade sustained, epic-sized Ponzi scheme, rivaled only by Roosevelt's concoction, the Social Security system. But Social Security is paid into under coercion and threat. Everybody handed their money over to Bernie voluntarily. And most who did so were college educated, sophisticated, successful and wealthy individuals, managers of family fortunes and trusts, and paid administrators of universities' investment portfolios and sizeable pension funds. All these "victims" had access to competent financial, tax, and legal advisors, undoubtedly routinely relying on those very advisors for guidance on all sorts of decisions. Yet they handed wealth to Madoff. None could explain exactly what Bernie did with their money or how he consistently generated above-par returns. Few wanted money, so Bernie avoided the payout pressure that breaks most Ponzi schemes; he needed only to print fake account statements. Trusting Madoff was inarguably irrational, so why did so many who, "should have known better"? Because someone whom they knew and trusted, trusted him. Yes, he had the aid of credibility of having served on the Board of the New York Stock Exchange. He had offices, trappings of wealth, charitable involvements, media recognition, all manufactured with the stolen money. But at the core, Bernie perpetuated his scam thanks to passed-along trust.

This reveals something very powerful about successfully selling inside the fortress walls of any closed community— and the very wealthy are a closed community. Their fortress walls are their reliance on peer-provided information. They trust each other and distrust all others. This is a strong fortress, difficult to penetrate; yet it is also extraordinarily imperfect and secretly weak, because once it is penetrated at any one point, with just one insider inhabitant, it is erased as a safeguard for all the other inhabitants. One to a few very quickly becomes many, then almost all. There are many such imperfectly fortressed communities; in fact, we all live in one or several. Among all the members of a church it is very common for small Ponzi schemes, mini-Madoffs, to flourish within the congregation. All that is needed is the trust of just one congregant; then all others defenseless. In a small, clannish industry or segment of an industry, the B2B marketer, the consultant, the software developer, the "expert" of any sort needs only the trust of one or a few of the well-known members, and all others' defenses against him disappear.

Further, the harder the trust of any one in such a community is to get in the first place, the more viral it is within that community, and the more valuable its viral nature is.

This is why it is so worthwhile to scheme to gain the trust of key centers of influence within any target group in which you seek to develop a clientele. Why it is so worthwhile to invest in securing that trust.

An Example of a Trust Virus Tactic in Action

This is a true experience of mine, from many years back. One day, in my mail, an envelope arrived, hand-addressed to me, with, in its sender's information corner, the name of a professional peer, another speaker. He and I lived in the same city, both belonged to the National Speakers Association, both engaged in some similar business activity, and he was a well-respected leader in our field. Although I was merely acquainted with the sender, not a friend, I certainly recognized his name, knew his reputation, and I was therefore curious about what he might be writing to me about, so I opened the envelope. That's important. With direct-mail, you can't win if your envelope isn't opened, and a great many aren't. In this case, had the business owner being promoted in this surreptitious way been overt and sent me an envelope or other mailer directly from him, I doubt I'd have paid any attention. On opening this envelope, I found a letter from this peer to me that began: "Dear Dan, I suppose you'll quickly wonder why I am writing to you about a plumber." That I did. It was odd. It kept my curiosity alive, so I continued reading the letter. That's also important. With direct mail, readership is required for success, but rarely achieved and usually taken for granted.

The letter went on to tell me a dramatic story of a bit of plumbing trouble my peer had found himself with in his home, immediately before hosting a party (to which I had not been invited). He couldn't reach the last plumber he'd used, and so he found this plumber—Al—in the Yellow Pages. So promptly, brilliantly, and professionally had this fantastic plumber served him that he had decided to send his endorsement letter to everyone he knew in our shared profession in Phoenix. So if I ever needed a top-flight plumber, I'd know to call Al. This doesn't end there, but I'm going to give you the minimum needed to see the tactical play. About a week later, I got a letter from Al, reminding me of my peer's enthusiastic endorsement, offering me a free "plumbing problem prevention audit," and enclosing a couple of refrigerator magnets. Of course, Al the Plumber engineered this entire thing, as means of leveraging a customer's gratitude and satisfaction into a circle of that customer's influence.

The technical term for this tactic is an "Endorsed Mailing #1," followed by a sequence of direct solicitations. Even with the tenuous connection between my peer acquaintance and me, it works because, after all, knowing about a really good, reliable plumber is a good thing, and I said to myself, *Well, if he's good enough for Joel, he's good enough for me*. This is a way to move from random referrals to organized, managed multiplying of satisfied customers.

This particular tactic is transferable to many different kinds of businesses and if you can find opportunities to use it, you'll very likely find doing so very productive, but don't miss the broader point this illustrates, of the power of trust gone viral, passed from one person to many, carrying you over a fortress wall.

CHAPTER 3

Underestimating the Difficulty of the Task

Dan Kennedy

It is my contention that more marketers fail for this reason than any other reason: They simply underestimate the difficulty of their tasks at hand. This occurs in many different ways, including:

- Unreasonable expectations regarding necessary investment in customer acquisition
- Inadequate preparation for sales appointments and presentations, i.e., "winging it"
- Acting on assumptions rather than collecting verified factual information
- Hastily creating advertising without research, tested and proven models, or copywriting skill (developed or purchased)

But far and away, the leading underestimation of difficulty has to do with the fears of the prospective customer, client, or patient. *Fears.* In settings where consumers must trust to buy, most underestimate the fear felt by those consumers. It's understandable. You look in the mirror and you don't see anybody scary, do you? You may not see somebody Hollywood handsome or super-model beautiful, but you don't see a scary monster. You think about the way you represent your products and services and deal with your customers, and you feel pretty good about it. You do, after all, have a lot of happy customers, a good reputation, and a good track record. You sleep just fine at night. You really don't see any reason people wouldn't trust you, let alone be frightened by you. It's almost unimaginable. In your presentations to customers, you use documented facts and statistics, you refer to respectable media, you have a clear and rational case, you have ample proof and reassurance to offer. Why would anybody be scared? The company you represent is old, stable, with deep roots, prestigious history, respected brand name, billions in assets. How could doing business with such a firm be frightening?

It makes little sense to you that people would be scared.

But fear is no more a product of rational thought than is trust. There are reasonably rational fears, say of bears or utterly dark alleys in bad sections of town or walking a thin tightrope 20 stories above the ground without a net on a windy day. The popular TV show *Fear Factor* exploits such situations. But there are also thousands of officially recognized phobias that are completely irrational yet shared by millions of people. Fear of certain foods in the refrigerator, of ever driving an automobile, of even a speck of dirt, even of leaving one's house. The TV show that aired for a number of years called *Monk* features a reluctant, germphobic detective, beset with obsessive-compulsive disorder, barely able to function. All his fears are irrational, but nonetheless paralyzing. You can forget all the rational reasons no one should fear you. They do. Most people are quietly, privately frightened by just about everything in their lives and every decision they make. Don't take it personally. People have shockingly little confidence in themselves.

You may be tempted to instantly question that last statement, believing your clientele superior in self-esteem and self-confidence. I have a long-time friend and occasional client, John Alanis, who operates an online training and coaching business at www.WomenApproachYou.com. It is for men who are shy, timid, or even fearful or feel lost at sea when it comes to approaching and meeting potential companions of the opposite gender. You might think his clientele would be poorly educated men, men in low-income jobs, or even physically unattractive men—perhaps young, inexperienced men. But a large number of his customers are well educated, accomplished men in professional careers and successful entrepreneurs. Many are divorced after long marriages and feel ill prepared for today's dating rituals. Even though these men may be confident in some settings, they are very unsure of themselves about this.

Of all the things people tend to be least confident about, successfully identifying somebody worthy of their trust—as advisor, vendor, or mate—is high, high on the list.

The Fears that Face Them

Most people desperately fear loss, therefore they fear change, which makes them avoid decisions. Most people describe their income or net worth as "*hard*-earned," thus hard to replace if lost or wasted. B2B buyers may feel their very job is put at risk by every decision, every purchase, and every embrace of a new or different vendor.

Most people have high recall of their worst misjudgments and mistakes. Most people have had what appeared to be very solid ground yanked out from under them as if it was a threadbare rug laid over thin ice. Many investors saw Enron or Madoff as solid ground. General Motors shareholders certainly thought GM and its stock was on solid ground. If not personally experienced, who doesn't have a family member or close friend who has somehow seen their long-held judgment and trust proven to be very, very poor?

My famous speaking colleague Zig Ziglar tells the story of the cat who hops up on the kitchen stove where a burner has been left on and scorches his paw. Zig says that the cat won't just avoid the stove in the future—he'll stay out of the kitchen! This is how everybody who feels they've been "burned" before acts toward advertisers, marketers, and salespeople. That's why you ARE scary. Not necessarily because of you, but because of many who have preceded you.

If someone feels irreplaceable money or status and position is at risk, and that same person is painfully aware of past failures of their own judgment as well as past experiences of "being sold a bill of goods" by a huckster or shyster, surely you can see that securing that person's trust will require Herculean effort, extraordinary sensitivity, excellent communication skills, and more. In trying to reach this fearful person, I've described a very difficult task. What most refuse to grasp is that this person is nearly every person!

The Problem Isn't Just Distrust of Salespeople

I'm afraid it is fact: the overwhelming majority of people don't trust salespeople. Anyone selling anything is up against that. But there's a deeper problem that most consumers are more hesitant about admitting and voicing, yet is nonetheless present. That ugly little critter is the fact that people don't trust themselves *with* salespeople.

> . . . Haunted by the ghosts of disappointments past.

It's said that when you climb into bed with somebody, there's an invisible crowd in there with you. Your partner's father or mother, first love, first evil bastard or bitch who broke their heart, ex-spouses, fictional characters from TV and the movies you're measured against. The ghosts of past mistakes are right there, in the sheets, with you and your partner. *Yeech.*

Similarly, when you, the marketer or salesperson, somehow sit down—physically or via media—with a potential client, customer, or patient, the two of you are not alone. Ghosts of past poor decisions and disappointments, financial losses, and embarrassments are hanging around. Every salesperson the customer feels took advantage of him is there to remind him he is not competent at judging individuals' veracity or propositions' value. Most people you'll be selling to won't be great judges of character; most of us aren't, especially when in lust over something we want. Most of us often find ourselves in situations where we must buy something we don't thoroughly understand and actually aren't competent to judge the virtues of A vs. B vs. C, and sometimes the best of us pick the wrong door to walk through. People with strong self-images, high self-esteem, and good track records of successful accomplishment are not cowed by the mistakes they have made, tend to think more about their achievements, and remain decisive. Most people, however, possess weak self-images, carry a lot of self-doubt and fear, and loathe and avoid decisions involving any risk. Their ghosts of disappointments and mistakes are ever-present and influential.

Many years ago, I had a conversation with a priest I had gotten to know, as fellow regulars at a neighborhood burger joint. I recall asking him about his celibate life. At that moment, a spectacularly attractive, young, busty blonde in a tight top walked past, enroute to the door. He said, "I am committed to my vow of celibacy—but it would be dangerous to put me on a desert island for many months with her as the only other inhabitant. Especially were she aggressive." Most people feel the same way about being with sales professionals. They feel it's dangerous because they can't resist a persuasive pitch, because they've made what they consider to be poor decisions under the sway of salespeople. In the recently sour economy, many people have outright told me they are not even opening email, opening mail, going to seminars, or tuning into a home shopping channel for fear they'll be presented something they can't resist, because they are determined not to spend any money right now, even if gold bricks are on sale for half price.

This is the mental and emotional state of a difficult to believe, high percentage of your potential customers. Consider this all piled up on one half of a scale: all the "danger—don't listen, don't buy" weight. On the other side, you need to pile up an awful lot of trust as counter-weight. Don't underestimate the amount needed!

I suppose, by the way, of all the difficulties I have with my private clients—and have had with clients over these many years—in developing advertising, marketing, and sales strategies for them is their easy underestimating of the difficulty of their marketing and selling tasks, due in part to underestimating the adverse mental and emotional state of their prospects. Hardly anybody thinks they are scary. Hardly anybody thinks of their clientele as weak-minded. Hardly anybody accurately assesses all the fears in prospects' minds.

You ought not be cowed or depressed by this; let your competition be victim to all this. You can and should use it as a foundation of understanding on which you construct a better, stronger, more comprehensive, trust-based positioning and presentation of yourself.

A Tactical Suggestion: The Positive Power of Negative Preparation

It is useful to build a comprehensive understanding of the difficulty of your task. Put down on paper a list of the general, commonly shared fears and anxieties—those I've just described and all others you can think of. Also, assemble a comprehensive list of the *specific* fears and anxieties your *particular* prospect may harbor, from his experiences, about your profession, product, or service. I call this the positive power of negative preparation: anticipating every hurdle and properly crediting each hurdle's height in the prospect's mind. For more about this, refer to Strategy #2 in my book, *No B.S. Sales Success in The New Economy*, an excellent companion to this book.

One More Warning: The Trouble with True Superiority

One of the grand old masters of marketing for professional services, Harry Beckwith, reveals the problem with true superiority in this, from his fine book *Selling the Invisible:*

> *With most professional services, you are not really selling expertise—because your expertise is [has to be] assumed,* because your prospect cannot intelligently evaluate your expertise.

You are going to get major reconstructive and cosmetic dentistry performed, perhaps investing $30,000.00, even $50,000.00, as I once did. You are interested, finally, in consolidating your life's savings from your patchwork quilt of CD's, insurance policies, 401Ks from two different employers, an IRA, etc., into one income-for-life plan, to facilitate retirement. You are in search of an expert mechanic for your exotic or classic automobile, or even just a safe, secure place to store it. You are planning a kitchen remodeling. How can you *really know* if the dentist, financial advisor, mechanic, architect, or contractor is really competent, let alone expert, reliable, and trustworthy, and certain to satisfy? Further, how can you *really know* if he is superior to others? You can't, of course. The proof can only be found by eating the pudding. You won't know definitively about that dentistry until, at best, after all the procedures are completed, but probably not for years. You won't know definitively about the financial strategies until—oops—it's too late.

This is why actual superiority is not much of a business or marketing advantage. My client, the Guthy-Renker Corporation, has in its Proactiv® acne remedy, factually, the best, most effective, and safest such product in its category, period. But you can't know unless, as acne sufferer, you (a) try other products and (b) actually use Proactiv® as instructed and (c) get rid of your acne and avoid it returning with Proactiv®. Therefore, this actual product superiority is not much of a barrier to cheaper price competition proliferating in the marketplace.

Entitlement Doesn't Work in the Marketplace

Many, many marketers, sales professionals, and entrepreneurs stubbornly deny this uncomfortable, unpleasant, inconvenient truth. They believe that the actual superiority of their product formulations, efficacy, warranties, services, personal commitment to excellence, or academic or experiential expertise *should* be a marketplace advantage. They insist on operating as if this were true because they believe it *should* be true. And they keep getting beat up, out-maneuvered, out-sold, out-earned because of their stubborn belief. Clinging to what *should* be is clinging to a sense of entitlement. Success hardly ever comes via entitlement. Cling to it at your peril. Insist to yourself that your M.B.A. or Ph.D., or longevity or other credentials; that your company's size and strength and stability; that your product's or process's actual superiority entitles you to marketplace advantage as you wish, but I am telling you that you are deluding and handicapping yourself. Like it or not, you are climbing your mountain with a huge, heavy false-belief boulder strapped to your back, weighing you down, slowing you down, increasing your fatigue and risk of injury.

You Simply Can't Rely on Entitlement in the Marketplace

Let's flip this coin. One of the biggest breakthroughs available to you is unstrapping that boulder and leaving it behind. One of the biggest breakthroughs available to you is deciding that you will not attempt relying on actual superiority in any way, shape, or form for purposes of attracting and interesting and acquiring clients.

Liberated thinking is powerful. Facing harsh realities is one of the best paths to power—given, true, creative, constructive response to these realities. In this case, you want to be superior but you do **not** want to rely on that fact in marketing yourself, nor permit yourself any sense of entitlement because of it.

Distrust Born of Un-Prosperous Times

"The average American family has lost 9% of their household worth in just the last three months of 2008—the fastest disintegration of wealth in more than seven decades. In fact, the majority of families were reporting a drop of 25% in their household worth in the past year alone. Pretty pessimistic stuff . . . . Our national confidence is in pieces, our personal expectations shattered. TRUST HAS COLLAPSED. We have little tolerance now for promises and pledges. We don't trust anyone anymore."

From: *What Americans Really Want . . . Really: The Truth About Our Hopes, Dreams, and Fears* by Dr. Frank Luntz (Hyperion, 2010), leading pollster and trend analyst, frequently seen on the FOX TV network.

CHAPTER 4

What Do Clients REALLY Want to Know?

Dan Kennedy

When a potential client, customer or patient is considering a new purchase or new relationship, they are trying to figure certain things out about the salesperson or provider. This is an important statement, because it contradicts the way most sell, and the emphasis of most sales presentations or marketing messages.

Most advertising is all about or nearly all about products. If you look at all the auto dealers' ads in your Sunday newspaper as example, you'll find each dealer's costly full-page and multi-page ads look nearly identical, and are all about photos of cars and prices. If anything is said about the dealer or his salespeople, it's a tiny mention; something about being in business since 1948, or having an award-winning service department. Sadly, a whole lot of advertising is much like local car dealers'. Most marketing messages conveyed through all media similarly focus on the product and its features and benefits. And most face-to-face selling is done by salespeople schooled in the same approach, and focused on the products they have to sell.

But is this aligned with what the customer *really* wants to know?

Some customers are pre-determined to buy a leather couch or a Ford Focus or a blue suit this weekend, and they can be swayed by availability and price to choose one place to go versus or ahead of another. Or, if predetermined to buy living room furniture, customers also can be attracted by product selection and price, and then convinced that leather is the way to go with a features-and-benefits presentation. But even in these cases involving "ordinary" purchases, if the customer was disengaged from comparing one place's products and prices against another's, and invited to think about different and more compelling reasons for preference, and about more significant questions, would he? With less ordinary purchases—say, a decision about a complete dental smile makeover or re-arranging one's life savings with a plan for guaranteed income for life, or remodeling several rooms in your house—the influence of answers to questions other than product features, benefits, and price is much higher. The more significant the purchase and/or the higher up in customer affluence you go, the more influence matters other than product and price. Yet most advertisers, marketers, and salespeople are universally and consistently focused on product and price.

In short, advertisers, marketers, and sales professionals stupidly and habitually or stubbornly, thoughtlessly and un-creatively continue to sell in ways *least* interesting to customers!

Into the Repair Shop We Go. Roll Up Your Sleeves.

To get better aligned with what the prospect wants to know, we shift the focus to trust. In most categories of products and services, purchases and relationships, there are actually far too many choices for most consumers to comparatively evaluate, and they don't. Instead, they look to somebody they feel they can trust to make most of the choices for them. The consumer doesn't typically educate himself and engage in comparative analysis of surgical techniques; he picks a doctor who makes those decisions for him. The last time my wife and I bought new, leather furniture for one of our homes, we did not research all the different manufacturers of leather furniture. We went to stores we knew and that had good reputations, we bought when we found something we liked by look and feel, and when we connected with a salesman we trusted. I am a fairly sophisticated businessperson, but I am not qualified to properly analyze and compare the thousands of mutual funds, the hundreds of bond investments, or the nitty-gritty details of commercial real estate deals. I invest in all three by having settled on expert advisors—all of whom are also salespeople—in these three areas, who I trust.

There are nine things that most of us are trying to figure out—consciously and subconsciously—before making a significant purchase or investment with a new provider. Only one of the nine focuses on product, one on price. Let's explore all nine.

Is This Guy "for Real"?

No President and Presidential candidate in modern times has come close to Ronald Reagan's success in getting voters to cross party lines and abandon long-held party affiliations to support him. "The Reagan Democrats" included union members defying the recommendations of their leadership, other blue-collar

The Nine Gates to Customer Commitment

1. *Is this guy "for real"?* (Authenticity)
2. *Is he telling me the truth?* (Believability)
3. *Is he knowledgeable and competent?* (Credibility)
4. *Is he appropriate for me?* (Feasibility of Relationship)
5. *Is he listening—or just "peddling"?* (Customized Solutions)
6. *Overall, can he be relied on?* (Safety))
7. *Do I understand (enough about) what he's going to do for me?* (Comfort)
8. *Am I making the best choice vs. other choices?* (Superiority)
9. *Am I paying a fair price?* (Value)

workers, and people who had never voted for a Republican in their lives. Even political adversaries like Tip O'Neil admitted finding it hard to work up "battlefield enmity" toward Reagan. Reagan may have been one of the greatest salesmen. If you talked with people who would ordinarily be in opposing political camps—like "working stiff" cab drivers or union construction workers, as I personally had occasion to do while Reagan was in office—what you consistently heard was what I call "admiration for authenticity." In different ways, they voiced that Reagan seemed real to them. What you saw and heard was the real guy, not concealing anything, not playing a part, ironically despite the fact that he was an experienced actor. I met President Reagan on three occasions, spent a half-hour or so backstage with him, and spent more time with people who knew him well, like Bill Bennett. My sense is the same as the cab driver's. He was for real.

I think a lot of sales professionals and others who are engaged in persuasion very erroneously feel they need to cover up who they really are, and play a part as if acting. Unless you are a true sociopath, this is quite difficult to do, and is usually sensed or felt by the other person. They may never be able to put their finger on the reason they wound up feeling a lack of trust, but often it's that they sensed the person being inauthentic. This does not mean, of course, that you can come to a meeting with a client in a pizza sauce stained T-shirt, sweatpants, unshaven from a lazy weekend, and sprawl in your chair, scratching your belly and belching. If *that* is the authentic you, there's work needed. This doesn't even mean you don't dress yourself or your selling environment for success—you should; or that you don't need to research prospects in advance so you possess knowledge that facilitates tailoring of remarks—you should. But if you have and exhibit no solid core, you'll suffer. One of the times I was working on this book was in the early months of the 2012 Republican Presidential primary activity, shortly before the Iowa caucus. If you recall, most people deemed Texas Governor Rick Perry entirely authentic, yet his reoccurring mis-statements, famous forgetting of the third of three federal agencies he wanted to eliminate, and occasional goofiness made people question his competence and readiness for the job. Mitt Romney was generally regarded as competent and capable, but grudgingly embraced by conservatives, most of whom felt him inauthentic. It might have been helpful if Mitt could loosen up and let people in, to get a better sense of who he is, but it would be a deadly error on his part to put on Governor Perry's denim shirt, corduroy slacks, cowboy boots, adopt his "aw-shucks"

Texas way of speaking, and hope to don friendlier authenticity as if it hung in a closet.

Walt Disney was a great marketer, great salesman, and great public spokesperson for his enterprises. He managed to be admired and beloved by his rank-and-file employees, his customers, and the public. Yet in private, Walt smoked, drank, could be mercurial, hot-tempered and, at times, unkind, and that was kept from the public. A vice-free Uncle Walt was presented. But at core, the real Walt was the real Walt behind the scenes and as publicly presented: curious, creative, fun-loving, with childlike wonder and enthusiasm, with great affection for children and animals, a good friend to his friends, a great storyteller—just the kind of guy most people would love to have as their next door neighbor, at their weekly poker or bridge game, or as their uncle. People sensed Walt's enthusiasm for everything he brought to them to be genuine, and it was.

Everybody has at least one character trait that is authentic and genuine, that can be magnified so the clientele's attention is focused on it, and that is generally beneficial in selling and, specifically, contributes to trust. For Walt, it was his authentic enthusiasm. For Reagan, it was clarity and plainspoken simplicity. Similarly, every company has a strength that can be placed as the centerpiece of all its marketing, that is generally beneficial and, specifically, contributes to trust. Chapter 21 discusses one of these: Leadership Position. It's important to figure out what your #1 thing is.

Very early in my business life, I thought it best to "put on costumes" and present myself in stagecraft-based ways. I was trying to overcome youth, inexperience, and low confidence with a carefully engineered presentation of self. It worked, but it was quite a strain. And as I made the transition to showing my authentic self, everything worked a lot better. For many years now, clients often come to meet with me for the first time at my home, which is not even close to being a mansion; I'm not a mansion kind of guy. We work in my large but unglamorous basement office, where I actually work every day, and it looks it. I don't dress as casually as I do when alone, but I don't dress up, either. I pick the client up myself in the morning at the closest, quite ordinary hotel, in (as I write this) my restored 1986 Jeep. We go to lunch at a little neighborhood joint. I talk candidly and openly and in the same style with the brand new client as I do with one of my many 20-year ones. I do not use artifice to impress, and it is clear I don't. This doesn't entirely rule out a little stagecraft here and there (see page 212, A Personal Trick.) But overall, as Popeye said, "I am what I am," and I let clients know it.

Ultimately, the client's first question—*Is this guy for real?*—is best answered by being authentic.

Is He Telling Me the Truth?

The second item, Believability, is also more sensed than ever known by the client. There are common, easily made mistakes in selling that sabotage believability. One, presenting everything about you, your product, your proposition as flawless and perfect. Another, being too easily pushed into making promises and commitments you initially did not make.

Ironically, being able to make fantastic claims in advertising can undermine believability. As an example, off and on over years, I've written advertising and sales copy for a client who teaches people how to invest in tax liens. This investment is backed both by real estate and by city, county, or state government guaranteeing collection of the lien and payment to the lien-holder before the property can be transferred by sale, gifting, or inheritance, so it is quite literally impossible to lose one's money. Further, returns commonly range from 8% to 16% and even more per year. So this is essentially the same as a passbook savings account at the bank in terms of safety, but paying interest far, far greater than at the bank. If you present all this in its best possible light, you have truth that seems too good to be true. The exceptional quality and value of this product actually presents more of a marketing problem than advantage. The cure, incidentally, is to create trust for the person, the teacher, rather than just for the product.

All the evidence in the world can't trump a context of believability attached to the person making the assertions. Who you have made yourself, in the mind of the prospective client, is far more influential than what you say.

In many fields, including this example's field, a strategy I call *"Preponderance of Proof"* is used to boost believability, typically using large numbers of fully identified, believable customer testimonials as well as academic or professional (and sometimes celebrity) endorsers. All the evidence in the world, though, can't trump a context of believability attached to the person making the assertions. For example, if I tell my regular readers, subscribers, and GKIC Members that I am going to present new strategies at a special seminar guaranteed to add at least $1 million to their net worth in 12 months, many will find that grandiose promise believable because (a) they have made money before, following my advice. (b) they know or know of many who have made money following my advice. (c) we have a trust relationship based on the ten factors in Chapter 2, and (d) I have a well-established reputation, track record, and story as a millionaire-maker. If I make that same assertion to strangers who do not know me, know of me, or have any prior relationship, I'm in for some tough sledding. What's important about that is I *can't* make up for the lack of (a)–(d) with slicker, better salesmanship. That's why creating your own context of believability and selling to well-prepared prospects is so beneficial.

Hurried, "slam dunk" selling—somehow hurrying a prospect from expressed interest to a sales pitch and a close—is, I think, a tough, stressful, unpleasant, and severely limiting way to make a living or conduct business. I'm not at all opposed to using effective, strong sales tactics, but I'd rather they be used in a setting most conducive to their success, and that is with a well-prepared prospect who has moved toward belief in the veracity of the salesperson in advance.

Is He Knowledgable and Competent?

The third question gets to: Credibility. This is foundational, but it should not be assumed. Just because you own a remodeling company and can present yourself effectively does not mean that you can drive a nail straight, and I know it. Suspicions and worries about competence get in the way of trust and sales a lot. Often, demonstration can be helpful here (covered in Chapter 17). Seeing work in progress to finished, successful outcomes can be very helpful, and showing it is an under-used strategy. At the end of a year, I got a very elaborate mailing from the Cleveland Clinic, a documentary in print of an endangered patient's difficult, complicated, and successful heart surgery—starting with diagnosis, through the operation, told in photos and print. It was convincing that these guys really know what they're doing, cross every "t" and dot every "i," are diligent, careful, and can be trusted.

Is He Appropriate for Me?

The fourth issue, Feasibility of Relationship, has to do with both facts and feelings. In my practice, for example, I have turned down clients and made them realize that a relationship with me wasn't feasible for them, because they had a real or heartfelt need for easy and fast access and an open line of communication, which is not how I work. They can only be happy with a different consultant and copywriter, even if that person is less capable and valuable than I am. In all kinds of advisor relationships, with doctors, dentists, accountants, lawyers, investment advisors, bankers, wedding planners, etc., different consumers have very different real or perceived needs, and each such consumer is trying to figure out: Will *my* needs be met by *this* person? Most people aren't very good at figuring that out, for professional or personal relationships, and they know it, and that makes them all the more hesitant about signing on to the next new one. I prefer very frank discussion of this with my clients, and for many, I'd suggest it as good strategy. I believe trust rises with candid conversation about what is most important to you in our kind of relationship, what I can and can't provide, what you can actually expect, and whether or not we can work effectively with each other.

Every consumer is trying to figure out:

Will MY needs be met by THIS person?

Is He Listening or Just Peddling?

Fifth, Customized Solutions contain a *very* direct link to trust. We are naturally and experientially suspicious of off-the-shelf, one-size-fits-all solutions to just about anything. Big brand-name manufacturers often figure this out. Once upon a time there was just Bayer® aspirin, the one pain reliever for everything. Now, check out the pain relief aisle (!) at your pharmacy. Look at the different kinds of Bayer® aspirin labeled and presumably formulated differently for different aches, pains, and ailments. Then check out all the other brands with different products for different purposes. In B2B, one of the most prevalent attitudes any marketer or seller confronts is: ". . . But MY business is different." Often this is absolutely untrue, but again, trust is not a rational thing. **You *automatically* enhance and accelerate trust the minute you present customized products, services, or information for the individual customer or at least for a small, precisely-defined group of people in which the customer belongs.** Conversely, you make trust harder and slower to come by if you stick to generic solutions.

As an aside, we all know that a custom suit is worth a lot more and thus fairly carries a much higher price than an off-the-rack suit. Every cowboy knows that custom-made boots fetch a much stiffer price than mass-manufactured boots. Pretty much every homeowner knows that having custom-made, built-in shelves or cabinetry costs considerably more than buying standard sized units at Home Depot. Every business owner already knows that having custom software engineered from scratch costs a lot more than off-the-shelf software. This pre-existent knowledge is a key to price elasticity in just about any marketing or selling situation. And it doesn't necessarily have to be difficult or complicated to capture this advantage. For example, when I first started selling my Magnetic Marketing System® by speaking to groups, I quickly discovered that it was distrusted and devalued by being generic and useful for any kind of business. So, if I was speaking to a group of Mary Kay, Herbalife, or Amway distributors, I altered the product's covers, titled it The Magnetic Marketing System® for

For many other powerful price strategies, get a copy of the book, *No B.S. Price Strategy* by Dan Kennedy and Jason Marrs. This book presents systems for more profitable pricing, for more effective presentation of price, tips on discovering where price elasticity exists or can be created in your business, strategies for combating commoditization, and more. It is an excellent companion to this book.

Direct Sales Professionals, and used pink, green and gold, or red-white-and-blue as the packaging colors respectively, and I added a small supplemental manual inserted into the main notebook, with examples specifically from these businesses. If I was speaking to real estate agents, the product was titled appropriately, and a small supplemental manual added. For each group, I dressed the outside of the product differently, and added a single, small custom manual. Otherwise, the product stayed generic. I found this erased the suspicions of a generic product and the group's ability to translate it to their specific needs, and it allowed for selling to a higher percentage of the audiences at higher price points, making each selling outing significantly more profitable.

Overall, Can He Be Relied On?

Sixth, consider Safety. Have you ever headed out to try a new restaurant you've read or heard about, pulled into its nearly empty parking lot, re-considered, left, and gone to a busier restaurant? Most people have. We are conditioned to believe there's safety in numbers, even that popularity suggests trustworthiness or value. I have long taught chiropractors and dentists with new practices to borrow or rent a half-dozen cars to park in front of their office, change up and rotate at different times of the day, to avoid passers-by or new patients confronting an anxiety-making, trust-diminishing empty parking lot. As people in the community become familiar with the presence of the office, it is very beneficial for the first impression they form to be of a busy practice.

We all want to be safe. Any suggestion we aren't can alter or reverse our behavior. Right after the 9-11 attacks on New York City, travel virtually stopped and very slowly recovered. I personally know of seminars devastated with cancellations, driven to great degree by spouses objecting to their partners' unnecessary travel. On 9-10-11, everybody felt that flying across the country at 30,000 feet up, in a metal tube built by the lowest bidder, was safe. On 9-12-01, a huge number *felt* otherwise. Similarly, the early 2012 capsizing of a cruise ship close to the coast in Italy spurred a rash of cruise booking cancellations, and stood squarely in the way of selling cruises, because, suddenly, people did not trust the cruise lines' ability to provide a safe travel experience. Incredibly, the parent company of the "Italian Death Cruise" hastily had what amounted to tele-marketing calls made to its survivors, offering, as apology, a 30% lifetime savings opportunity on future cruises. For those survivors, I doubt savings was motivational in the absence of safety. I'd love to have heard the discussion in the meeting that led to that marketing decision: *Let's see, these people have their luggage and belongings at the bottom of the ocean, narrowly escaped death, have barely toweled dry: Let's call 'em on their cell phones. We've got a great excuse for a sales call!*

People cannot trust you if they don't feel safe in doing so. Conversely, creating a sense of safety can be very powerful. I was at Disney in Florida with a group not long ago, and one of the attendees turned his 14- and 12-year-old daughters loose for several evening hours while he and his wife had dinner with our group. I quietly asked him if he would do so at a shopping mall back home. "Of course not," he said, "but this is Disney." Disney has a hugely successful time-share business called Disney Vacation Club, selling interval ownership at premium prices with little resistance. In fact, the salespeople never really "close the sale"; they actually do let people buy. The time-share industry is notorious for promised amenities never getting built, shoddy construction, abandonment of developments by builders, and even bankruptcies of companies, and most sales professionals in this field must work hard to overcome prospects' fears about such things. Hardly anybody raises such matters—or thinks such dark thoughts—when forking over $30,000.00, $50,000.00, or more for a Disney time-share.

During the zero-yield years, from about 2009 through my writing this book, a lot of "mattress money" moved from what the most conservative senior investors thought safest, FDIC insured bank CDs, to annuities and to gold bullion. I was working then with Matt Zagula, developing marketing for a group of about 60 top financial advisors in the annuity field all associated with a multi-brand company. I also had a friend who was a top agent with one of the old-line, long-established, well-known companies, New York Life. He told me he was getting a lot of "gimmies"—existent clients and their referrals and even "cold" prospects calling to buy annuities, no persuasion required, because they believed New York Life to be an acceptably safe alternative to a bank. If asked, he was able to use many trust triggers, like Longevity, Credibility, and Leadership Position, and present a host of reassuring facts about New York Life's mammoth cash reserves and wise avoidance of investing in the sub-prime mortgage derivatives market. The group of financial advisors Matt and I were assisting was not so fortunate; it had to more aggressively advertise, market, and sell.

You might argue that these two examples argue for brand identity, and further, draw on generations of accumulated trust, and your business lacks those assets. You would be correct and incorrect at the same time. It is true that Disney has been in peoples' lives and their parents' lives for generations. It is true that New York Life is a very familiar brand. But the real issue here is not who they are, but that they *stand for safety* in the public's mind. There are many ways you can lay claim to that same positioning without waiting 100 years to get there. Here are two tactical examples:

Rent the Trust Triggers You Lack

Tactic #1: You can rent the known, respected, trusted brand. In the public seminar field, a client I helped early in the development of what became America's biggest-ever success rally entity, putting on 25+ events a year in sports arenas, pulling 10,000 to 35,000 people to each, began with no recognized brand name or reputation, and personally, he was an unknown speaker who had been toiling in oblivion. For people to buy tickets and take a day away from their work or businesses, they need a sense of safety, that their time and money won't be wasted. My client started out by putting the venerable, respected, and celebrated elder statesman of success motivation, Zig Ziglar, on every event, with top star billing, done to such extreme that most people thought and said they were going to a Zig event. For this target audience, Zig brought the trust triggers of Familiarity and Safety. Without Zig, my client would have spent a great deal more on less effective advertising and marketing to fill these arenas, handicapped by marketing without Familiarity or Safety. Just about every industry, profession, and community has trusted elder statesmen who can be rented, often at very modest costs.

Substitute for the Trust Triggers You Lack

Tactic #2: Safety In Numbers can be a persuasive substitute for Safety tied to one of the other trust triggers like Longevity or Familiarity. Figure 4.1 shows a portion of a multi-page promotional magazine put out by a client of mine, The Scheduling Institute, which trains dental practice staffs (and staffs in other kinds of practices as well) to more effectively convert the in-bound query calls from potential patients to kept appointments. Its CEO, Jay Geier, is a brilliant marketer as well as an expert in improving the growth, profitability, and success of dental and other professional practices. His company has grown rapidly and is dominant in its field, but the growth has been almost entirely driven by targeted marketing delivered to dentists at their home addresses, not by splashy advertising, big presence at industry trade shows, and other brand-building means. So his

FIGURE 4.1: Jay Geier Promotional Magazine Example

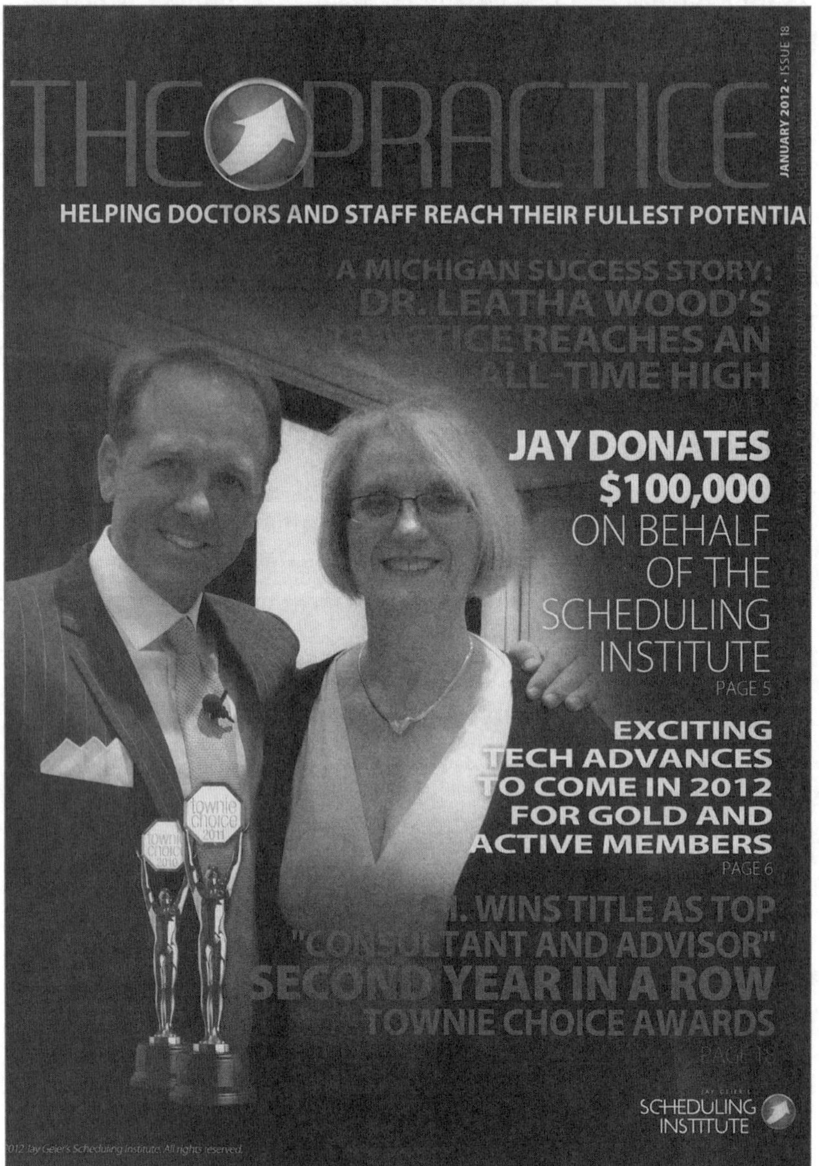

FIGURE 4.1: Jay Geier Promotional Magazine Example, continued

Scheduling Institute is not New York Life or Disney. It does not have Longevity or Familiarity. But this graphic depiction and copy play the Safety-In-Numbers card perfectly. *If all these doctors are bringing Jay's trainers into their offices, they can't all be dummies; how has this gotten by me? Shouldn't I get on the bandwagon? Catch the wave?* Where there would otherwise be skepticism about an unfamiliar entity, thus a sense that investing in their services is a risky unknown, this information replaces skepticism and risk with Safety and, as an added benefit, urgency.

Do I Understand What He's Going to Do for Me?

Seventh, Comfort—means knowing and understanding enough of why and how your product or service works to feel an intelligent and informed buying decision is being made. It's impossible to feel Safe if you secretly feel stupid. It is important to keep in mind that most people *are* eager to delegate responsibility to a trusted stand-in, in matters of finance, health, many major purchases, child-rearing, gift selection, etc., but they have to feel comfortable doing it. Sometimes that hurdle is low: Male executives still routinely ask their female secretaries or assistants to pick out gifts or order flowers for their wives merely on the grounds that a woman knows what another woman will like. Low trust hurdle there. Most parents are a bit more circumspect about the martial arts academy and sensei they are going to turn their child over to, with the goal of a safer, smarter, more confident, better disciplined kid. Higher hurdle. Many parents and their children are even more patient and engaged in picking the university that son or daughter will attend, often trekking to visit several different options. Higher hurdle still.

Am I Making the Best Choice?

Eighth on the list is Superiority. Most of us want the best, or at least the best we can afford, and we are persuaded and reassured when the expert advising us or the product or service we're buying has a claim to "best." Within GKIC Membership, we have people like Diana Coutu of Diana's Gourmet Pizzeria (www.dianasgourmetpizzeria.ca) who competes in international pizza chef competitions and brings home medals; Lloyd Irvin, a martial arts instructor and local academy owner who also coaches several MMA champions (www.lloydirvin.com); and Craig Proctor, a sales and business coach to real estate agents, who maintained top-ten status in the entire Re/Max organization for a decade. These people have gone out of their way to get "street cred" that equates to Superiority. They have been able to lay claim to Superiority positions: for Diana, "award-winning" gourmet pizza; for Lloyd, "champion maker"; for Craig, the only real estate coach actually doing and succeeding at what he teaches. Personally, I use my Price Strategy as a demonstration of Superiority, making it clear that I am the highest fee, highest compensated freelance direct-response copywriter in the country. In the years I was actively promoting myself as a speaker, I leaned on the fact that Zig Ziglar and I were the only two speakers appearing on every SUCCESS EVENT during the year, year after year, as a Superiority claim.

Am I Paying a Fair Price?

Ninth is Value. People want to know that they are paying a fair price, and most people prefer the idea that they are getting very good value. Even affluent consumers who don't base choices on price still have value concerns. My friends who sell high-end mattresses, from $5,000.00 to $35,000.00, who you will meet elsewhere in this book, need to make such prices good and justifiable values. That means selling to the right people: Someone with chronic back pain giving him poor sleep and daily fatigue will find more value in a well-selected and prescribed mattress solution than a person with no pain, who sleeps like a log, even on the floor. That also means putting price in context of the total hours and percentage of life spent trying to get good sleep, adverse affects of poor sleep on health, longevity, career or athletic performance, and, perhaps, the deservedness of the individual buyer. All the other things people want to know factor into their perception of Value.

No one likes feeling they are overpaying and few are comfortable with simply squandering money. Most multimillionaires I know are both self-indulgent and frugal. I, for example, stopped flying commercial some years ago, and fly only by private jet, whether on business trips or vacation. It is, frankly, outrageously expensive, particularly if compared to a ticket on JetBlue scored at www.Priceline.com. I joke that it is justified because I get free parking at the airport. It is self-indulgent, but I feel I've earned it and deserve it after doing about 15 very tough road-warrior years and building a successful business and fortune from scratch. I can rationalize it, often, by the high value of my time saved from travel by other means and invested instead in billable hours working for clients, starting at $2,000.00 to $3,000.00 per hour, but often topping four times that much. Getting home the same day and starting my productive work at 7 A.M. vs. being stuck in the Memphis Airport Hilton overnight and dragging myself home, tired and irritable, at 2 P.M. the next day has real cash value in my business life. But I also try to be and feel frugal about this arguably unfrugal exercise: I buy my charter jet hours in bulk with pre-payment in order to get a discount, I use different classes of aircraft for different length trips in order to control costs, and I usually

> If you have special interest in attracting or now work with affluent clientele, Dan's book *No B.S. Guide to Marketing to the Affluent* will prove very valuable.

build multipurpose trips—book-ending a few days' vacation with business activities, for example. I find this sort of frugality with unfrugal expenditures and indulgences common among the affluent. It gives you insight into an important fact about what everybody wants to feel they are securing: good value.

A Valuable Tactical Exercise

I've just laid out nine broad, generic things most buyers want. It would be good to invest a little time in thinking about how each one relates to your clientele and to your presentation of self and services or marketing of your company, with some specificity. Further, there are likely additional, different desires, perhaps never straightforwardly enunciated by your prospects, that are important to your clientele. Building a complete list of such desires to use as your messaging checklist on an on-going basis is a worthy exercise. Also, using it to review all your present advertising, marketing, and sales presentations for unaddressed desires could lead to immediate improvements.

CHAPTER 5

How NOT to Be Another Salesman

Dan Kennedy

I can't think of a bigger handicap in selling than to be seen as, perceived as, thought of, or felt as another salesman. This must be avoided at all costs!

People are threatened by salespeople and feel uncomfortable and anxious in their presence. There are four chief reasons for this: one, they've been conditioned since childhood to feel this way. What most people hear from parents, educators, and other adults about salespeople and about selling just isn't good.* Two, they've had bad experiences before, being pushed into

*Note: this generally does not apply to people whose parents were in selling as careers or as extra income endeavors and had a good attitude about it. Such people make far better prospects. However even they, and other professional salespeople, instinctively put their guard up in the company of a salesperson.

buying things by aggressive salespeople that have subsequently been disappointing or even embarrassing. Three, they doubt their own decision-making ability, judgment, and willpower. Four, they may, at any given time, be trying not to spend money, and at those times any salesperson is at odds with their purpose.

For all these reasons, it is useful and beneficial *not* to be felt as a salesperson. Conversely, there's rarely any benefit to being seen as another salesman. So, if there's no benefit, but there is likely harm, clearly you want to avoid this. Yet, most salespeople are as easily identified as salespeople as is a stranger, arriving in a small town.

If It Looks Like a Salesman, Walks Like a Salesman, and Quacks Like a Salesman, Hey, It's a Salesman!

How do you spot a salesman in the forest, at 50 yards away?

Assume I am on stage, speaking to a large group, and you're there, in the front row. Suddenly there's a commotion behind you and a man rushes down the aisle and onto the stage. He is dressed in matching blue shirt and pants, black shoes, and his belt has a holster and a handgun. He quickly puts handcuffs on me and hustles me off the stage, out of view. What do you assume he is?

Now assume you are leaving a theater, among the last to leave, walking down a dark side street to a parking garage a few blocks away to retrieve your car. Out of the shadows steps a man, wearing a hooded black sweatshirt, black jeans, a piece of lead pipe in his hand. As he moves toward you, what do you feel? Alarm, of course. You feel threatened. And what would you like most at that moment? To be somewhere else.

If you don't want people assuming you are a threat to them, you can't appear as a salesperson. If you don't want to elicit alarm, you can't seem like a salesperson.

One of the financial advisors in Matt's group brought his newly remade packet of professional literature to our coaching meeting, and asked my opinion. I "vomited" all over the very first page his prospects were to see when opening it. This page proudly presented all his plaudits and awards from several different financial companies, for achieving "Top Producer" and "Million-Dollar Producer" status. With this, he shot himself in the foot—twice. Not only did he announce, "I'm a Salesman," he trumpeted the fact that he is a Damn Good and Persuasive Salesman. This has the same affect as encountering a big, scary bear in the woods, then hearing the bear announce that he's desperately hungry. How fast can a timid hiker run in the opposite direction?

A friend who was a car salesman once told me that it seemed people always got anxious and nervous when he took them into his office, even if they'd been relaxed and friendly with him out on the lot looking at cars. He chalked it up to unavoidable anxiety about "talking turkey" about a car to buy and its price. When we went into his office, I immediately saw another reason for everybody's sudden leap in blood pressure: they were seated, backs to the door, facing him at his desk, and above him, on the wall, a row of framed certificates and plaques, and a shelf of trophies—all attesting to his prowess at devouring his prey: top salesman awards. I had him take all his trophies and plaques home and replace them with oversized framed photos of happy families posed with him and their new cars, and re-arrange the office so everything was at an angle, so the customers' backs weren't to the door. Years later, my colleague Sydney Barrows (www.SydneyBarrows.com), co-author with me of the book *Uncensored Sales Strategies*, coined the term Sales Choreography® for all this, and she is the reigning expert on creating environments most conducive to low-anxiety, high-trust selling in offices, clinics, showrooms, and stores.

Anyway, here are . . .

The Top Ten Ways People Know You're a Dangerous Salesman

1. The shelf of trophies, the wall of plaques or equivalent display
2. Being too easily and readily accessible
3. Being too pliable
4. Being too eager
5. Being "pushy"
6. Obviously trying to hurry the prospect
7. Being over-confident and glib, with a quick-triggered answer to everything
8. Pushing products from a pushcart (vs. diagnosing needs, offering custom solutions)
9. Evading or altering questions
10. Using sales tools

We've already addressed #1. Points 2, 3, and 4 are interesting, because they're such common mistakes. Most salespeople and businesspeople think they should, or, worse, must be instantly, easily, and always accessible. The problem with this is how badly it lowers your status, which makes you untrustworthy as an advisor. I teach: there's no long line waiting patiently to consult the wise man at the bottom of the mountain. Positioning matters to trust. A lot. So, there must be a process that people go through to gain access, and some delay in getting access, unless your business phone number is 9–1–1. Similarly, the person so pliable that they agree with any request quickly loses customers' trust. If you quote four weeks for production and delivery of high-end furniture and the prospect says "Geez, I was really hoping to have it all tomorrow," and you hastily acquiesce, you more likely killed the sale than made it. Or, if you do close that sale, you may leave such an aftertaste of distrust you won't sell furniture for the other rooms in the home or get referrals. And, should you surrender to a promise you can't keep, all future benefit of the customer relationship is lost. Excess eagerness telegraphs need and desperation, and needy salespeople make prospects nervous. Any or all of this behavior stamps SALESMAN in red stencil on your forehead, and you might as well add: NOT TO BE TRUSTED.

Points 5 and 6 are more classic, obvious errors. One of the all-time great sales trainers Bill Gove used to give a speech titled '"People Love to Buy—But They Fear & Hate Being Sold." People have to be given the opportunity to come to trust at their own pace. A good experience I like to give sales and marketing people is a visit to the stables at the racetrack where my racehorses live and work. When a group of strange visitors arrive, some horses immediately come to their stall gates and crane their necks to see them, eager to be petted and fed carrots. Others stand a few steps back, cautiously evaluating the person approaching their stall. Others stand far back and must be patiently coaxed forward, and the impatient person who tries reaching for their halter to pull them forward fails. A similar but even more dramatic experience I can't give most seminar attendees is a trip two hours south, to the farms, to go out into the fields and try to get loose horses and, especially, babies and yearlings, to come forward. Prospects behave much the same way toward salespeople and buying decisions.

Point 7 is another counter-intuitive caution. Many think that the more memorized their presentations, the more swift and certain their responses to every question and objection, the better. But the fact that you've heard "Objection #22" six million times during your career should be kept to yourself. For the prospect, it's an original, personal concern. The glib response is perceived as a hasty, thoughtless, practiced response—not to be trusted as authentic or sincere. Points 9 and 10 link to this. People are quite familiar with "objection handling," and with sales tools.

Let's do some quick comparisons:

SALESMAN has a brochure. An EXPERT has a book.

SALESMAN has a fancy slide presentation. The DOCTOR engages in dialogue, diagnoses, and prescribes, often making his points on a pad of paper.

SALESMAN has a scripted, polished spiel. When interrupted, he often picks back up where he left off, like a tape recorder with a pause button. An ADVISOR gives thoughtful responses.

SALESMAN has products. The CONSULTANT has solutions.

SALESMAN has a "close" and tries to close the sale. The DOCTOR has a prescription. The CONSULTANT has an Action Plan.

Trust-Based Marketing Requires Selling via Media Without Screaming "Salesman"

In print and direct-mail media, we use a number of different formats to diminish the appearance of salesperson-in-print. These include: advertorials, tear sheets, magalogs, newsletter-logs, and mini-books, (described and shown in a special online file, a free extension of this book, accessible at www.NoBSBooks.com/Trust); in broadcast, infomercial formats that mimic news, or documentary programs, or talk shows; online, webinars. In Matt's business, we did very well for a time repositioning free workshops for retired and soon-to-retire investors as "An Evening with the Author." This does not mean this media is neutered and not permitted to deliver strong sales messages. Just because we title it as a book or present it as special report does not mean it can't really be a sales letter.

In 2011, acquaintances of mine—very astute financial/investment information publishers—conducted one of the most successful ad campaigns ever for a newsletter. You most certainly saw it, heard it or received it in the mail. It directed you to an online video presentation, two hours in length (!), at www.EndOfAmerica.com. When the invitation to view the video was presented and the video began, it did not wear salesman clothes, and it did not announce that its purpose was to sell you a newsletter. It presented itself attired as a Paul Revere sounding an urgent alarm, a bold and heroic truth teller revealing secrets you desperately needed to know, for you and your family's sake. I am told this campaign brought in over three-quarters of a million new subscribers in just 12 months. That may be an industry record. All astute marketers studied it. And since subscribing to a financial newsletter is the purchase of advice and guidance, pure and simple, this campaign lived or died by trust.

Also in 2011, the publisher and membership organization of entrepreneurs I'm most closely associated with, GKIC, conducted one of the most successful online info-product launches to date—generating millions of dollars of revenue, for a home study course on influence and persuasion, titled "The DNA/Game-Changers System," and simultaneously attracting thousands of new members. You can see a condensed replay of the entire launch campaign online, and get more information about GKIC at www.DanKennedy.com/Trust. What is significant is that two forms of trust-based marketing fueled this campaign. One, hundreds of affiliates were organized to promote the viewing of my free online videos to the lists of people they had trust relationships with, and these affiliates included such highly-respected business experts as Tom Hopkins and Brian

Tracy. We borrowed/rented their trust relationships, a tactic I discuss in several other places in this book. Two, we delivered a series of my content-rich, provocative, and entertaining video presentations over a period of days plus a climactic, "live" multi-hour broadcast in advance of the offer; in fact, there was no way to buy the product until after these videos. This facilitated fostering trust in me and in the value of my information before a proposition was ever made.

If you compare these examples to the way most people attempt to attract buyers for most goods and services, you'll see a clear and profound difference. Most hold up a product, service, or proposition and holler, "Come buy this—and here are all the reasons, features, benefits, discounts and incentives to do so," and then they fight to overcome a great deal of resistance, including clutter, competition, skepticism, and price issues. In my product examples, we said, "Come and see some fascinating and valuable information available nowhere else." Then, with trust brewing, we presented an offer.

You may be quick to argue that you are not selling financial or investment newsletters or business how-to materials. Were this a four-day seminar instead of a 200-page book, I could regale you with examples nearly identical to the two I just cited, from clients or GKIC Members in the following businesses:

- Acne Treatment
- Animal Remediation (Google it!)
- Back Pain Relief (Chiropractors)
- "Better Sleep" Beds & Mattresses
- Charities
- Cosmetic Dentistry
- Cosmetic Surgery
- Dental Implants
- Disney Vacations & Cruises

- Dog Obedience Training
- Estate Planning (Attorneys/Law Firms)
- Financial Services
- Genealogy
- Health Clubs & Gyms—Fitness Programs
- Investments
- Juicers & Other Kitchen Appliances
- Karate Schools
- Lama-Farm Investing (yes, really)
- Life Insurance
- Marriage Counseling
- Mobility Devices & Home Remodeling for the Handicapped
- Nutritional Supplements
- Ophthalmology
- Parenting Courses
- Quilting—For Fun or Profit
- Reverse Mortgages
- Sheds (Custom Backyard Sheds)
- Trout-Fishing Excursions
- Vacation Home Rentals
- Weight Loss
- Wine-Tasting Parties @ Local Wineries

The Power of the Principle of the Delayed Sale

Most of these named businesses require and involve establishing trust in the provider before successfully presenting a proposition. *By first being a provider of information*, the trust-based marketer intentionally (and courageously) delays presenting propositions and asking for money, in favor of building authority, affinity, credibility, fascination, and as outcome, trust. This is what I call "the principle of the delayed sale." I have not yet found a business where it can't be beneficially applied. But . . .

. . . the sales impulse is damnably difficult to resist.

I tussle with corporate clients often, advising them to deliberately delay the sale in favor of developing trust with new customers or clients, even to the point of holding leads back from a sales force or dealer network until the prospect can be developed. Few companies' leaders have the intelligence and backbone to engage in such restraint. And for anyone who is doing the selling, when someone with a pulse and a wallet appears in person, by phone, even as visitor to a website and reveals interest, the nearly irresistible impulse is to leap upon them and try to rip out their wallet immediately, lest they escape, or get eaten by a competing beast.

If for no other reason this impulse should be resisted, it is because delaying the selling fosters and builds trust. That reduces all resistance, including, importantly, price or fee resistance; it expands price elasticity. It makes the selling and buying less stressful for you and the client, which better facilitates referrals at a faster pace, which reduces advertising and marketing costs, and boosts profitability.

If you ask Everte Farnell, he will tell you how powerful delaying the sale has proven for his businesses, remodeling and construction, and animal remediation (www.evertefarnell.com). If you ask Sean Greeley, who sells area-exclusive business development services to operators of gyms and fitness centers at fees as high as $100,000.00, he will tell you that he deliberately delays these sales (www.fitnessmarketingsystems.com).

And, let me tell you what has always occurred in my office, even in earlier days when I was still proactively seeking speaking engagements, consulting opportunities, and writing assignments, and we fielded a good number of cold, fresh inquiries from potential clients calling with typical new client questions—like: *Is he available to do "x"? How much does he charge?* If anybody in my office answered such questions or gave in to pressure to put the caller through to me or promise them a return call, they were shot. Not fired. Shot. My process has forever been deliberate delay of the sales conversation. In the most recent ten years, it goes like this: My assistant *instructs* the prospective client to submit a one-to-three page memo via fax describing their business and matter of interest that she will forward to me with my weekly in-bounds for review. Then either she or I will follow up with them. In most cases, when I get that memo, I draft a letter of response and have it sent with a package of selected, relevant books and other materials. My letter typically addresses fees and other compensation issues. If the inquiry is about my copywriting services, my letter explains that all new client relationships begin with an initial day of diagnostic and prescriptive consulting, at my standard base fee. Ultimately, the letter invites next steps by the potential client, often scheduling the day via my assistant; sometimes getting a brief, preliminary telephone appointment set with my assistant, almost always one to three weeks out. In the interim, the client is encouraged to get familiar with my work via the materials sent and certain websites. By the time I am actually speaking with or meeting with a new client, he has had to make two successive requests, set a specific phone appointment or pay a fee and travel to the day with me, and read and possibly view or listen to information from me—and he is virtually pre-determined to retain me if he can. Trust in me has been strengthened three ways:

1. I did not behave like an eager salesman.
2. I had a set, definitive process in place for moving forward.
3. I "forced" the client to become (more) familiar with me in advance of any sort of sales conversation.

I have known many people in many different businesses who were too fearful—who believed it could not work in their businesses, who thought they would lose people, who believed they had to be immediately accessible—to try the delayed sale principle and prove it to themselves. I admit, bail bondsmen, hospital emergency rooms, and tow truck operators are on a short list of businesses where delaying the sale isn't often practical; these businesses can, however, develop an informed customer in advance of need.

The micro-mechanics of this are one thing. The critically important objective is, as Matt Zagula puts it, to show up like no one else. This ties nicely to a key principle from my *Renegade Millionaire System*: the majority is always wrong, so opportunity often lies in the opposite direction. Each time I have personally entered a new field of endeavor, or developed marketing for a client about to do so, I made a point of thoroughly understanding all the industry norms, customary practices, commonly-followed advertising, marketing, and sales models, and then strived to find utterly contrarian, opposite strategies. In every instance, I want to show up like no one else, and definitely like no salesman in the field.

Tactical Exercise: Differentiate or Die!

Differentiate or Die! is the title of a book by the great ad man Jack Trout, but it has broader application than advertising. Differentiation, preferably to the extreme of a category of one, is evermore important in an increasingly cluttered selling environment. Two good tactical exercises are:

1. List every industry norm and customary advertising, marketing, selling and other business model or strategy in your field that your clientele would experience with all your competition, and creatively seek differentiation.
2. List every way in which your customers or clients would spot a salesman in their forest, and creatively seek differentiation.

CHAPTER 6

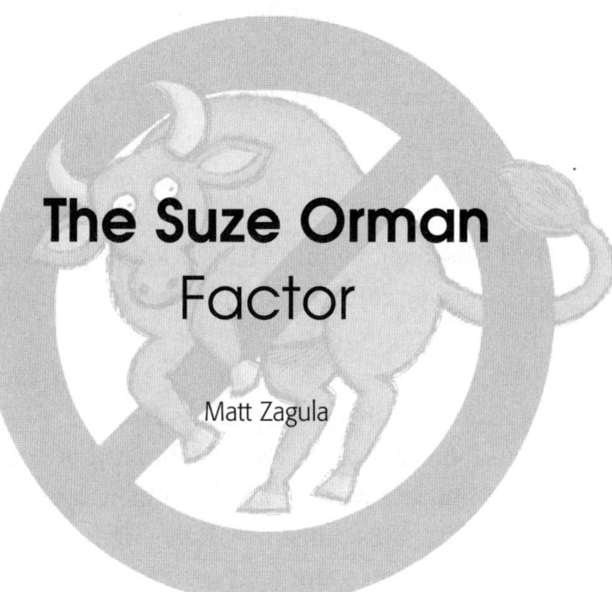

The Suze Orman Factor

Matt Zagula

If you are a financial advisor, I'm sure that headline immediately grabbed *you* because you believe you are ten times the financial advisor Suze Orman ever was! And I truly believe that you really are much more knowledgeable and skilled at helping "real" clients than she. But guess what, I'd pick her marketing positioning over yours all day long because she would totally kick your ass (mine too).

Consider the speed at which Suze could gain tremendous wealth by launching the Suze Orman Secure Retirement Fund? How long would it take her to grow that fund to $1 billion in assets? I'm guessing not too long. Why? She's a celebrity *and* a market-accepted authority on personal finance. To buck her in our industry by saying she isn't all that and a bag of chips has a much higher probability of ticking off a prospect than making them more attracted to a financial advisor who diminishes her ability and knowledge. It is very counterproductive to bad-mouth a loved whale (not that she is a whale in physical size but a whale in the marketplace's belief in her and her knowledge). Great marketing and trust building is gained more rapidly through ethical alignment with the loved whales in your own industry. Don't try to position yourself as better; instead, agree and expand. The internet guys get this—they are a syndicate, of sorts. Ryan Deiss isn't saying, "Hey, I know more than Frank Kern." Nor is Frank going to say that about Ryan—nothing is gained—they all compliment each other and offer their audience multiple paths to learn. Dan Kennedy traveled for years on the SUCCESS tour with great speakers like Zig Ziglar and all of the speakers on that tour were competing for the dollars in that arena but nothing would have been gained by saying "hey don't buy his stuff cause mine is better"—the person who says that is viewed as an arrogant jerk. Instead, be an advocate for your whole community and align ethically and truthfully with the loved whales. Later on, I'll explain how you can work with anyone you want.

Back to Suze, love her or hate her, she has masterfully positioned herself. So the real question is: can an advisor copy Suze Orman's market positioning in their hometown? Here's how:

Suze is perceived as an authority because she has written a whole series of books on every imaginable financial topic. It's crazy how the word "author" is actually in the word authority. Have you ever heard someone say, "Oh, he's *the guy who wrote the book* on so and so"?

When I think of authority, I think of expert witnesses. My father was a very successful trial lawyer. I believe a big part of his success can be traced back to his genius in finding and hiring "the guy who wrote the book" as his expert witness. Imagine a scenario where the other side's expert witness is referring to the *William's Pediatric Guide* to prove their case and my dear old dad's expert *is* Williams, the author of the book, telling them why they are wrong. The guy who wrote the book is *the* definitive expert.

Suze is also a celebrity. She's on TV all the time. Being a celebrity is powerful. The public places great value in celebrity status. Look at what celebrities earn. It's not a stretch to say celebrity status = wealth. Plus, celebrity wealth creation often happens rapidly: You know, Lady Gaga was doing bar gigs a few years ago. And no greater celebrity wealth creation example exists beyond Oprah Winfrey, who is a billionaire as a direct result of her celebrity status.

Like Suze, I'm on TV, too, in a 30-minute show also known as an infomercial. The show enhances my authority and it creates a level of celebrity for me in my cable TV viewing market. Last month we brought in $12.52 in revenue for every $1.00 spent on our "show," and this isn't including the value of the support the show lent to our other marketing methods. I'm certainly no Oprah, but a 12-to-1 ROI works for me. I air this "show" mostly on the FOX channels, which have the highest credibility with my market. I sometimes buy short-form commercials on these same channels. I also advertise more like an authority and celebrity than a service provider. In most of my advertising, I feature one of my books and my status as a published author, seen on TV.

Both celebrity and authority can be created. Both can be manufactured through effort and/or purchase. Am I on TV because a talent agent discovered me? No, I'm there because I paid to be there. Did my last two books publish because of my amazing writing skills? Wrong again. I paid to play in the author's arena. Now, I am very proud of what I have created and the content is perfectly in line with my planning beliefs, but the exposure was bought.

However, not all exposure is bought. I write a monthly article for *Insurance News Net* magazine because the editors there checked me out and know I know advisor marketing and advertising. I didn't buy that exposure; I earned it. So, exposure can also be earned.

Business is really all about power. To be great in business you have to be perceived as having power. And the public equates trust with power. Someone, somewhere, came up with the idea that "the customer is king." But the customer doesn't really want to be the king. The customer wants to find the person who is the best at what they do and hire them to be their king. So you need to be the king and you need to position yourself accordingly, which brings me to my final point: You can spend a lot of money manufacturing celebrity and authority and still absolutely blow it if you fail with exclusivity.

How easy do you think it would be to get an appointment with Suze Orman? I'm guessing it would be about as hard as getting an appointment with President Barack Obama. Assuming it was even possible, do you think Suze would come to your house to meet you? Do you think her assistant would work around your schedule and agree to have Suze meet you in the evening or on a Saturday afternoon because you're busy at work? Of course not. You are just lucky she will meet you at all and that meeting will suit her schedule and conform to her rules.

Living marketing legend, business guru, and my co-author here Dan Kennedy says: "Customer service does not mean customer *servitude.*" Suze offers you a clear road map to success. Honestly, most business owners won't follow her lead because it's a lot of work, it costs money and <u>MOST</u> significant of all is that they lack the internal belief system to accept a position of authority and celebrity. If you, however, are the exception and can easily see yourself as your area's authority and financial celebrity, what a tremendous opportunity this chapter just handed you, on a shiny silver platter: to totally dominate your local market.

Even in crowded spaces you can differentiate. For instance, my consulting client Chris Hobart has done just that in his bank-dominated market, Charlotte, North Carolina. Chris is quite well-known, by design. He has mastered the art of public relations and utilizing media to elevate his status. Chris has been quoted in *The Wall Street Journal,* hundreds of *Associated Press* news articles, and recently, *Men's Health* magazine. He also has been interviewed about financial topics on *MSNBC* and *CNN,* as well as on local news stations. Chris's media exposure offers him and his firm a high level of celebrity. Consulting with Chris was fairly easy because for him it was about amplifying a solid message and a proven track record of exceptional client care and results. It was about helping a good, humble, and hard-working guy—who does great work for his clients, who didn't want to brag too much—understand that his celebrity needs to be displayed and leveraged. Chris is a take-action man; the day after our consultation he put our new game plan in motion. Chris looks totally different than other advisors in Charlotte who have a planning bias toward safe money. Now his marketing reflects that. *MSNBC Money* could call about 100,000 advisors closer to their studio but they call Chris and they do so for good reason. He's exceptional at his craft. This is fantastic but need not be a category of one. Chris's good friend Rob Russell, who is a fantastic money manager in Dayton, Ohio, specializing in safety of principal and alternative investments, was able to study Chris's path to PR and adopt it in his market, quickly becoming his area's obvious choice for high net worth asset management services. The key here is to learn from the folks in your industry who are doers and then, by all means, do.

I can say with great certainty that business owners who consistently take home $1,000,000.00 or more annually, do things differently. Many of my consulting clients are in this prestigious and exclusive group and none of us are using "off-the-shelf" marketing materials from marketing organizations or materials created by the manufacturers of the financial products we sell. We all use compliant, simplified marketing explanations that make it obvious that we are different from the herd of financial salespeople out there. If you want to break away from the pack in your industry, be very aware of how you show up and then leap to the next level of sales and productivity in your business.

CHAPTER 7

Publish or Perish

Dan Kennedy
with Matt Zagula

Matt Zagula pointed out to me that the word "author" is in the word "authority."

There is no more essential a tool of authority than authorship. You can certainly get to celebrity without it, although the Kardashians and even Snookie have books published they're down on as authors. One suspects Snookie might only read a book if she runs out of crayons, yet she is officially the author of a *New York Times* best-selling book. On a more serious note, the actress Suzanne Somers, best known as the ditzy blonde on the sitcom *Three's Company,* made herself into a widely accepted authority on women's health and alternative health as the author of books on these subjects. I'm not suggesting you need to write and publish a real book like theirs or this one and its family of No B.S. books, although there may be reason and opportunity for you to do so. Here, we'll talk about the authorship and publishing of pure promotional tools.

One of the very first things I've done every time I've entered a market is write and publish a book on a subject of specific interest to that market. These books have never been for the bookstore shelf—only for direct distribution to my target audience, in some cases advertised, in other cases used, essentially, in place of or in support of other marketing materials. I have also written and published a newsletter for each market, special reports and "white papers," and, of late, online content pieces as well. All the other information pieces are beneficial, but nothing trumps a book. In my case, each of these situations has been national or global and B2B. The niche target markets for which promotional books were created, in order, were professional speakers and members of the National Speakers Association; chiropractic physicians; chiropractic physicians and dentists; direct marketing industry companies' owners and executives. Eventually, I went very broad, as with this book, and from creating just self-promotional material to paid content. Now, I contribute to or entirely write five paid subscription monthly newsletters I contribute to or write in entirety for GKIC members, and a sixth that is sold by a different publisher. But this exact same strategy for establishing Authority in a target market applies to a *local* business.

I began teaching local, small-business owners to use their own published information—in most cases in the form of simple "free reports," as magnets in place of directly advertising their goods and services—way back in the first version of my *Magnetic Marketing System,* in 1983. Since then, over $100 million of that System has been sold, and hundreds of thousands of business owners have benefited from this radically different approach. (You can get the current edition of the System at www.DanKennedy.com/store.)

Even if you are the proprietor of a local hardware store, landscape company, home remodeling company, etc., and want differentiation and competitive advantage over big box stores; consumer preference for and trust in you for advice and product recommendations for big home improvement projects; and price elasticity, you *need* to write and publish your own book as well as other information media such as newsletters, special reports, how-to guides, and more. Anyone who seeks trusted authority and advisor status will publish, or perish. Such tools give you opportunities to not only advertise differently than everyone else, but to advertise something that is different from what all your competitors are advertising. The same tools can also accelerate trust in prospects.

That's why Matt Zagula has authored and had published several books on money, finance, and investment, like his *Invasion of the Money Snatchers,* and why, when opening a second financial advisory practice in a neighboring city and state to his own, with a celebrated local sports hero as a key associate, the first thing he did was secure a lease on a prominent office building; the second thing he did was to put together a book specifically for this market. I'll let him tell the story:

> Although I never developed a huge passion or love for sports, I have seats on the 48-yard line, on the club level, for all Pittsburgh Steelers' home games. Rocky Bleier, the four-time Super Bowl champion from the Steelers sits right in front of me, and has become a good friend of mine. My passion is for business, specifically for solving my clients' problems and becoming their hero. Passion for an activity can be contagious, and I guess that's why Rocky approached me about us going into the financial planning business together in Pennsylvania. Imagine, a financial firm with this champion from the Pittsburgh Steelers, in Pittsburgh! Obviously, my answer was: Yes. When

we decided to do this, Rocky was not a financial advisor. He was and is a motivational speaker who shares his inspiring life story and success principles with many corporate and association audiences nationwide. My creative team and I took his stories of inspiration and life principles and converted then into financial-related messages, to provide the content for a small book, *Don't Fumble Your Retirement*. We did this by transcribing Rocky's main speech and adding a little content, photographs, and captions. This serves as a symbol of Authority, and a credible bridge between Rocky's celebrity and the serious matter of safeguarding someone's life savings and assisting them to achieve a financially secure retirement.

Rocky and his son are actively involved in the practice, and Rocky meets clients at workshops and at the office, but even if that wasn't the case, and he was available only in a more traditional celebrity-endorser role, he would be very valuable in the Pittsburgh market. Most people underestimate the power of celebrity, and the influence of celebrities, and many businesspeople feel securing celebrity endorsers or associations with celebrities beyond their reach, although Dan Kennedy frequently assists business owners with doing so, for national or local advertising; but all that's beyond the scope of this book. Local businesses can often find a local celebrity who is very affordable, who is just as valuable to them as a national celebrity with no relationship to their community. But the point I want to make is that you always want to combine "Trust Triggers" in your marketing media and tools. In this case, we didn't settle for just Celebrity. We married Celebrity with Credibility and Authority (*Author-ity*) by creating this book with Rocky as its author.

This is a powerful way to practice my #1 success strategy: Show up like no one else!

FIGURE 7.1: "Authority" Book developed by Matt Zagula for Rocky Blier

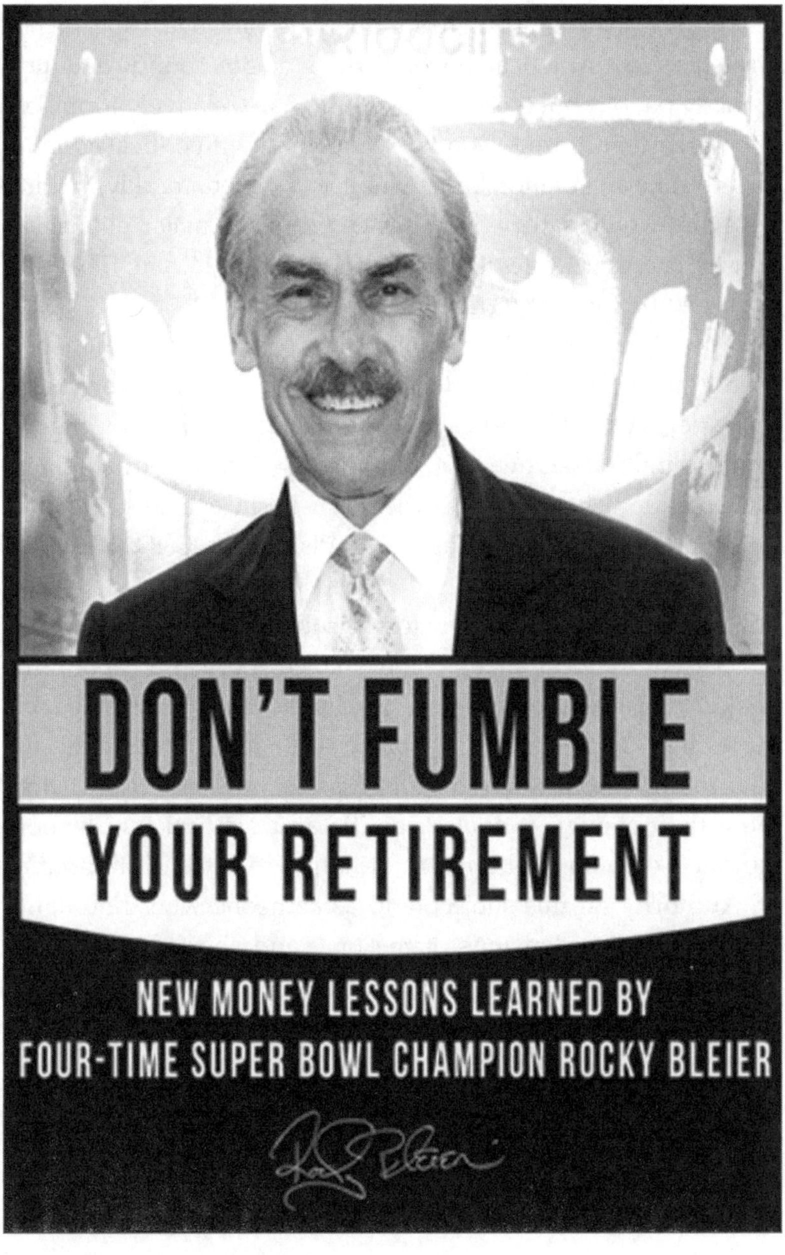

Don't Turn Molehills into Mountains

It's important to grasp that Matt fast-tracked this process, and that we are not asking you to suddenly become Shakespeare, nor write the great American novel. Writing a book sounds daunting to many people, but these kinds of books are relatively formulaic and narrow-purposed. Don't be concerned with critical acclaim, mass public acceptance, best-seller lists, or even, frankly, writing style that would satisfy the critical editors of a major publishing house. These are sales letters put into book format. They are governed by the Trust Triggers presented here.

Your book should be aimed at a certain target audience, written to speak to their interests, and to create trust for you as the expert authority best capable of meeting their needs aligned to those interests. Often this will be very narrow; not long ago, for example, I helped the owner of a Lasik eye surgery clinic develop a book about "Eagle-Eye Vision for Golfers," which he then distributed to golf pro shops at country clubs, sporting good stores, and golf instructors throughout his area. He also advertised in local media, and mailed postcards about the book's availability online to a purchased list of golf magazine subscribers in his area. The book was thin—fewer than 100 pages—and also a thinly-disguised sales letter, yet it presented more than enough factual, scientific and medical information, educated opinion, and other information to establish himself as an Authority on this subject, and as someone who thoroughly understands the demands of the long and short game in golf. He even got a "name" golfer competing on the PGA Senior Tour to write the book's Foreword (noted on its cover and in its advertising), for a very small fee.

In many cases, these books are written in conversational style, much like you would tell the same information to a prospect, so they are often sourced from transcripts of recordings of your speeches or workshops, your actual, or role-played, one-to-one sales presentations to a prospect, or from simply having someone who understands the objectives of the book interview you at length about your knowledge. One of the companies who offers turn-key book development and publishing that Matt and I often work with (with our clients, or refer clients to), Advantage Publishing, has a Talk Your Book® service that works exactly like this: It's an organized, expertly conducted, multi-hour interview, supplemented by whatever other recorded or printed marketing information you might have, all put in the hands of a skilled ghostwriter. Often you need only spit 'n' polish the manuscript written for you.

Don't magnify the difficulty. You *are* an expert. You know your business and you know how to explain, present, and sell your product or service. You likely have a "bank" of past and present advertising and marketing materials. All the raw material for a book built to be a strong, trust-based marketing tool already exists. Think about this more as repurposing, assembling, and organizing, not "writing."

Tactical Advice: How to Get Your Book Done, Right, Fast (Even if You Think You Can't Write)

You can approach this as a do-it-yourself project. Most printers can produce a book. You can model other books for appearance. You can copyright your book (and other marketing materials) easily and inexpensively via services like LegalZoom.com. And you can get samples of books built for promotional purposes rather than as "book books" from the smartest marketers in your field, by answering ads offering free books, and by visiting health food stores (where promotional books are common). You can find and hire a ghostwriter who also has sales copywriting experience: A good source is the "jobs board" and directories of American Writers & Artists, Inc., at www.awaionline.com. I, myself, ghostwrite several books a year for clients.

The other method is to work with a "one stop shop"—maybe the previously-mentioned Advantage Publishing Group—which can take your material, use interviews, do research, provide ghostwriting, cover and interior graphic design, copyright and trademark assistance, related website development, and other services in a turn-key package. If you would like a referral to such vendors and other resources for authors, feel free to query my office via fax, (602) 269-3113. You will also find a good range of vendors serving authors and publishers at the Information Marketing Association, www.info-marketing.org.

Why Promotional Publishing Is So Important

I went to the giant home and garden show held at the exposition center in Cleveland, hoping to find a trustworthy vendor to address several specific matters. One: a back-up generator for my home. I found four different booths where generators were being sold, and the owner of each company present. It turned out, they were all selling the same manufacturers' generators; Kohler and General Electric. One owner instantly defaulted to talking about price and his prices being lower than everybody else's. Another instantly launched into a mind-numbing, confusing, and intimidating technical explanation of how the things work and how parts made of this metal are better than parts made of that metal and how many quibitzbits different doohickeys put out and why one had an automatically cooled whatchacallit. I tried steering them to talking about their expertise in diagnosing and prescribing for my needs, but they would have none of that. Each one sent me away with look-alike brochures and business cards. None bothered to capture my name and contact information for follow-up. As salespeople, they all sucked. As marketers, they are all incredibly stupid—paying big bucks to be there, having a well-qualified prospect serve himself up, but have no differentiation story to tell (but price), no way of creating Authority, and not even attempting to set an appointment or engage in follow-up. Pitiful. All too common. If only they understood Matt's #1 principle: *Show up like no one else.* Instead, they just showed up.

Imagine if one of these four vendors was the author of a book, say, *How To Protect Your Home & Family in Times of Crisis: The Consumer's Guide to Back-Up Home Generators*, that he gave me, maybe with a DVD as well, and a diagnostic form to talk me through and fill out, capturing my contact information. When I got home and went through all the literature I had gathered at the show, I would have three dinky, look-alike product brochures about generators and I'd have his book, positioning him as an expert Authority. Which of those four do you think wins? I would much rather trust the expert who "wrote the book on" back-up generators than the sales guys who gave me tri-fold brochures with business cards stapled to them. I am also more likely to keep the book and trash the brochures than vice versa. And if I get follow-up material or a call from the assistant to "the man who wrote the book," I'm more likely to give attention to it than follow-up from the sales boobs. When I do invite him or one of his technicians to my home to then prescribe what I need, I'm less likely to question that recommendation or the price than I would be an ordinary salesman or dealer. (By the way, could there be a less trustworthy word than "dealer"? Yet, there it is, right on one of the little brochures: Authorized Dealer.)

My friend and long-time GKIC Member Ben Glass is a lawyer with a large, thriving practice in northern Virginia, and a business coach to thousands of lawyers nationwide. For both businesses, he has written and published a number of books, using some as something to advertise instead of advertising his practice or services (like all other attorneys do), and using other publications purely as trust-based marketing material provided only to interested prospects.

For his law practice, for example, he has authored, published, and promotes simple, little books titled *Robbery Without a Gun: Why Your Employer's Long-Term Disability Policy May Be a Sham; Five Deadly Sins That Can Wreck Your Virginia Accident Case;* and *Why Most Medical Malpractice Victims Never Recover a Dime.* For each, there is a website: www.RobberyWithoutAGun.com, www.TheAccidentBook.com, and www.TheMalpracticeBook.com, respectively. Ben also writes and publishes special reports on related subjects, and a monthly newsletter sent to all clients as well as all the prospective clients who visit these websites and obtain these books.

For his business coaching, and training other attorneys, Ben has written and published a meatier 172-page book, *Great Legal Marketing: How Smart Lawyers Think, Behave, and Market to Get More Clients, Make More Money, and Still Get Home in Time for Dinner.* That book's main site is www.GreatLegalMarketing.com. In the book, Ben uses offers of various special reports to turn readers into actively responding prospects—for example, at www.RegisterTheBook.com, readers can get a copy of his report: "Why the Billable Hour Is a Bad Business Model."

Ben is an outstanding example of a trust-based marketer making full use of the benefits of authorship and publishing. *He* wouldn't be caught dead acting like the poor salesmen standing in their booths with nothing to say to establish Differentiation or Authority, and no tools other than a run-of-the-mill brochure.

To be candid, lawyers are not my favorite people. Yet I have quite a few who follow and profit from my marketing leadership, Ben included. Some are in my coaching groups or as private clients. They are the good-guy lawyers, so I feel OK about helping them. The smart ones do not let ego or entitlement cloud reality. Just like the four guys selling the same home generators, they know the public perceives them as interchangeable commodities, just alike, and that they need to set themselves apart and elevate their status in their potential clients' minds. Further, they know they are viewed skeptically; most people don't have warm, fuzzy feelings toward attorneys, but when the right situation occurs, need to find one they feel they can trust. What Ben has done with authorship and publishing, with his books (note plural), special reports (plural), and websites (plural), and what he shows other attorneys to do is exactly the right counter to the negative forces of both commoditization and consumer distrust.

CHAPTER 8

All Media Is NOT Equal

High-Trust vs. Low-Trust Media
Online vs. Offline Media

Dan Kennedy

What IS media?

For sales professionals, it can replace or augment manual labor, in prospecting, in follow-up with recalcitrant leads, in personal promotion and public relations, and in post-sale follow-up. For companies, it is the toolbox for advertising and marketing. It's important to understand that there is no best, better, good, bad, worst media. Both the axe and the scalpel are perfect tools—but for different purposes. Some media are more conducive to trust than other media. The facts about this may be contrary to your beliefs, opinions, or personal preferences. The first—factual information—is essential to marketing success. The latter—unfounded beliefs and opinions, personal preferences—are often enemies of marketing success.

Even companies that spend huge sums on media often do so blindly, randomly, absent of accountability or facts, and without considering the link between their media choices and the overarching goal of high trust. A 30-second TV commercial in the broadcast of the 2012 Super Bowl cost from $2.5 million to $3.5 million: For one company, this is a bargain; for a different company, the most foolish of investments. Media choices must be strategic and situational, factoring in your target clientele, *their* preferred means of being made aware of and interested in new ideas, information, products and services, *their* trust triggers, as well as a measurable return on investment. For the cost of one of these Super Bowl ads, we might secure several weeks of intensive radio advertising with host endorsement on a popular syndicated show squarely aimed at a specific target audience—for example, on Rush Limbaugh, reaching politically and fiscally conservative people, many of whom own businesses or are self-employed in selling; on Dr. Laura, reaching values-driven, concerned parents. Or we could obtain carefully chosen mailing lists of buyers of products indicative of likely interest in ours, hire a top pro (like me!) to craft several versions of a direct-mail piece, and conduct a thorough split-test encompassing millions of recipients. Or we could produce and air a 30-minute TV infomercial. Or employ an elite team of social media, Google AdWords, Google Spaces, Facebook advertising, and YouTube experts, practitioners, and service providers to conduct an aggressive online marketing campaign for months, maybe an entire year. I could go on citing other options.

In weighing options, you weigh objectives: Brand building, ego gratification, entrancing Wall Street (should you be at helm of a publicly traded company or future IPO), motivating dealers or franchisees or salespeople in the field, direct return on investment. But don't forget the objective Matt and I are advocating here, as the most valuable of all: trust.

Online vs. Offline

This is often framed as either/or, and I want to present a different alternative. But let's begin with some facts that are very surprising to many:

- The 2011 Epsilon Research Channel Preference Study shows that direct mail is still *the* United States and Canadian consumers' top, preferred choice for receipt of information in a variety of product and service categories, including health, financial, and household products despite 66% growth in consumer use of Facebook, and despite direct mail's reputation as stodgy. To many peoples' surprise, this preference extends to the 18 to 34 age group, although it is even more pronounced at ages over 50. In specific comparison, 26% of consumers rank direct mail as more trustworthy than email, and 50% say they pay more attention to direct mail than email. 65% say they receive too much email each day to open it all. Interestingly, consumers also report an emotional boost from receiving direct mail, with 60% saying they enjoy seeing what's in their daily mail.
- Of all media, including print, direct mail, broadcast and online, the *least trusted* channels are social media and blogs. Only 6% identified social media as trustworthy. Newspapers got a 21% trust ranking; direct mail, 18%.
- Another current study reported in *Direct Marketing News* shows that a whopping 98% of consumers retrieve mail from their mailbox the day it is delivered, and 71% sort through it and read items of interest the same day it is received. If you compare this with the dismal, dropping open rates for email—at single digit percentages for most marketers and campaigns—it's clear that there's really no comparison at all!

- In B2B, one of the most telling facts is that Google, one of the world's largest internet companies, has to use direct mail to sell its pay-per-click ad media. Can you spell "ironic"? I have a private client selling Google Spaces marketing services to local businesses—entirely via direct mail. There are over 100 different niche-industry training, consulting, and coaching companies in the Information Marketing Association (www.info-marketing.org), ranging in size from $1 million to $30 million in annual revenues, and all but a handful publish and mail monthly newsletters, and more than half rely on direct mail as a primary marketing media for acquiring clients and/or marketing conferences.
- In the nonprofit world, direct mail trumps all other media for new donor acquisition and for quality of acquired donor, measured by size and frequency of donations, by no less than 3 to 1 to as much as 15 to 1, as reported by various leading charities. Organizations that I support, including The Salvation Army, Smile Train, Food Banks in two cities, and a number of animal charities all have direct-mail as their workhorse. Last year, I wrote and executed a direct-mail campaign to a small donor list on behalf of a local animal charity, and raised more money for it in 20 days than all of its work with online media produces all year. The backbone of this nonprofit is its monthly newsletter, printed and mailed. If you took direct mail away from charities, you'd see a halving or quartering in revenue size nearly overnight, massive lay-offs of paid employees, cutbacks and cancellations in programs and services, and many shutting down altogether.
- In toto, use of direct-mail advertising, marketing, and sales rose by 5.8% from 2010 to 2011, with over $48 billion invested, according to the USPS, reported in www.DeliverMagazine.com

Of course, the tendency of companies, marketers, and sales professionals is to abandon direct mail in favor of easier, cheaper online media they *think* that *everybody* prefers. So here is what you need to know about choosing the media you use to communicate with your prospects, clients, and customers. You *don't* choose based on your own preferences. You *don't* choose based on peer pressure. You *don't* choose based on ease. You choose only based on what works best in meeting your objectives.

I find that "old" media very often best meets the objectives of my clients—often to their surprise. While the herd stampedes to "new" media, my clients are mailing like crazy, putting speakers and sales teams on the road doing events; utilizing telemarketing, in permission-secured environments; using broadcast fax; at the local level, using merge-mail programs like Val-Pak; newspaper FSIs (free standing inserts); direct mail; and good, old-fashioned, grassroots marketing, the subject of one of the newest books in this series, *No B.S. Guide to Grassroots Marketing for Local Businesses*, co-authored with Jeff Slutsky.

Here's a good "old-school selling" example. Bruce Strachan, one of the most successful P&C insurance agency owners in the Midwest, told me, as I was finishing this book, that he and a group of ten other top P&C brokers from around the country came to the consensus—after two years of serious effort, investment, work with experts—that social media was bunk, in their business. None could track any significant revenue to it. Other media was profitable for new client acquisition, notably direct mail as well as telemarketing to business prospects. But not online media. They agreed as a group to waste no more time or money on it. Bruce went on to tell me of guiding his son in starting in the business by pushing him to set appointments with business owners by phone, also cold-calling on a client's business neighbors, and networking in business groups. "Five direct conversations a day. Five by five days a week, 25. Five by 20 days a month, 100. Five by 20 days a month times 12 months, 1,200 a year. I tell him: that's the way you are *guaranteed* to build a six-figure income. Old school, but it works, and it is paying off for him." Bruce and I discussed why direct relationship marketing works in his business but online marketing doesn't. We agreed that (a) his is a trust business, and trust can't be established and built with business owners and executives any way but person to person, (b) dragging people online or dealing with them there invites commoditization, price shopping, and price resistance, and (c) it is difficult if not impossible to create differentiation through expertise and expert advice online. He said that it might be fine if you want to sell cheap insurance to rate-shopping consumers in a price war with Progressive, Geico, and State Farm, but if you want affluent individuals or business owners as clients, you will create those relationships offline.

Don't get mad at me. I didn't say any of this. Bruce did. And Bruce's agency has had consistent growth every year, year after year, for many years, in both good times and in a sour economy. He happens to be my agent, for business, classic car, and other insurance needs. And I've never rate-shopped him, nor would I, because I value the trust I have in him to provide expert advice.

The lessons here are:

> **You need to be very clear about the kind of client you want, in mind-set terms, not just in factual or statistical terms.**
>
> **You then need to create your trust relationship with that client in the way(s) that are preferred and valued by that client, and that serve your own interests most productively.**

For the record, I am *not* universally "anti-internet." Although I famously, steadfastly refuse to use it personally, I am reasonably expert in it as a marketing media, customer service tool, and educational tool, and I devise marketing for online media for most of my clients. Last year, everything I developed for marketing via websites, email, online video sales letters, webinars, Facebook, YouTube, etc., generated hundreds of millions of dollars in revenue. I typically integrate online and offline media, but I do not shun online. Many of the most respected experts in online media are GKIC Members and followers or clients of mine, notably including Perry Marshall, author of *The Ultimate Guide to Facebook Advertising*, Timothy Seward, the CEO of ROI Revolution—which manages Google Adwords campaigns, even marketers who just about live online, like Frank Kern, Ryan Deiss, and Matt Bacak. These leading experts understand that the internet is nothing more or less than a collection of advertising and marketing media to be deployed in appropriate situations. So, for the record, I am not anti-internet. However, I'm *very* anti-internet when it is inappropriate for the task at hand or being favored for all the wrong reasons.

The very astute CEO of the giant Tupperware organization, Rick Goings, says what is commonly called social media is, in his mind, "*anti*-social media." He says their business is the real social media: people gathering in living rooms, around the kitchen table, at the backyard patio, in the break room at their workplaces. And that is the driving force of their growing, profitable, successful global empire. As disclosure, I'm a very happy stockholder in Tupperware, and have a very healthy respect for Rick. Tupperware has certainly modernized its business, yet its core is easily traced to the 1950s, and the company has wisely preserved and honored that, and resisted seduction by trendy and popular new media.

One of my many clients, Alan Reed, owns a dairy farm with an old-fashioned home delivery business with more than 3,000 accounts, having grown every year, for consecutive years, a retail operation, and even a nationwide mail-order ice cream business.

He does *not* hold his yearly Customer Appreciation Farm Days Homecoming virtually, on Facebook. Thousands of customers with their families plus their friends and neighbors (prospective new customers) come to the farm in person, to picnic on the grounds, take hay rides, meet and take photos with the cows that provide their milk and ice cream, and meet Alan and his family and staff. Their company does have a robust online presence, including their own websites with video, a Facebook page, and more. But they also mail a monthly paper-and-ink newsletter, use direct-mail for new customer acquisition, and create personal relationships between Alan and Holly and delivery drivers and customers. Many of their customers are cheerfully paying premium prices because they trust the Reeds to provide higher quality, hormone-free, chemical-free milk, butter, and ice cream. Check them out at www.reedsdairy.com.

My point is that a lot of businesses that may not seem at a glance to revolve around trust either do or could be substantially re-invented and strengthened by making them do so, therefore all media decisions must take trust into account.

In Matt Zagula's business, *the product is trust*. Matt and his financial advisor brethren aren't asking Boomer and Senior clients just to make a purchase; they are asking them to hand over their life savings and put their retirement security on the line. What these advisors *must* do can be replicated in many other types of businesses to great benefit. Many of these advisors also make good use of online media; others incorporate it out of defensive posture because competitors are there; others have it in place merely to satisfy the need of consumers to check if it's there. But the drivers of these seven-figure income advisors' businesses are: newspaper, radio, and TV advertising; informational seminars; books; and person-to-person meetings. The kind of trust they must create cannot be fostered in cyberspace. I believe many other business owners, private practice professionals, and sales professionals should put their emphasis on this very same approach: Use trusted media to create interest, get interested prospects into group settings where expertise can be demonstrated and interest deepened efficiently, then move to one-to-one relationships.

Media Integration, for One and All

Figure 8.1 shows two simple diagrams, depicting two approaches to online and offline integration.

A giant corporation could use these. A single, self-employed salesperson could use these.

FIGURE 8.1: Media-Integration Flow

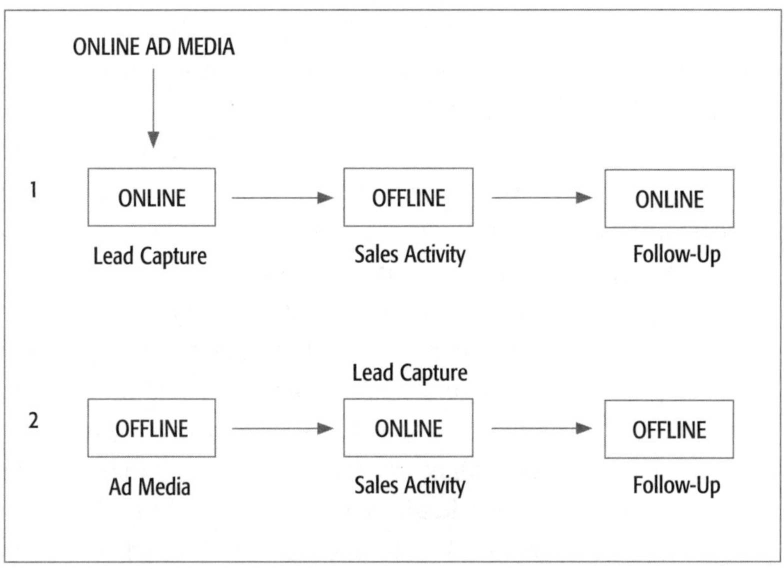

Number 1 begins online, so interested prospects might be brought to a website from any number of online sources, such as Google AdWords, SEO (Search Engine Optimization), Facebook, YouTube, etc. There, at the site, the prospect's full contact information (not just email) is captured, perhaps via a double squeeze page (see Chapter 9) and an information-based incentive that requires offline delivery. In this manner, we qualify prospects and move the conversation with that prospect offline. We may send direct-mail pieces; printed or recorded material; we may drive prospects to an in-bound call or utilize outbound telemarketing; we may bring the person to a seminar, a showroom, a store, or arrange for a salesperson to meet the prospect at his home or office. We captured the interested prospect via online sources and media, but we moved our actual selling offline. Finally, we may move stubborn, unconverted leads back online, perhaps to webinars, video-assisted sales letters, customer discussion forums, and alternative offers at other sites. And we may also deliver post-purchase support, service, and subsequent offers online, via a membership site, email, and other online media. Thus the integration flows: ONLINE-OFFLINE-ONLINE.

One of the main reasons for the first type of media integration is avoidance of what Matt Zagula describes as "the Google slap," described in Chapter 10.

The integration flow shown in diagram 2 begins offline, bringing interested prospects to a website with direct mail; Val-Pak and other merge mail; print media ads; newspaper FSIs; even broadcast. There are many marketers using low-cost postcards with relatively simple messages to drive prospects to their online media. Once there, the prospect may get to "meet" the marketer via video, may have access to such things as product demo videos, click to live chat, be invited to live or automated webinars, and outright sold a product or service. I have clients in various fields selling different items from $20.00 to $20,000.00 directly from online sales presentations. Prospects who do not purchase from this online media are taken back offline, and may receive sales letters and other direct-mail pieces, outbound telemarketing, and/or be turned over to local dealers or salespeople. Here the flow is: OFFLINE-ONLINE-OFFLINE.

Most businesspeople leave enormous sums behind, by settling for simple and simplistic media systems, often either all online or all offline, or static rather than dynamic, and with far too few sequential steps. The trust trigger of Familiarity is best achieved with complex multi-media, multi-step marketing campaigns.

Offline Media's Superiority in Creating Trust

While online media gives us a lot of capability for patient and persistent follow-up at nominal cost, there is abundant evidence that it is still offline media that best produces high trust. Walter Cronkite is no longer "the most trusted man in America"; TV news and all of TV is fragmented, so there can never again be *one* leading trust figure in the media, connecting with one-third of Americans. But still, TV, radio, and newspaper rank far higher with most demographic groups than any online media, even those featuring peer reviews, as trusted sources of information. Advertisers in these media benefit by association, even though there's no endorsement. I can assure you from the work Matt Zagula and I have done with his own financial advisory practice and in aiding many others across the country that advertising on local Fox News and Fox Financial News is a rising tide that lifts all other marketing boats. I can't divulge specific statistics without violating confidences, but I can tell you this isn't opinion or vague feeling; it is evidenced with empirical data. We also know for fact that even faux broadcast media, such as a bought and paid-for radio talk show hosted by a financial advisor, done properly, can both directly drive business to him plus lift response to other advertising and marketing. There is no online equivalent to this, at this time. Network and cable TV, radio, as well as newspapers and other print media have a "halo effect" for their advertisers unmatched by online media. Often, it can be extended from one media to another. For example, an opening sentence like, "You've probably heard my financial alerts aired during the Glenn Beck program on WKNR . . ." may heighten readership and thus improve response to a direct-mail piece sent to the right list. It uses the Affinity and Familiarity trust triggers. A book written by you or representing your company, delivered to a Boomer-age prospect benefits from the Credibility trust trigger to an extent no online presentation can. There is some implied or borrowed authority from being heard on the Beck radio program or being the author of a published book that is not available from any online advertising or marketing media. Sorry, but a blog is not equal to a book, nor your own "internet radio/TV program" equal to being seen within a Fox Financial broadcast, in leveraging the Credibility trust trigger.

Since our objectives—and hopefully yours—are more complex than just "let's sell something as cheaply and easily as possible," we have to evaluate, compare, value, and choose media on a more complex and sophisticated basis.

I need to mention that the media landscape is in constant flux, and developing effective uses of different media is an on-going process. This is one of the many good reasons to take me up on the **free offer on page 273,** to experience GKIC Membership, including the *No B.S. Marketing Letter* and other timely communiqués, learning opportunities, updated online courses, and other resources. GKIC is a central clearinghouse for cutting-edge discoveries about media, marketing, and business strategy drawn from its tens of thousands of Members in diverse businesses worldwide, its Independent Business Advisors operating local chapter groups in many cities, relationships with hundreds of leading authorities and niche industry marketing advisors, and hundreds of thousands of dollars of research—

plus my own in-the-trenches work with my private clients. All this is distilled every month, to deliver, by various means, what GKIC Members need to know to get optimum results from marketing their businesses.

There is benefit to viewing marketing media through a different prism than most do. The most common idea is that media deployed is salesmanship multiplied, narrowing its purposes to getting customers and making sales. That leaves it somewhat akin to a Flintstones car. Fred's little buggy with round wheels and holes in the floor for foot power will work as a mode of transportation, but obviously an automobile can be much more sophisticated, powerful, and useful. Media can be used for trust building as well as for creating equity, not just income (per Chapter 1).

CHAPTER 9

Creating Trust ONLINE—Pipe Dream?

Matt Zagula

A squeeze page technically is a very simple "mini" website offering only relevant information (a video, a white paper, an e-book or better, a physical book) in exchange for information about the requesting website visitor; often referred to as the visitor's opting in.

Think about it this way: Prospects have sought out your information, received your opt-in "gift," and have given you permission to continue to communicate with them based on their interest in what you are offering. They have asked you to communicate with them, share information with them and guide them in making a decision—for which, of course, the answer will ultimately be your product or service. They have invited you in, somewhat like inviting you in physically to their home or office. Dan Kennedy has been talking about this for nearly 30 years as "Welcome Guest Marketing." More recently, another popular marketing guru, Seth Godin (a bit late to the party), has presented it as "Permission Marketing." From a trust standpoint, which builds trust better?—(a) broadcasting a message, in this case in a big, broad-based, splashy website OR (b) pushing your way through a prospect's door OR (c) being invited in by the prospect and asked to provide advice?

So, instead of having a big brochure website for my business as a whole, I have a number of different squeeze page sites, each one directly targeted at a particular type of prospect I want to attract and get an invitation from, to begin a one-to-one dialogue, online and offline.

To get a better idea of what this type of squeeze page looks like, take a look at mine at www.wartimeveteran.com. Since the page is obviously targeted to wartime veterans, someone on Google looking for IRA tips isn't going to end up on this site. But a wartime veteran looking for help paying for long-term care is exactly who I want to visit, who I want to ask for more information and who I can continue to send information to on this specific subject.

The information is sent to the visitor who opted in by an autoresponder (a system that automatically sends email messages on a pre-set schedule). For this site, that means 17 very personal letters explaining the problems wartime veterans face getting these financially attractive benefits, and some of the secrets to unlocking the benefits. Notice, I said *some* of the secrets; ultimately, the message in the solution is as simple as hiring me. These 17 emails are sent at a rate of one every other day over the course of 34 days. At the end, we offer another series of letters explaining "new generation" estate planning with asset protection built in from long-term care; I believe that sequence is 26 letters long. If you add up all the correspondence, the recipient can get 57 emails from us and multiple offers to attend our live workshop events so they can meet us face to face, get a copy of our recent book, and learn more about our services. This online sequence of communication is supplemented by delivery of information offline, such as my book, other printed material, CDs and DVDs, integrating both online and offline media. The key is that all of it is structured as one to one, from me to the prospect, not delivered as a broadside for everybody and anybody.

The key to doing online marketing right is the material must have significant content value, be written in a conversational tone, and be geared toward developing a relationship based on two critical things:

1. I'm a good guy who is here to help you and not jam a product down your throat.
2. I'm an expert and all this information I just gave to you proves it.

Go ahead and check it out, but don't swipe it, because it is copyright protected; plus, it's really important to send a message out that is congruent with your personality and business—not someone else's. So, to build trust online, here are the steps to do it right:

1. Set up a squeeze page site. If you want to keep it simple, check out www.bluehost.com, which offers easy-to-use templates and includes everything, including your domain name, for $6.95.
2. Set up a database and autoresponder. An easy service I found to do this is www.aweber.com, offering up to 5,000 contacts for only $49.00 a month.
3. If you want to really make a premium site, use online video like I did at www.themillionareadvisor.com; we left it up and running for your review but have taken the opt-in out since that campaign is over. This site is not for my own

advisory business, but is a B2B site, aimed at other advisors nationwide. Take a look at how the video flows. The message is spot-on (written by Dan, of course), the video very supportive to the message. It brought in over 2,000 opt-ins, and we were asking: How much money do you make? So it wasn't easy to respond since it was intrusive, asking for personal data. The video was done by Andrew Eckelbad, who works mainly for online video ninja master Frank Kern, and the voice was provided by my friend Bill Hammond, famed Elder Law Attorney and coach to Elder Law Attorneys nationwide. Video can be amazingly easy these days. Just buy the Kodak HD handheld camera for less than $200.00 and set up an account at www.ezs3.com.

If you are tech-challenged like me, you can check out www.guru.com and hire a web designer. Last time I checked there were 699 freelance consultants available, starting at $20.00 an hour, and a lot of them are quality providers.

The Choice: Brand/Image Like Almost Everybody Else or Interested Prospects Inviting You In

In today's world you *do* need a web presence. But a brand-building website can be a waste of money. Instead, you build your bank of value by religiously building a list of prospects who are interested in subjects that you are expert at. Then send them material online and off that consistently reinforces your expert knowledge. A process like mine brings to bear many good trust triggers, such as Familiarity, Consistency, and Authority. You develop relationship and trust directly with each person. Eventually, it'll be their time, and when they are ready there will be no question who they are going to call. Trust building isn't a sprint, it's an ultra-marathon, and to win you have to control *your* behavior and expectations. People must be allowed to move at their own pace. If you go used-car salesman on them and try to rush them to buy now, they will run, as you are exposed as another salesman. If you allow them to move to you at their own pace and stay present in their mind on your topic, then when they are ready, you'll be the only logical choice.

CHAPTER 10

Don't Get Google Slapped

Matt Zagula

McDonalds dominates the hamburger-selling business why? Consistency. If you are down south in Naples, Florida, and order a Big Mac, it'll taste the same as the Big Mac you ate in Flint, Michigan. Is it the best tasting burger in town? No, but the customer knows what he or she is getting. There are no surprises with what they are served. The customer knows how it is going to taste, what the exterior of the building will look like, and how their "meal" will be packaged—always done in a consistent way.

Consistency, NOT Conformity

In many respects, consistency is the key ingredient in creating trust. So, my newspaper lead generation insert looks and says much of the same that is written about in my book and discussed in my public seminars, and my staff and I use the same terminology—most of which we created—and the visuals throughout my office all have a very consistent look, tone, and message. Nothing will surprise a prospective client because there is a consistency to what we say, to what we do, and how we show up—always in the same way, saying the same core values of our planning philosophy over and over, in print and in what we verbally say.

This kind of consistency is very beneficial. It is reassuring to clients or customers, whether they are choosing what foods to eat or where to eat, or choosing a financial advisor. However, this kind of consistency within your business's marketing should not be confused with *conformity* with your industry as a whole. Conformity only aids your competition, particularly if you are the biggest or most aggressive advertiser.

In his *Renegade Millionaire System,* Dan Kennedy challenges people to deliberately violate as many of their industry's norms and common practices as possible, and points out how much famous success has come from doing so: Walt Disney, Herb Kelleher and Southwest Airlines, Lee Iacocca and Chrysler, Howard Schultz and Starbucks are some classic examples that are Dan's favorites. I took this to heart in creating separation from other financial advisors, and even my entire industry, in crafting my own business approach. As a result, I also created a strong defense against the Google Slap. I'll describe how this works in my business. I think the need for such a strategy in just about any business will be evident.

Nothing Stops Trust in Its Tracks Faster Than the Google Slap

In my practice, we often integrate financial products with very specific trusts. Estate planning and elder law planning trusts really fall under three categories: irrevocable, revocable, and a hybrid trust commonly referred to as "a defective grantor" trust. We are very careful to never mention any of these trusts by their technical name because of the very dangerous possibility of being Google Slapped!

Here's a little background on this crucially important matter; I tend to spend time with a lot of diverse professionals. A Google slap to my online internet marketing friends means something totally different than what I want to discuss here with you, business owner to business owner.

For internet marketers, a Google slap has to do with how Google's algorithm changes and how a site's optimization rises or falls based on their new ranking criteria. For the internet guys it's a hard blow, because they work very hard to get "optimized" only to be slapped down by new Google rules. So, a slap to them costs them a lot of money.

That said, the Google slap you and I can receive is every bit as expensive and costly. Let's talk about how Google and the other search engine sites can hurt your business. We'll look at something very common in my business, the financial and estate planning profession: Life Insurance.

As you can see in Figure 10.1 on page 110, a Google search offers the searcher 189 MILLION resources to review/study/ponder/consider—to "think about."

So, think about a prospect sitting in front of me who should buy life insurance. He gets out of the meeting telling me he needs to "think about it." He goes home, jumps on Google and searches life insurance and he goes to work doing his "due diligence." By the time this prospective client, whom I've miserably failed by not closing (FYI, closing is a GOOD thing—it's truly client / customer advocacy), finishes his review of these 189 MILLION resources, articles, and needs-based calculators, he'll likely be dead.

FIGURE 10.1: Google Search for Life Insurance

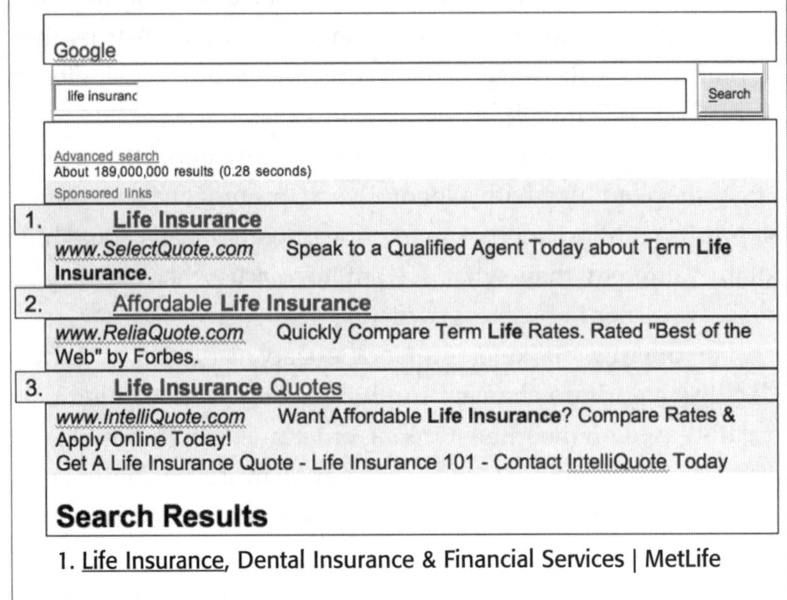

Two Key Points

1. Google is NOT your friend—nor is Yahoo!, MSN, or the search engine your neighbor's 13-year-old kid is creating this week that will be the next big tech thing of 2013.
2. The slap YOU get is YOUR own fault. Ouch, a self-inflicted and costly wound.

Google creates this do-it-yourself, 24/7 on-demand resource that is often harmful and certainly confusing for our prospects and clients. It's also a self-inflicted wound for you if you let your selling process lead the client right to the point of needing "self-validation" of your concepts, your pricing, and your offer with other options to chose from. If you let yourself fall into a category of many, to be compared against other products, services, or professionals, you invite the Google slap or other evils that operate in similar fashion—questions asked of friends or relatives or co-workers, driving about from showroom to showroom or store to store, procrastinating while collecting information from others "like you." This is how prospects go astray. This is the point where the trust you've been building up in advance of the sale is blown to pieces. Let me explain . . .

People, specifically your prospects, identify with certain terms, phrases, and even single words. You must be very cautious of your words. Let's say the prospect hears me say the word "trust," as in a "Revocable Living Trust" or an "Irrevocable Living Trust." They've heard that before, so in their minds they want to do their "due diligence" despite the fact that they are not qualified to do so; they want to validate my idea for themselves, and be sure that my plan is good for them. They lack the law degree, the education to understand the core concepts, *but they know that word,* so it's a starting point to "research" from. In addition, they also want to make sure they are getting the best deal, which downgrades me to a seller of a widely available commodity. Go ahead and Google "Life Insurance," and see how many of those millions of hits are about getting the best-priced premium payment. In the financial industry we struggle with retirees and those soon-to-be retired because they are stuck, like a deer in the headlights, with just too much information available to them and too much time to "think about it."

Some version of this can occur in just about any field. The automobile sales industry did it to itself, starting way back with the advent of "The Blue Book" that gives consumers the prices they should pay for a car. Because almost all auto dealers advertise price and try to close on price, they made themselves a commodity, and today, all the resources at consumers' fingertips on the internet further encourage the idea of interchangeable sameness of dealers, make nothing of the expertise of the sales consultant, and guide consumers to choice by price (although both Dan and I know highly-skilled auto salesmen who circumvent all this with trust-based marketing and typically sell at margins 50% higher than their peers). Every field wherein the kind of suicidal behavior common to the auto industry can occur is now very subject to the Google slap. Doctors, lawyers, interior decorators, home remodelers, real estate agents, catering and event planning companies, website developers—virtually every provider of a service to consumers or B2B—is vulnerable.

Here's the Foolproof Way to Avoid the Slap

Write a list of common terms used in your field, and known to consumers. Here's a quick partial list, as an example, from my industry: mutual fund, annuity, life insurance, living trust, power of attorney, Irrevocable Trust (I could keep going with this but you get the idea). Then, simply, rename your planning process or your product to avoid or replace these terms. Yep, it's that easy.

Sy Sperling did it for the toupee. He renamed the process "The Strand-by-Strand Hair System" for his hair replacement company, The Hair Club for Men. He changed the perception for millions of customers about his entire industry, resulting in him selling his company for $210 million to the Regis Company in 1976.

So, a secret to achieving far greater success, and the ultimate defense from the "think about it" prospect is to change the way the world looks at your product, your process, or, if it applies, both. In my office, we ALL call gifting and wealth transfer plans

"Protected Gift Accounts" (PGA). Go ahead and Google that—you won't see much. Hey, by the way, if you are a financial advisor, please don't go slapping that onto your website since I'm trying to help you out here. Don't mess me up, OK—fair enough? So, while advisors nationwide are speaking to the possible benefits of on-going gifting plans, we are talking about a totally new and better way to transfer wealth through our specially designed PGA—ultimately we get to a place with our client where we all understand there is going to be some form of gifting but we did not trigger the common terminology within the prospective client's mind that may create resistance. Instead, we went a different way that allowed us the time we needed to explain the concept without the preconceived resistance we may have received if we explained it in the traditional way.

BE AWARE: This in no way changes my firm's obligation, nor any seller of a product, service, or information, to disclose all the relevant details about the products or promised deliverables the client will ultimately receive. Full disclosure is always our professional and moral obligation. That reality fully realized, we need not, in the process of turning a prospect into a client, believe we have an obligation to say certain words, phrases, and terms that will lead them to Google. Your job as a great client (customer) advocate is to help those who trust you to cut through all the information clutter and pick an appropriate solution to their most pressing problems that your product or service solves and get them the desired result they are seeking. Part of that obligation is to hold their hands through the planning process . . . tightly . . . so their fingers don't type in www.google.com.

Dan Kennedy took elements and strategies common to the direct marketing industry and assembled them into his proprietary Magnetic Marketing System®, made usable for non-direct marketing businesses, small local businesses, professional practices like mine, and sales professionals, and has sold over

$100 million of his "un-generic-ized" product. Our friend Dave Dee, a reformed magician and mentalist and skilled salesperson, similarly took practices that have common, generic terms (such as cold reading, mind reading, ESP, intuition, etc.) and put them together into his own Psychic Selling System® Training. Disney twists itself like a contortionist to avoid use of the rather toxic, generic terminology of the "time-share" industry, in selling its Disney Vacation Club.

Nobody needs to be bound by the "correct" or common language customarily used to describe *anything*—whether a clinical or technical process, a place, a product, or a service. In the next chapter, you'll see how Familiarity can be an influential trust trigger. It's nearly the twin sister of Consistency, and should definitely be incorporated into a complete, trust-based marketing approach. But, in this one particular situation—avoiding the Google slap or its equivalents—familiarity is *not* your friend. As with all trust triggers, care is required in effective use of Familiarity, and in avoiding its *evil* twin, Conformity.

CHAPTER 11

How Familiarity Breeds Trust

Dan Kennedy

A lot of advertising and marketing is about grabbing attention. GoDaddy.com's very racy Super Bowl commercials starring scantily-clad racecar driver Danica Patrick. Everything the Kardashians do seems to attract attention. The remote-control-surfer-stopping celebrities we routinely use in TV infomercials. Geico's hamsters in rowboats, Allstate's Mr. Mayhem. In some cases, these gimmicks do drive sales. In others, they fail miserably, although it takes big, dumb companies two or three calendar quarters to figure it out. The infamous Taco Bell Chihuahua comes to mind—millions spent, no measurable increase in sales.

You can snare attention with the oldest rhubarb—a giant headline like this:

SEX,

Tiny type beginning:

Now that I have your attention, let's not talk about sex, but about something even more important: life insurance . . .

Yes, you grabbed attention. But will you be trusted?

"The sound of an ambulance siren *instantly* triggers alarm. A magazine article's provocative title *sucks us in* with mystique. *One glance* at the latest iPhone summons lust. **Trust, however, is a fascination of a different sort. This trigger is more complex . . . more nuanced, more fragile, harder to earn, easier to lose.** . . . Other triggers often guide our decision-making by provoking us in some way. Alarm thrills us with immediacy or change. Mystique stimulates with curiosity. Trust, however, guides everyday decision-making in a different way: familiarity and comfort."

Sally Hogshead, in her book *Fascinate: Your 7 Triggers to Persuasion and Captivation.*

I am a big fan of Sally Hogshead and her work in the area of fascination. Matt Zagula and I brought her in to work with an elite group of financial advisors we coach, and I hope to find other opportunities to work with her. Almost all marketing or sales has to begin with magnetic attraction in order to gain attention, then move the person forward from mere, temporary attention to interest, just to give us enough time to capably tell a complete sales story. Interest is linked to fascination. Thus, the chain is: **attention to interest by fascination = opportunity to make a sales presentation and attempt closing the sale**. But if you are about more than the quickest, one 'n' done, slam, bang, thank-you transaction, and are either committed to developing long-term client relationships and/or are involved with complex sales of high-priced goods or services, then a more complex chain is required: **attention to interest by fascination, to involvement for familiarity and trust, to opportunity to acquire a trusting client.** The difference between these two marketing methods is illustrated in Figure 11.1 on page 118.

It is relatively easy to accelerate the first chain of events, and all seven of the fascination triggers Sally presents can do so. But it is much harder and more hazardous to try accelerating the second chain, although I am going to talk about ways to do that here, and would also refer you to Chapter 12 "The Unmatched Power of Affinity." In any case, understanding the link between familiarity and trust is important; finding ways to deliberately utilize it, powerful.

One of the most common examples of the role familiarity plays in trust is how often we act on peer referrals or accept peer opinion as factual information. Most people trust the word of a familiar friend, neighbor, or co-worker more easily than that of a stranger—even though their co-worker is just as ignorant about the matter in question as they are—but the stranger may be a bona fide expert with credentials, who has devoted his life to studying the subject. Doctors will tell you that their life is full of "wrestling" with patients committed to medical advice they got from Aunt Lulu, who got it from a former vacuum cleaner salesman turned alternative health expert, who managed to make a book about "secret cures" and get himself on *The View*. This happens because Aunt Lulu watches *The View* every day of her life and, for no sensible reason, trusts its hosts and trusts

FIGURE 11.1: Basic vs. Trust-Based Marketing

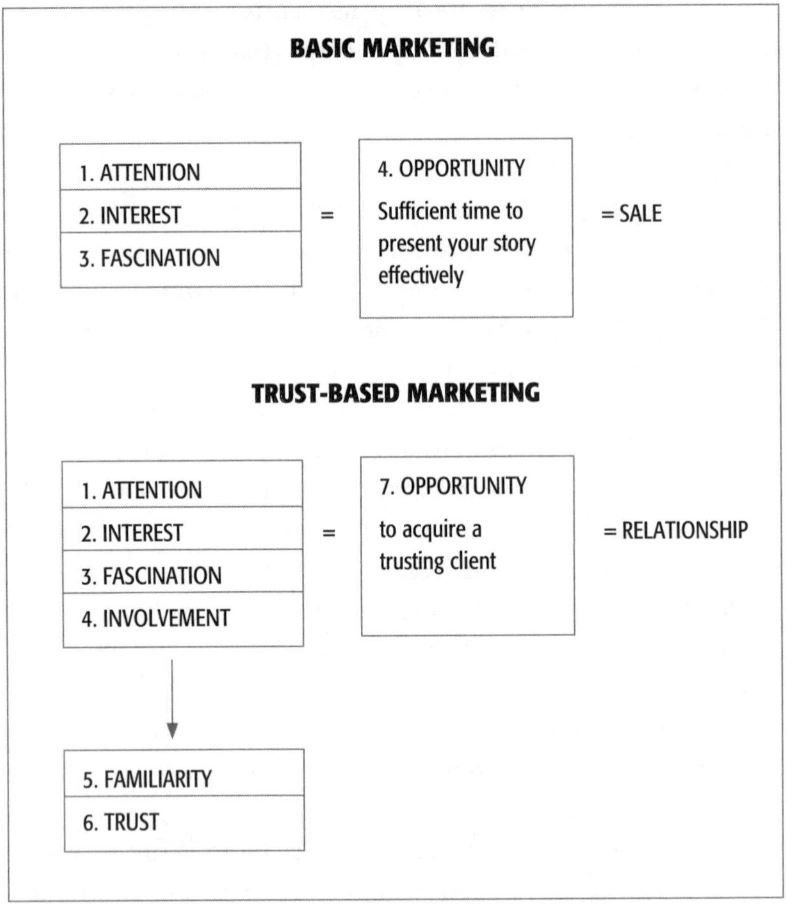

BASIC MARKETING

1. ATTENTION 2. INTEREST 3. FASCINATION	=	4. OPPORTUNITY Sufficient time to present your story effectively	= SALE

TRUST-BASED MARKETING

1. ATTENTION 2. INTEREST 3. FASCINATION 4. INVOLVEMENT	=	7. OPPORTUNITY to acquire a trusting client	= RELATIONSHIP
↓			
5. FAMILIARITY 6. TRUST			

everybody they introduce her to and everything she hears there, and because the patient has grown up with Aunt Lulu and trusts her. It's *all* driven by familiarity. *Not* by rational thinking.

When somebody decides to buy home furnishings or appliances, get home repairs done, hire a lawn service, or hire a babysitter, they may very well ask their neighbor who they buy from or use. It's a shortcut, but is it really a trustworthy one? After all, what research did the neighbor do? Did the neighbor aggressively shop around, have a background check done, check other customer references? The neighbor likely did none of those things. She either took the same shortcut and got a referral from another neighbor or randomly responded to a flyer in her mailbox. Again, people trust for the wrong reasons. But the neighbor or co-worker is familiar.

A smart home services company—say, a carpet cleaning business operator—can *manufacture* familiarity in a neighborhood in advance of soliciting its homeowners simply by having a billboard-style van emblazoned with its name and slogan driven around the neighborhood at different times of day for several Saturdays in a row, and parked on the street in different places from 4:00 to 6:00 P.M. when people are coming home from work on week nights. Then, when they send sales letters into that neighborhood, they get appreciably better response than they would without the shenanigans with the van. This is not theory. It's well tested. Why does it work? Familiarity. A certain comfort and trust level is created simply because the company's van has become a familiar presence in the neighborhood. Sure, there's also assumption that neighbors are using the company, but be careful not to over-think this; what makes the strategy effective, more than anything else, is familiarity.

Another bought-and-paid-for place strategy that often works fabulously, although it's costly, is advertising constantly on one popular and trusted host's radio program. Broadcasters like Rush Limbaugh and Glenn Beck have been full-on market makers for a number of fledgling products and companies. These hosts have an extremely high trust level with their audiences—the same core audience tunes in every day—so being there two or three times every day as an advertiser has a similar effect to parking the carpet cleaning van in the neighborhood day after day, week after week. Most of these radio ads are also direct-response ads, and the response to them may start out small but build over weeks as the audience's familiarity with the advertiser grows. But what only a tiny number of especially astute marketers utilize is that familiarity's power transferred from the radio advertising to other media, notably, direct mail to the lists of that same host's newsletter subscribers, ads at the host's or show's or affiliated local stations' online media, ad buys at Amazon adjacent to the listings for that host's books, and so forth. That's the equivalent of the direct solicitation of the homeowners after the carpet cleaning van has become a familiar presence in the neighborhood. If you are, for example, a regular listener of one of these hosts and begin getting direct mail from one of the regular advertisers on the show, it's probably not random coincidence. It is bought and paid-for familiarity being leveraged into direct solicitation.

This gets to my personal **strategy of omnipresence**, meaning—in a target audience of prospects in a defined market—being bumped into every time a prospect turns around. That's why I write and promote books like this one (on average, one to three new titles a year); write articles for other industry thought-leaders' newsletters and syndicate them for free; write articles for magazines like *Success Magazine* as well as dozens of trade journals; speak at important business conferences; and develop my own media platform of newsletters, online media and courses, and audio programs. I have trained and cultivated relationships with "marketing gurus" in hundreds of niches, from chiropractic and dentistry, to the restaurant industry, to the financial services fields, etc.—everywhere there are small-business owners with interest in smart marketing. That individual business owner in any of those fields hears me mentioned by industry leaders he trusts, reads my articles in the newsletters of those leaders he trusts, hears about my book from the leaders he trusts, buys a book—a trusted media itself, sees that I'm speaking at an event he trusts—effective whether he attends or not. Soon, I'm familiar. At some point, he is directed to or finds his way to an introductory offer similar to the one on page 273 of this book. He then begins getting my own newsletter, accessing my own online content, getting information from me, and getting to know me and my background, philosophy, and personality. More familiarity. *Every few days*, one way or another, or more than one way, he sees me in his world, hears from me, thinks about me. This is a means of growing trust, or more accurately, letting trust grow. Seeds of trust are planted, fertilized, nurtured; trust grows; ultimately, you have a harvest.

It admittedly requires patience, but it is about having an assembly line's conveyor belt bringing trust-matured prospects to you at a steady clip. As some are reaching you at your end, others are being put on, way, way, way at the other end, and there are some on every inch of the belt between there and here, all moving toward you apace.

Please stop for a few minutes and think about that term: ***trust-matured***. How many trust-matured prospects do you have coming to you every day like clockwork, thanks to your system? If you captain a company, how many trust-matured prospects is your national lead development system delivering to your local stores' or dealerships' doorways or sales force's hands? (If you leave prospecting to salespeople, you waste their best skills and sabotage their morale.) If you or your salespeople are working with "green" and "cold" prospects who aren't trust-matured, you or your people are undoubtedly working harder than necessary for inferior results, and likely succeeding only at exchanging labor for income, not at building equity. A system for developing trust-matured prospects can transform a business.

As a result of this approach, when a new client raises up and requests a consulting day or to engage me for a marketing or copywriting project, I frequently hear these statements, which I've separated here for clarity:

1. I've been hearing about you from people in my field for months/years.
2. I've been reading your stuff for months/years.
3. It seems every leader in my business makes mention of you.
4. It finally occurred to me: Why not move upstream to the source?
5. I'm finally ready and wonder if there's a way I can work with you.

In 99% of these cases, I subsequently sell and conduct my business with zero resistance to fees or working arrangements. In my case, that means I can insist all clients from anywhere in the United States or abroad travel to me rather than me having to go to them; even group coaching and mastermind meetings, seminars and conferences are often put in one of my home cities for my convenience. Clients accept that I take no unscheduled, direct in-bound phone calls; they must get on the schedule weeks to a month in advance for a phone appointment on one of the two days each month I take care of all telephone calls. For my copywriting, they pay large fees plus on-going royalties, a compensation arrangement secured by, maybe, one out of a few hundred ad copywriters. Etcetera. It's all "my way." Further, my strategic advice is mostly accepted with little argument, an experience few consultants or copywriters enjoy. The clients who fail at that are quickly jettisoned and just as quickly replaced.

Of course, you are immediately discounting all this because you aren't me, and your business is different; that's very poor thinking on your part.

Small = Speed to Familiarity

The best way to accelerate this kind of familiarity is by focusing on a very small target audience or market. In 1981, for example,

I made myself omnipresent, familiar, famous, and well trusted in the chiropractic profession—fast—over just several years. At the time, there were about 35,000 chiropractors, one weekly journal they all read, one big convention attended by nearly 25% of the profession, and about a dozen very influential thought leaders. Had I instead gone after the medical profession, I'd have been in a vast ocean, instead of a small pond, trying to become familiar to hundreds of thousands of doctors, many cloistered and segmented into different specialties, with dozens of different trade journals, hundreds of conferences, and hundreds of thought leaders. Small equals speed, especially if you have spare resources. A guy with one van can make his carpet cleaning company familiar to a small neighborhood in several weeks. To achieve the same level of familiarity with the same guerilla strategy for all of the city of Dallas will require a large fleet of vans and several years—if possible at all.

This is the reason Matt and I work with top financial advisors in their local communities to develop relatively small, target prospect groups, organized by advertising, obtaining referrals from happy clients, and by direct mail, and then being omnipresent in their lives, via every media possible. This includes sending at least one newsletter at least once a month. To our top clients we provide a mini-magazine for this purpose, shown in Figure 11.2, sent along with the individual advisor's insert—example in Figure 11.3, and the entire program is implemented by a master in the newsletter field, Jerry Jones. There are other, excellent done-for-you newsletter services for many different kinds of businesses, and if you are interested in a referral, you are welcome to fax an inquiry to me directly at (602) 269-3113. This is just one piece, though. These advisors use the newsletter, email, and social media communication, networking with and outreach through other influencers, carefully chosen local charity support and involvement, having published and promoted their own books (which Matt and I also assist with), paid-for local radio shows, commercials and sometimes long-form, half-hour infomercials on their local FOX or FOX Financial cable channels, and periodic public seminars and closed, clients and friends events. They become a very, very familiar presence within the small pond of their making.

All this combines the strategies of omnipresence and integrated media with a number of trust triggers—notably Authority and Familiarity—with trust-favorable media. It's a powerful combination just about any local business, practice, or sales professional can use.

There's Science Behind All This

In her book *Fascinate!*, Sally Hogshead refers to research, dating back to 1876, into "the exposure effect"; there is actual neuroscience at work. A certain kind of repetition that produces **familiarity actually rewires the brain** to trust in and exhibit preference for the familiar. Scientists have since documented this as the reason we may like a song more after hearing it a few times than at first, and why we feel as though we personally know or have personal relationship with certain celebrities. Bette Midler wasn't the only person crying the night she serenaded Johnny Carson on his final show, nor he the only one wiping a tear from his face; huge numbers of viewers got teary-eyed with him as Carson sat on the stool and told his audience of his retirement. We felt loss akin to that of loss of a close friend or beloved family member. Why? Familiarity. He had been a most familiar presence in our homes, night after night after night, for many years. Many people ended almost every day with Johnny.

Carson chose not to capitalize on his relationship with us as a commercial spokesperson much at all, but his sidekick Ed McMahon did, and was a very productive endorser for a wide range of products over the years, including the Publishers Clearinghouse Sweepstakes.

I can tell you from all my work in advertising, utilizing hundreds of celebrities in varied print, direct mail, TV infomercials, radio and online campaigns that—often to the surprise of incredulous clients—just the presence of the celebrity, without specific and direct endorsement or use of testimony, raises response. Celebrities with high familiarity to the audience targeted by the advertising work best.

"The exposure effect" actually produces trust. The more we're exposed to something or to someone, the more we trust it or them. And the more we like it or them. Big brands build this with big audiences over long periods of time, by committing big ad budgets and big resources to it. But most of us can play the very same game as small ball and win. A small budget invested in a small target group of people can have the same effect.

FIGURE 11.2: Mini-Magazine Example—Page 1

LL&H®

Life, Liberty & Happiness®

FREE
Cutting-Edge
Health &
Wellness Info

Wolfgang Puck's
Sauteed Shrimp
WITH SHERRY, DIJON
MUSTARD AND
TARRAGON

RECONNECT
yourself

In *Praise*
of the
COMMON
COLD

FINANCIAL
NEWS &
NOTES
The Truth
About
Annuities...
FINALLY!

tid•bit:
a choice or
pleasing bit
of anything

Happy
Birthday!
Cary Grant

U.S.A. $3.99
CANADA $5.99
FOREIGN $6.99

51631142723251

FIGURE 11.2: Mini-Magazine Example—Page 2

Welcome to…
Life, Liberty & Happiness®

Welcome to 2012! We're excited you're with us. This month, Wolfgang Puck shares yet another great dish, Cary Grant adorns our cover as the January birthday celebrity, and, please join us in welcoming our new humor columnist Mark Bazer. As always, we hope you enjoy this little gift from us.

~Enjoy and happy reading!

We're Never Too Busy For Your Referrals!

If you enjoy *Life, Liberty & Happiness®* mini-magazine and our *News From The Office™* newsletter, we'd be happy to send it to a friend, neighbor, or family member, so they too can benefit from the information inside this monthly communication to our clients and friends.

Feel free to share the enclosed Referral Cards with this magazine, or, just have them contact our office! We promise to take great care of your friends, family, or colleagues, while giving them the respect they deserve.

table of contents

2-LL&H®

Life, Liberty & Happiness®
Volume I, No. III

Jerry A. Jones, Editor-in-Chief
Melody Petersen, Design

Life, Liberty & Happiness® is published monthly by
Novus Venalicium, Inc.
PO Box 4102
Salem, OR 97302

Comments? Fax to:
(503) 218-0557

Statement of Purpose

Life, Liberty & Happiness® (LL&H) Magazine's mission is to inspire, entertain, inform and assist readers in taking care of their families, finances, freedom and health. To this end, it includes the latest, most accurate information available from America's finest writers, educators & chefs, all bundled into an easy-to-digest format.

Life, Liberty & Happiness® is meant for entertainment purposes only. The stories contained within reflect the individual views of the authors and do not represent the opinion of the publisher, or its affiliates.

Consult with a physician before making changes in diet, activity level, or changing lifestyles.

FIGURE 11.2: Mini-Magazine Example—Page 3

CARY GRANT ~ *January 18, 1904*

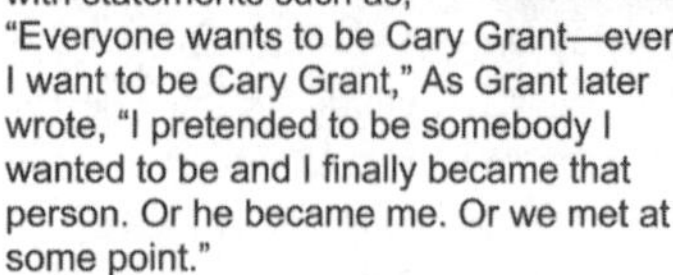

Archibald Alexander Leach (January 18, 1904 – November 29, 1986), better known by his stage name Cary Grant, was an English actor who later took U.S. citizenship. Known for his transatlantic accent, debonair demeanor and "dashing good looks," Grant is considered one of classic Hollywood's definitive leading men.

He was born in Bristol, England. An only child, Leach had an unhappy upbringing. His mother had suffered from clinical depression since the death of a previous child. Her husband placed her in a mental institution, and told his nine-year-old son only that she had gone away on a "long holiday." Believing she was dead, Grant did not learn otherwise until he was 31 and discovered her alive in a care facility. When Grant was 10, his father abandoned him after remarrying and having a baby with his new young wife.

After joining the "Bob Pender Stage Troupe," Leach performed as a stilt walker and travelled with the group to the United States in 1920 at the age of 16, on a two-year tour of the country.

When the troupe returned to the UK, he decided to stay in the U.S. and continue his stage and vaudeville career, which would benefit him in Hollywood.

Paramount gave their new actor a list of surnames to choose from, and he selected "Grant" because the initials C and G had already proved lucky for Clark Gable and Gary Cooper, two of Hollywood's biggest movie stars.

The Awful Truth (1937) was a pivotal film in Grant's career, establishing for him a screen persona as a sophisticated light comedy leading man.

Never self-absorbed, Grant poked fun at himself with statements such as, "Everyone wants to be Cary Grant—even I want to be Cary Grant," As Grant later wrote, "I pretended to be somebody I wanted to be and I finally became that person. Or he became me. Or we met at some point."

Grant was a favorite of Hitchcock, who called him, "the only actor I ever loved in my whole life."

Grant was the first actor to "go independent" by not renewing his studio contract, effectively leaving the studio system, which almost completely controlled what an actor could or could not do. In this way, Grant was able to control every aspect of his career, but, at the risk of not working. He decided which movies he was going to appear in, he often had personal choice of the directors and his co-stars and at times even negotiated a share of the gross receipts, something uncommon at the time.

Grant remained one of Hollywood's top box-office attractions for almost 30 years.

Grant did not think movie stars should publicly make political declarations. He described his politics and his reticence about them this way:

"I'm opposed to actors taking sides in public and spouting spontaneously about love, religion, or politics. We aren't experts on these subjects. Personally I'm a mass of inconsistencies when it comes to politics. My opinions are constantly changing. That's why I don't ever take a public stand on issues."

"I'm opposed to actors taking sides in public and spouting spontaneously about love, religion, or politics. We aren't experts on these subjects. Personally I'm a mass of inconsistencies when it comes to politics. My opinions are constantly changing. That's why I don't ever take a public stand on issues."

LL&H®-3

FIGURE 11.2: Mini-Magazine Example—Page 4

From... Wolfgang Puck's Kitchen

Back to Basics: Sauteing

Sauteed Shrimp with Sherry, Dijon Mustard and Tarragon

After all the effort you've put into getting through the holiday season, it's time to allow yourself some instant gratification in the kitchen. That's why I want to help you get back to the basics by talking about one of the easiest and quickest cooking methods around: sauteing.

The French "saute" literally means to jump, and that's a perfect way to describe how hopping-quick sauteing can be. All it takes to saute the right way is to start with good-quality ingredients that are naturally tender enough to cook quickly; make sure they're in uniform, small pieces that will cook evenly; and then prepare a quick sauce based on the glaze of delicious juices left in the pan.

Yes, it's that simple. But you still must pay attention to details.

The most important detail is the heat, and that means you need the right pan. A good, wide saute pan will have enough surface area for the food to move around freely in a single layer without crowding. This will allow moisture to escape, so the food cooks by direct contact with the pan rather than by steaming. And the pan should be heavy and made from a material that conducts heat well and evenly, such as stainless steel or anodized aluminum. Many cooks prefer stainless-steel pans with bottoms containing a sandwiched layer of aluminum or copper, which holds and conducts heat well. Some cooks also prefer nonstick pans, which enable them to use less oil.

Whatever kind of pan you use, preheat it well before you add a touch of oil. Then, when the oil is good and hot, in goes the food.

If you watch professional chefs saute, you'll often see them lifting their pans to toss the ingredients around. For home purposes, stirring continuously with a wooden spoon or spatula to keep the food moving will be fine. Once the food is done, add flavorful liquids and seasonings to the hot pan, quickly stir and scrape to "deglaze" or dissolve the flavorful deposits that have formed on the pan's surface, add cream or butter if you'd like a touch of richness, season to taste, and serve the sauteed food and sauce together.

One of the best ways I know to master sauteing is a dish I've been making for almost 40 years: Sauteed Shrimp with Sherry, Dijon Mustard, and Tarragon. Follow the recipe and, in minutes, you'll have a terrific appetizer to offer with some crusty bread for soaking up the sauce. Or, serve the shrimp and sauce over pasta or rice, add a side of steamed fresh vegetables, and you'll have a main course that's all the more gratifying for having taken you little more than an instant to prepare.

4-LL&H®

FIGURE 11.2: Mini-Magazine Example—Page 5

Ingredients: Serves 6 as an appetizer, 4 as a main course

This tasty dish, using fresh shrimp, can be an appetizer or entree.

3-to 4-dozen medium-sized fresh shrimp, shelled and deveined
Salt
Freshly ground black pepper
4 tablespoons mild-flavored oil, such as safflower or canola oil
2 medium shallots, minced
1 small bunch fresh tarragon leaves, minced
1/2 cup dry or medium-dry sherry
1/2 cup heavy cream
1/2 pound unsalted butter, cut into small pieces
2 tablespoons Dijon mustard
1 tablespoon minced fresh chives
Freshly grated nutmeg
4 to 6 fresh sage leaves, torn into small pieces

Preparation:

Season the shrimp with salt and pepper to taste. Set aside.

Divide the oil between two large, heavy saute pans. Heat the pans over high heat until the oil flows freely in the pans and shimmers slightly. Divide the shrimp between the pans and saute, stirring frequently, until the shrimp turn uniformly pink and look plump and firm but still slightly translucent, 6 to 7 minutes. With a slotted spoon, transfer the shrimp to a warm plate, cover with aluminum foil, and set aside.

Divide the minced shallot between the 2 pans and add 1/2 tablespoon of the tarragon to each pan. Saute, stirring continuously, until the shallots begin to turn transparent and just slightly golden, 2 to 3 minutes. Divide the sherry between the pans and stir and scrape with a wooden spoon to deglaze the pan deposits; then, pour the contents of one pan into the other. Stir the cream into the sherry and simmer briskly, stirring frequently, until the sauce is thick enough to coat the back of a spoon. A small piece at a time, whisk in the butter. At the last minute, reduce the heat to very low and whisk in the mustard, taking care that the sauce doesn't boil, which would turn the mustard grainy. Adjust the seasonings to taste with a little more salt and pepper.

Arrange the shrimp on serving plates or on top of beds of cooked pasta or steamed rice. Spoon the sauce over and around the shrimp. Garnish with chives and serve immediately.

LL&H®-5

FIGURE 11.2: Mini-Magazine Example—Page 6

Financial News & Notes From the Office

The Truth About Annuities...Finally!

It seems everywhere you look today there's an opportunity to purchase an annuity for your retirement dollars. Banks sell them, brokerage house representatives sell them, the guy who insures your car can probably sell them, too. But the real question is, are annuities any good for you, your money and your retirement? And if they are good, who is qualified to find you the right one for your unique retirement planning situation?

First things first. Are they any good and should you own one? Yes...and NO!

Let's start out by identifying annuities that are less desirable due to high fees and uncertain performance:

Variable annuities appear interesting since they offer some of the benefits of a fixed annuity, mixed in with mutual fund investing. The problem comes when you peel back the cover and look at the cost to own them. First, you have mutual fund fees, which include easy-to-figure-out expense ratios. (A mutual fund's expense ratio is its management fee.)

Next you have fund turnover, which is the trading that goes on inside mutual funds. This is not a cost that's easy to figure out, and it's not published like a mutual fund's expense ratio is. This lesser known – but often much more costly – expense can drive fund expenses up dramatically. Add the costs of mutual fund ownership onto a mortality expense that typically is 1.2%, and you've got yourself a really costly retirement planning vehicle.

Let's consider a variable annuity with average fund expense ratios of 1.1% and an annual turnover ratio of 150% (meaning the portfolio is bought and sold one and a half times throughout the year). John Bogle, the founder of Vanguard mutual funds, wrote that a 100% turnover rate adds approximately 1% of expense to the investor. When you add this up, you have an expense ratio and turnover cost of 2.5%, then you add on the insurance expense of 1.2%. All in, the cost to own it is 3.7%. In other words, for every $100,000 invested, the first $3,700 of productive gain goes to fees and expenses, NOT into your retirement account.

> Be VERY aware of the "too-good-to-be-true" variable annuity.

Be VERY aware of the too-good-to-be-true variable annuity. From time to time I will hear from a prospective client that they found an annuity that goes up 5% every year OR the gain that year in the mutual funds, whichever is better. Now, let's consider that offer. It's perfection – who wouldn't want to own that asset? But does it strike you as way too good to be true? Yeah, I thought so. Me, too. There are strings attached; this isn't the real deal. It's the sales pitch, minus the reality of how the vehicle works. Nothing is perfect, but if something is presented that sounds so good it's almost a miracle – run away! Do not

6-LL&H®

~ continued on page 12

FIGURE 11.2: Mini-Magazine Example—Page 7

In Praise of the COMMON COLD

I come in praise of the common cold.

I've been fighting one the past week and a half, and, honestly, it's been nothing but a pleasure.

Every symptom has arrived right on schedule, been on top of its game, stayed its allotted time and then respectfully made way for the next stage.

Oh, hey there again, morning sore throat. You're so adorable in your attempt to make me suffer. I trust your little pal runny nose is on its merry way!

What is more comforting in its predictability than the progression of an honest cold -- scratchy throat into sneeze into seemingly unlimited supply of mucous into relentless hacking into phlegm into teaching your son the word phlegm into lingering cough into newspaper column?

In a world in which the super bug from India promises imminent death to all, the common cold is downright retro. They should sell ironic colds at Urban Outfitters.

As soon as I knew my cold was upon me, I took appropriate action and rushed straight to the doctor so he could prescribe me ... a box of tissues.

(The only thing that can ruin the good vibes of a common cold is leaving your nose maintenance in the hands of toilet paper.)

If the common cold has any downside, it's the first day you have it. You have to first confirm you have a cold, then you have to reschedule that week's plans, then you have to cancel all your credit cards.

And, at least on the first day, you have to show up at work -- to establish your cold's legitimacy in the eyes of co-workers and bosses and to do your part to maintain the train as a enclosed chamber of germs.

But if you get four or more "You sound awfuls" at the office, you're home that day by 3:45, the latest. Then the fun starts.

And nothing is more fun, at least at age 36 with two kids, than a couple of days spent on the couch alone and being semi-miserable.

The most benign of illnesses, the common cold is, ironically, the most legitimate reason to stay home from work. You can't really prove to your boss you have a migraine or that your sciatica is flaring up, but you wear your common cold all over your face. And nobody in your office wants to be around that face.

Of course, they should want to be around your face. If I ran my office, there'd be a raffle whenever anyone had a cold. The winner would get to nuzzle with the person with the cold in hopes that he or she would catch it. If handled correctly, there would an ongoing, fairly distributed common-cold rotation.

Perhaps my affection for the cold has to do with age. Wait, this is it? Just the common cold now? Are you sure you're not going throw a kidney stone or a hernia my way, too? Well, OK, I guess I owe you one.

If I have one regret, it's that I didn't savor the colds of my youth. In between my hacking, I plan on instilling that value in my sons -- and nuzzling with them real tight tonight.

LL&H®-7

FIGURE 11.2: Mini-Magazine Example—Page 8

Use It Or Lose It ~ A workout for your brain

SCRABBLE® BRAND GRAMS

SCRABBLE® is a trademark of Hasbro in the US and Canada. ©2011 Hasbro. Distributed by Tribune Media Services, Inc. All rights reserved

O1 O1 X8 W4 B3 R1 K5	1st Letter Double	RACK 1
E1 O1 Y4 R1 T1 P3 T1		RACK 2
E1 I1 O1 L1 L1 F4 W4		RACK 3
E1 U1 Y4 F4 R1 T1 P3	Triple Word Score	RACK 4
E1 E1 I1 U1 L1 V4 S1		RACK 5

PAR SCORE 275-285
BEST SCORE 357

FIVE RACK TOTAL ____
TIME LIMIT: 25 MIN

DIRECTIONS: Make a 2- to 7-letter word from the letters in each row. Add points of each word, using scoring directions at right. Finally, 7-letter words get 50-point bonus. "Blanks" used as any letter have no point value. All the words are in the Official SCRABBLE® Players Dictionary, 4th Edition.

JUMBLE

THAT SCRAMBLED WORD GAME
by Mike Argirion and Jeff Knurek

Unscramble these four Jumbles, one letter to each square, to form four ordinary words.

PUTER

©2008 Tribune Media Services, Inc. All Rights Reserved.

INGIC

TOORRA

www.jumble.com

MASTIG

We're broke. They all flew away

WHAT HAPPENED WHEN HE INVESTED IN A BEE FARM.

Now arrange the circled letters to form the surprise answer, as suggested by the above cartoon.

Answer: HE "   "

SUDOKU

Sudoku is the popular number placement game. It's fun and simple to play, with the aim of the game being to fill in the entire Sudoku grid so that each row column and 3x3 grid contains the numbers 1 to 9 in them once and once only.

	5		1				9	
		6		8				
8		1	9			2		5
6					8			
3				4				2
			6					9
		7			9	6		3
				2		7		
	2				4		1	

Game and Puzzle Solutions on Page 11

8-LL&H®

FIGURE 11.2: Mini-Magazine Example—Page 9

CROSSWORD PUZZLE

ACROSS

1 Word after boom or Bean
5 Dickens's Uriah
9 *Jake LaMotta, e.g.
14 Aleve target
15 Fall birthstone
16 "All systems __"
17 *Mexican neighbor of New Mexico
19 Feature of "butte" but not "but"
20 Like lava flows
21 Austin-to-Dallas dir.
23 British golfer Poulter
24 *Skiers' patron
28 NYC hub
31 Tolerate
32 2008-'09 Japanese prime minister Taro __
33 Sans serif typeface
35 Expansive
37 Ye __ Tea Shoppe
41 *Like Hammett's falcon
43 *Piece of advice
45 Information storage unit
46 Choice word
48 __-wip: dessert topping
49 Bear: Sp.
51 Brand for a 58-Down
53 Follow-up film: Abbr.
54 *Labrador was added to its provincial name in 2001
59 Pie __ mode
60 Suffix for glob
61 Home builder's subcontractor
65 Get started
67 *Beijing dialect
70 Upright
71 "They're __ again!"
72 Desert tableland
73 Greetings from the answers to starred clues
74 Lord's partner
75 Tiny power source-

DOWN

1 Filled tortilla
2 Cuatro times dos
3 Ace
4 Classic grape sodas
5 Philly's signature sandwich
6 N.T. book after Galatians
7 Seine contents
8 Backup strategy
9 Agricultural cubists?
10 Yellow metal, in Mexico
11 Seat of Greene County, Ohio
12 Samantha of "Doctor Dolittle"
13 Set of drinks for the table
18 Lacking capacity
22 "Cool!"
25 Umbilical terminus
26 __ la la
27 Not a soul
28 Doorframe part
29 Start to unravel
30 Scot's skirt
34 Dined on, biblically
36 Witch's incantation
38 Old Ford models
39 "__ Dinah": 1958 Frankie Avalon hit
40 La Salle of "ER"
42 Asian Olympics city of 1988
44 Like some patches
47 Blue
50 Squeaks and creaks
52 Equivalence
54 Big wheel
55 2010 Supreme Court appointee Kagan
56 Staked amount
57 Himalayan country
58 Steadfast belief (and parent of each answer to a starred clue?)
62 Acre's 43,560 square units
63 Bygone U.S. gas
64 500 sheets
66 Octopus's defense
68 Inbound flight posting at 28-Across
69 Joke around with

LL&H®-9

FIGURE 11.2: Mini-Magazine Example—Page 10

Reconnect Yourself

By Wina Sturgeon

By the time you reach middle age, many people have passed through your life. A few stay as lifetime friends. Others get lost as time goes by. Occasionally you think of them, wonder whatever happened to them, and maybe even regret the loss of contact.

The pace of life today is so fast and hectic that it's hard to stay in touch when locations, jobs or other circumstances change. The greeting cards stop, the phone calls dwindle. Finally, you both lose contact. But often, when that happens, a little piece of your life disappears.

As we get older, family and friends always become more important. They are the anchor that connects us to the mainstream of life. No mid-ager really wishes to disappear into a solitary existence where their major exposure to the outside world is only through television programs. But we often slip into that lifestyle without even realizing it. This year, make a decision to not allow that to happen to you. Reconnect with people who have passed out of your life; people that you genuinely would like to communicate with again.

There's a method to doing this in a way that will pay off by enriching your life. Don't do it in attack mode, rushing to contact everyone with whom you've ever spent any time. Start first by making a list. If you've saved any old cards or correspondence, bring it all out and go through it (this is also a great opportunity to get rid of pieces of paper you no longer value). Go through these mementos, putting to one side those from people you'd really enjoy hearing from again.

Next, make a list of old friends who occasionally come to mind. Write down their names. It could be a former neighbor or co-worker, an acquaintance with whom you exchanged phone numbers but never contacted, or anyone else you've wondered about over the years. But be discriminating: Don't wrack your brain for the names of everyone you've ever met. Only include those on your list whose names give you a memory of pleasure, a remembrance of a personal connection or bond. Don't include "frenemies" with whom you had a relationship of one-upsmanship, jealousy or backstabbing - not even to check out whether or not they've changed. That would be an extra hassle you don't really need in your life.

Next, if you don't have current contact information, go online and look them up. Try first just entering their name and city in a search engine. If that doesn't give you the information, look in local phone books to see if the person still has the same phone number and address. Don't use "finder" services that say they are free, but actually demand money to find someone; they often don't work and won't refund your money when they don't. If the person isn't listed in the white pages, try Facebook, looking at the picture and location to make sure it's not someone else with the same name.

Next, instead of telephoning, write a letter. A sudden phone call out of the blue after years of silence is just too abrupt, and may come at a bad time. A letter gives your old friend the opportunity to remember you and also decide if they wish to renew the relationship. In addition, a letter shows more of an effort than a phone call.

One final bit of advice: Be careful about writing to old romances. They may be married or they may be bitter about your former relationship. The best thing is a simple card with a line to the effect that you've thought of them often and hope they are well, along with your address and phone number. The response - or lack of it - will tell you everything you need to know.

10-LL&H®

FIGURE 11.2: Mini-Magazine Example—Page 11

Free Cutting-Edge Health & Wellness Info

MAYO CLINIC MAYO CLINIC HEALTH LETTER RELIABLE INFORMATION FOR A HEALTHIER LIFE

HARVARD MEDICAL SCHOOL Harvard Health Newsletters

Finding reliable, cutting-edge health information on the Internet can pose a challenge for experience web surfer or, the novice. The online world is full of unreliable, even misleading and dangerous clutter and old, outdated information.

Not only is finding solid health and wellness info online difficult, once found, you have to answer the question, "Who's information do you trust?"

Fortunately, there are many reliable, very well-established resources where you can find relevant and recent material on a variety of topics you may find useful in living healthier.

The editorial team at AD® researched and found several reputable, both free and paid "online" options, where you can retrieve material and receive emailed news for just about any health question you can think of. Here are our top results:

- UC Berkeley Wellness Letter @ www.berkeleywellnessalerts.com
- Mayo Clinic @ http://healthletter.mayoclinic.com
- Harvard Medical @ www.health.harvard.edu/healthbeat/Subscribe.htm
- Johns Hopkins Health Alerts @ www.johnshopkinshealthalerts.com
- WebMD.com

As always, online learning and researching health info is just the beginning. Be sure to consult your trusted healthcare advisors on what is best for your unique situation.

Here's to 2012 being your healthiest year, ever!

GAME & PUZZLE Solutions

Jumbles: ERUPT ICING ORATOR STIGMA

Answer: What heppened when he invested in a bee farm — HE GOT "STUNG"

SUDOKU

7	5	4	1	3	2	8	9	6
2	9	6	4	8	5	3	7	1
8	3	1	9	7	6	2	4	5
6	1	5	2	9	8	4	3	7
3	8	9	5	4	7	1	6	2
4	7	2	6	1	3	5	8	9
1	4	7	8	5	9	6	2	3
9	6	8	3	2	1	7	5	4
5	2	3	7	6	4	9	1	8

CROSSWORD PUZZLE

T	O	W	N		H	E	E	P		B	O	X	E	R
A	C	H	E		O	P	A	L		A	R	E	G	O
C	H	I	H	U	A	H	U	A		L	O	N	G	U
O	O	Z	I	N	G			N	N	E		I	A	N
			S	A	I	N	T	B	E	R	N	A	R	D
J	F	K		B	E	A	R		A	S	O			
A	R	I	A	L		V	A	S	T		O	L	D	E
M	A	L	T	E	S	E		P	O	I	N	T	E	R
B	Y	T	E		E	L	S	E		R	E	D	D	I
			O	S	O		A	L	P	O		S	E	Q
N	E	W	F	O	U	N	D	L	A	N	D			
A	L	A		U	L	E			R	O	O	F	E	R
B	E	G	I	N		P	E	K	I	N	G	E	S	E
O	N	E	N	D		A	T	I	T		M	E	S	A
B	A	R	K	S		L	A	D	Y		A	T	O	M

SCRABBLE BRAND GRAMS SOLUTION

W4	O1	R1	K5	B3	O1	X8	RACK 1 =	77
P3	O1	T1	T1	E1	R1	Y4	RACK 2 =	62
L1	O1	W4	L1	I1	F4	E1	RACK 3 =	63
P3	U1	T1	R1	E1	F4	Y4	RACK 4 =	95
E1	L1	U1	S1	I1	V4	E1	RACK 5 =	60

PAR SCORE 275-285 TOTAL 357

LL&H®-11

FIGURE 11.2: Mini-Magazine Example—Page 12

The Truth About Annuities...Finally! ~ continued from page 6

buy into an offer that defies logic.

Lifetime immediate annuities can also be undesirable, because if your life is short you can lose money. That said, term certain immediate annuities can offer you peace of mind and certainty that the check that was promised is in the mail. Buying an immediate annuity requires specialized knowledge and an advisor who is in the know. Rates can vary significantly.

So, are annuities good?

Yes, they can be a great "safe money asset" to own. There are hybrid annuities available that gain interest when the market goes up, and they don't lose money when the market goes down. Commonly referred to as **indexed annuities,** these unique contracts also offer additional add-on benefits such as guaranteed lifetime income withdrawal benefits that can create guaranteed retirement income (for you and for your spouse) that you can't outlive. In essence, it's retirement income insurance that kicks in if your balance goes to zero. Naturally, this is a very attractive offer as long as you are aware of the strings attached and the rules of the contracts that deliver those results. Again, a complete disclosure is needed to make an informed decision. But this hybrid is attractive as long as the strings attached are acceptable to you. Which brings us to our final point...

Who is qualified to advise you about these unique retirement planning instruments? Safe money advisors who specialize in income planning – NOT your bank or a brokerage house. Why not? Simple. The bank channel is focused on the limited products the bank represents, and the brokerage house is aligned with the fee-heavy variable annuity. A good safe money advisor also knows how to "ladder" annuities to create the highest retirement cash flow possible to supplement your retirement income.

tid•bit: a choice or pleasing bit of anything, such as news or gossip.

There is a privacy about it which no other season gives you.... In spring, summer and fall people sort of have an open season on each other; only in the winter, in the country, can you have longer, quiet stretches when you can savor belonging to yourself.
– Ruth Stout

I like these cold, gray winter days. Days like these let you savor a bad mood.
– Bill Watterson

FIGURE 11.3: Advisor's Insert Example

Teresa Bear
Certified Financial Planner™
Certified Public Accountant
4864 E Baseline Road, Suite 109
Mesa, AZ 85206
Call (480) 503-0050
www.JCGrasonMesa.com

Present this card to
receive your
Complimentary
Dinner and Wealth
Preservation Consultation

My experience with Teresa Bear and her team has been fantastic. Because of that, I'd like to introduce my friend, ______________________________, to you.

Please extend the same professional and compassionate service you offer me and my family! Also, please be sure they receive your New Client, Get-Acquainted Offer:

Complimentary Dinner and
Wealth Preservation Consultation

Thank you!

Sincerely, ______________________________

CHAPTER 12

The Unmatched Power of Affinity

Dan Kennedy

Believe it or not, porcupines huddle together at night, taking care not to get too close and be stabbed by each other's quills.

Huddling is almost universally popular. Probably instinctive. Everybody is unconsciously looking for like-minded or comfortably similar folks to huddle with. This is why every immigrant group that has come to America has congregated in its own, culturally distinct neighborhoods. It is why there are "blue collar" taverns and "white collar" bars, and rarely do "blue collars" invade and hang out in the "white collar" cocktail lounge. It is more common for "white collars" to go "slumming," but as a little adventure, not a habit. (Curiously, strip clubs are the only such establishments where there is a very diverse demographics stew of customers.) There are also "cop bars" where mostly cops hang out; dying now as the newspapers die, but there used to be reporters' bars, where the newspaper journalists hung out. One in each city, walking distance from the newspaper's offices. Young people with kids tend to be most comfortable living in neighborhoods with other young people with kids, and choosing each other as friends. In this case, it's somewhat forced by the neighborhood's proximity to the schools, but then seniors tend to find living in such neighborhoods uncomfortable and tend to voluntarily relocate and, well, huddle together. I am an entrepreneur and a marketer, and I find socializing with what I call "civilians" challenging, uncomfortable, and awkward, and I am most comfortable with other marketing-oriented entrepreneurs. If such segregated huddling is a cliché, you will find that you, too, are a cliché. In this behavior is a major pathway to trust. It *shouldn't* be—reinforcing the very important fact that people often trust for all the wrong reasons—but it is. Porcupines tend to most easily and quickly trust other porcupines.

Matchmaking

You are aware of the big, online matchmaking sites, like www.Match.com and www.eHarmony.com. Maybe you've seen some of the bigger niche ones, like ChristianMingle.com. You may not know, however, that there are find-a-date/find-a-mate sites for horse owners, dog lovers, people over age 50, people interested in diverse sexual fetishes, even for married persons seeking no-strings affairs with other married persons. All this activity, by millions, searching for people like them.

Some years back, I had a client who brought prospects to a showroom, and employed four salespeople. Many prospects came in at pre-set appointments, but still got placed with whatever salesperson was next up, and empty-handed at the moment, a common practice. One of these salesmen was an ex-Marine who looked like a Marine, and had Marines memorabilia in his little office. Another had a big family; 8 children, 22 grandchildren. The business was located in the northwest, and another was a big boating and fishing aficionado. And so on. I devised a series of questions to be gently asked when the appointments were set, with the disclosure that we liked them to have their showroom experience with a consultant they might share common interests with. Perhaps surprisingly, most people cheerfully answered the questions. The client then assigned the prospect to the salesperson with whom there was best affinity. The results were simply amazing. The no-show rate for appointments dropped considerably, the closing rate of the salespeople improved, and the average transaction size increased by more than 20%.

I got the idea from another situation, explained to me by the CEO of the highest-priced and most effective in-bound telemarketing company in the Midwest, at least at the time of this story. Their success rate of converting prospects calling in from various advertising efforts mounted by diverse clients to buyers or donors was double to quintuple that of any of their competitors. I spent a day with him, to learn why. Three of the reasons aren't pertinent to the point here, but I'll mention them quickly, to present a full and fair picture of the superior results. One was an extremely well-disciplined approach, including scripts, supervisor eavesdrops on calls, and daily pre-shift coaching. Two, they charged clients more so they could better pay staff and reward performance, thus getting higher caliber staff. Three, they were selective about the clients they took. But the fourth reason is the most interesting. They used "flexible scripts" permitting authentic conversations, and they matched their telemarketers to the callers by affinity. For example, all the telemarketers assigned to taking calls from an ad campaign about high performance golf clubs were avid golfers. All the telemarketers taking the calls for an evangelical Christian nonprofit, raising funds for missionary work in distant lands, were evangelical Christians, and so on. The telemarketers disclosed their affinity as early in the calls as possible. The CEO told me this was logistically difficult and complicated, but well worth it.

At a time I did a major consulting project for Weight Watchers International, I noticed, in monitoring and assessing one of their in-house call centers, handling about 300,000 inquiry calls a year, that the slightly overweight, "pudgy," if you will, middle-aged women out-performed younger and thinner women and men in converting calls to appointments—even though, obviously, the callers couldn't see them. But they had authentic empathy and it was heard; this is evidence that trust can be a fragile thing.

So, how can *you* use this knowledge of the power of affinity in a practical way? Try to think of yourself as a matchmaker.

You can try to target your marketing and selling to clientele with whom you have the greatest possible affinity. And there need be no relevant and direct connection between the affinity and the nature of your business for this to be of benefit. For example, consider the chiropractor whose personal passion was restoring old cars. He painstakingly compiled a list of antique auto club members and car show participants and owners of classic cars in his area, and at some expense, rented lists of subscribers to "car-freak" magazines in his area. He purchased a quantity of a book about car collecting and restoration called *The Cobra in the Garage*. He sent a letter and the book in a big envelope, including a photo of himself with his latest restored car, and segued to his passion for restoring health, fitness, vitality, and pain-free living to folks in his area. He invited them to an office open house—with his car on display outside—or to request additional, free information about different subjects: back pain relief, headache relief, etc. He also sent a "what to do in case of a car accident kit" to be kept in car glove compartments. This was a complicated, costly campaign, reaching about 210 prospective patients. In immediate response, to the open house or the other offer, it pulled 18 people (a *very* respectable 9% response rate), 2 immediately becoming patients, 2 more later. Over a year's time, another 7 patients came from the campaign. In total, over $64,000.00 in revenue was generated. The campaign cost about $5,000.00. Tracking referrals from those patients as well, over the next 2 years, the gross revenue rose to over $130,000.00.

This is easier on a national level. One of many companies selling gold bullion and other precious metals and gold coins to investors—just like the ones all over cable TV news broadcasts during recessions—chose to focus on full-page ads in magazines having to do with hunting, fishing, guns and other outdoor sports, the ad featuring a photo of the company's President in hunting regalia, carrying his rifle, accompanied by his dog, with note of his having won a major sporting contest. The rest of the ad was straightforward about investing in gold. This was a very successful campaign for two reasons. One, he reached the right audience—many reading guns and sporting magazines are over 50, politically conservative, and more likely to invest in precious metals than the general public. Two, his affinity with those readers; it shouldn't, but it does foster trust.

A related strategy is to be sure to use and tell your story. I have two relatively unique and instructive experiences: First, for 9 consecutive years, I spoke 25 to 27 times a year to very large audiences, often 10,000 to as many as 35,000, on day-long programs with an eclectic parade of former U.S. Presidents, Olympic and pro athletes, Hollywood celebrities, iconic CEOs, and other top sales and business speakers like Zig Ziglar, Brian Tracy, and Tom Hopkins. At these events I sold my Magnetic Marketing System®, for small-business owners and sales professionals. As I was always the last speaker of the day, I hung around while the stampede of buyers was accommodated, got questions answered, signed autographs, and chatted. These were all strangers, most of whom had never heard of me and didn't know me from Adam's housecat, yet had just hurried to spend $278.00 on my package. During the speech, at different points, I (barely) mentioned that I have, in my past, struggled mightily and gone through bankruptcy, and had a severe stuttering problem as a kid. I also read three brief testimonials, one from a Mary Kay agent, one from a real estate agent, and one from an auto salesman. In every city without exception, people lugging the bag of my stuff bought at the back-of-arena tables were waiting in line to tell me they or their child stuttered, they'd been through bankruptcy like me, or to tell me they were in network marketing or direct selling or real estate or selling cars like the people I'd mentioned. I can't prove they bought because of that, but I'm certain that little bit of affinity—that they heard while thousands of others listening never noticed it—helped. I call this technique when doing group presentations "planting affinity seeds."

The other somewhat unusual and instructive experience has to do with one of my businesses as a whole—the business you connected yourself to by buying this book (and next, hopefully, by accepting my free gift offer on page 273.) I have tens of thousands of readers of my books, courses, monthly newsletters, and weekly bulletins, all drawn by an exceptional interest in more effectively marketing their businesses. And I deliver that professorial instruction, but not dryly. I let my readers, subscribers, and members "in" to pretty much everything in my life experience, past and present. Many get a book of autobiographical essays, *Unfinished Business*, which tells a lot about me. Others pick up things here or there, from comments I make in the newsletters or from the stage at events. I've been at this for about 35 years, so I've had a lot of experience with the influence of all these personal disclosures—bankruptcy, drinking problem (also ancient and done with), diabetes, divorce and recovery from, the stuttering, somewhat dysfunctional siblings, and so on—as well as happier personal interests, notably, my involvement in harness racing, and ownership of classic cars. Which do you think I get more correspondence about? My marketing advice or all the personal stuff? It runs neck 'n' neck, 50/50. And at events, what do people want to talk with me about—marketing advice, or their business, or one of these personal affinities? Many want to quietly tell me their recovery story or show me their car photos or talk about having gone to the harness races at a county fair in their hometown with their parents when growing up, or owning a horse. In this same business, I have what I call my "Lifers"—readers, subscribers, and members with me for 7, 10, 15, even 20 years. What 80% of those have in common is some sort of personal affinity with me. I am very cognizant of this power of affinity.

For everybody—for you—your personal story has magnetic power and trust-building power. You should take the time to learn more about storytelling, and for starters I suggest movie mogul Peter Guber's book *Tell to Win*, and my own audio program, *Personality in Copy/Customers for Life*, available at www.DanKennedy.com/store.

Birds of a Feather Really Do Flock Together

I worked on this chapter while sitting on the balcony of a suite at Disney's Boardwalk Resort in Orlando, overlooking its boardwalk and lake. I was being closely watched by several little gray, spotted birds perched above me. One got brave enough to land on the glass-topped cocktail table next to me, cock his head, and curiously study me. These little birds are all around the boardwalk in plentiful supply. Also there, sea gulls. And also there, ducks. They all help themselves to popcorn and crumbs dropped to the ground at tables by people at eating establishments all along the boardwalk. But they never get together. The gulls perch atop pier pilings. The ducks float in the lake close to the pier; waddle about together on the pier. The little birds fly about in groups, and cluster on empty tabletops, chairs, and in the eaves of the hotel room balconies. No gulls at the balconies. No little birds on the pier pilings. Three kinds of birds, each kind together with its own kind.

I watched all this knowing it to be true of people, too. People feel more comfortable, safe, and at ease with other people like them, and just as these birds do, tend to form little groups, societies, and cliques that are exclusive, not inclusive. We could fill a book just with lists of these affinity-based groups. There are loosely united groups like university alumni, members of a country club, parents of kids that attend the same school, members of special interest clubs—car clubs, gardening clubs, etc., Tea Party activists, members of professional and trade associations. There are more tightly-knit groups like the Wednesday night poker group that has met at Bob's house for 31 years running, the volunteers in a particular PTA, or the supporters of a local charity. And on and on and on. Humans acting just like the birds. This behavior is so ingrained, it followed people from the physical world to cyberspace, with communities within communities, as in Facebook; with tools on smartphones that help you, as one TV commercial running as I wrote this put it, "so you can organize your friends into circles (little groups)—just like you do in real life."

This innate *and* chosen behavior offers three kinds of enormous leverage to the trust-based marketer: one, being part of different groups, being "one of them," so you are more quickly and easily accepted as trustworthy by them. Two, making certain to uncover and identify every affinity group to which your best clients belong, and gaining access to them via your client's introduction and endorsement. Three, giving your prospective clients good opportunity to see that you are trusted by and serve other people just like them. This third leverage is really quite easy to do, with my marketing concept invention, "Find yourself here."

Tactical Opportunity: A Trust-Based Marketing Tool: "Find Yourself Here . . ."

On the following pages, I've reprinted a sample of an actual brochure developed for a client in the hearing aid industry. It is typical of this tool—what I call the "Find Yourself Here" brochure—which I often build for clients in all sorts of different businesses. The idea behind it is profound: People thinking about buying your product are very reassured by discovering that it is "for" people *just like them*, for a specific reason, and that people *just like them* like it, for that specific reason. A brochure like this one allows the prospect to find himself, and learn the specific reason* people *just like him* like the product.

In this case, there are five different kinds of people someone might match himself up with:

1. Active Seniors
2. People Still Working
3. Seniors Determined To Remain Independent
4. Especially Active and Involved Grandparents
5. People Who Take Their Health Seriously

As you'll see when you examine the sample, there are reasons why the product is "for" each of these affinity groups, so when

*As an incidental note, there is an approach to advertising copy called "Reason-Why Advertising," credited to John E. Kennedy, dating to 1904. This school of advertising focuses on presenting beneficial and persuasive reasons why a product should be purchased. The most powerful reason I've ever found is that the product is precisely and perfectly matched with you, with the individual.

the person finds his group, he learns the specific, personally relevant reason why people in that group, who are just like him, like the product. In many cases, pages like these are integrated with pages of consumer testimonials organized into the same affinity groups.

Figure 12.1 are examples from work for a private client of mine, name withheld. All the copy is copyright-protected.

In a similar brochure for a weight-loss company's program, there are eight:

1. Busy Women
2. People Who Have Tried And Been Disappointed By Other Diets
3. People Who Value Professional Advice
4. Professionals, Sales Professionals, and Executives
5. People Who Take Their Health Seriously
6. People Who Prefer Nature's Medicine To Drugs And Surgeries
7. People Who Hate To Exercise
8. People Who Want Fast Results

In a financial advisor's "Who Relies On . . .?" piece there are four. In this example, I'll give you the summary of the reason why for each*:

1. Active, Healthy, Vigorous Seniors—Why? Because men, women, and couples "on the go" have lots of good reasons to plan in advance.
2. Seniors Facing An Uncertain Diagnosis—Why? Because once a diagnosis comes from your doctor, it can be very scary.

*Courtesy of a client of Matt Zagula and mine, The Financial Dynamics and Estate & Elder Planning Center of Virginia, who owns copyright thereof. You can see more of their outstanding marketing at: www.FinancialAndEstatePlanning.com.

FIGURE 12.1: Brochure Sample—page 1

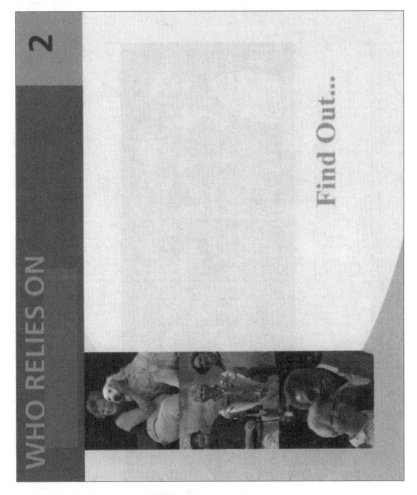

3. The Child with Power of Attorney—Why? Because being appointed with power of attorney for a sick family member is a tough place to be.
4. Single and Widowed Seniors—Why? Because many single and widowed retirees want to take care of themselves and do not want to become a burden to their families or friends if disability strikes.

FIGURE 12.1: Brochure Sample—page 2

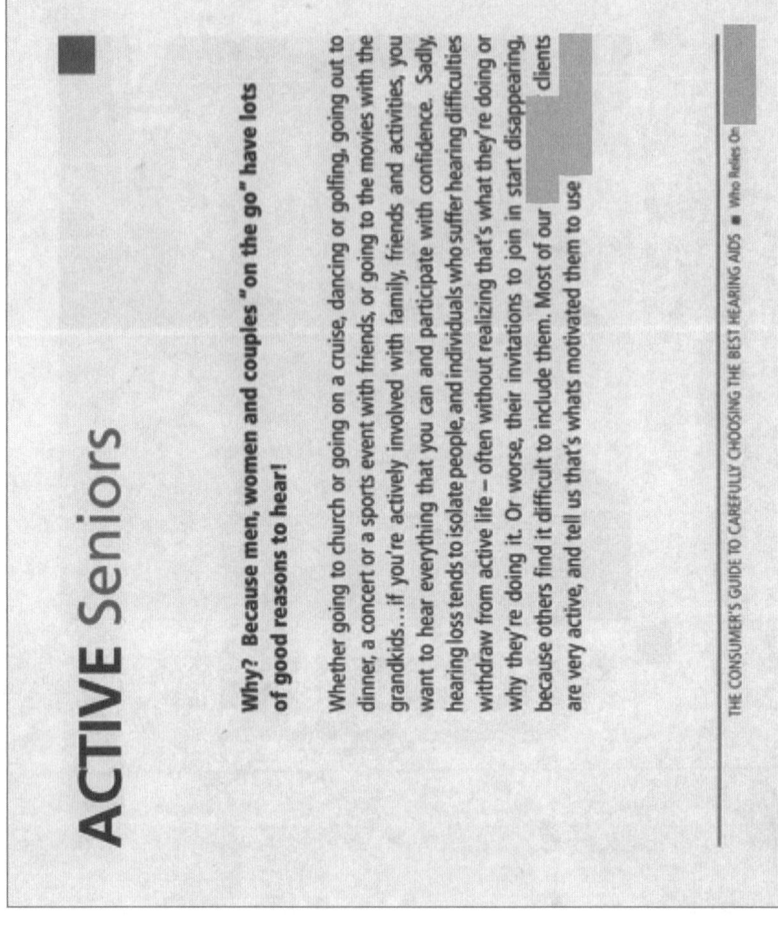

ACTIVE Seniors

Why? Because men, women and couples "on the go" have lots of good reasons to hear!

Whether going to church or going on a cruise, dancing or golfing, going out to dinner, a concert or a sports event with friends, or going to the movies with the grandkids....if you're actively involved with family, friends and activities, you want to hear everything that you can and participate with confidence. Sadly, hearing loss tends to isolate people, and individuals who suffer hearing difficulties withdraw from active life – often without realizing that's what they're doing or why they're doing it. Or worse, their invitations to join in start disappearing, because others find it difficult to include them. Most of our clients are very active, and tell us that's whats motivated them to use

THE CONSUMER'S GUIDE TO CAREFULLY CHOOSING THE BEST HEARING AIDS ■ Who Relies On

FIGURE 12.1: Brochure Sample—page 3

PEOPLE Still Working

ESPECIALLY SALESPEOPLE, OFFICE WORKERS, EVEN DOCTORS, NURSES, LAWYERS AND ACCOUNTANTS...AS WELL AS CAB DRIVERS, SCHOOL BUS DRIVERS...

***Why?* Because they NEED to hear well, in order to perform well in their jobs.** These days, 60 is the new 40, 70 the new 50, and many who rely on are choosing to continue working and want to do so with confidence, and with the respect of everyone they work with. Nobody wants to be "the old person on the job," who has to be coddled or helped! There are also studies that indicate that an employee's hearing difficulties are a 'secret' reason they lose their jobs or are asked to retire before they are ready. People in every imaginable occupation come to us, to keep them able to do their jobs, at their best!

THE CONSUMER'S GUIDE TO CAREFULLY CHOOSING THE BEST HEARING AIDS ■ Who Relies On

FIGURE 12.1: Brochure Sample—page 4

SENIORS Determined *to remain independent*

Why? **Because many families start talking about the need to get Dad or Mom into an assisted living or nursing home environment when it seems Dad or Mom is "slipping" mentally, is having memory problems, is unable to follow and participate in conversations --- and, often, these are actually *just* symptoms of hearing loss…easily improved by hearing aids!+**

Better hearing makes an individual seem "sharper"…gets you "back in the game," fully participating in conversations and activities – so we often hear from our clients or their sons and daughters: "It's as if you rolled the clock back and made Mom ten years younger!" Hearing is also an important health and safety issue related to your independence. Whether it's about continuing to drive your car or safely use public transportation, live alone in your own home or apartment, or travel alone – you'll be safer and more sure of yourself if you can clearly and correctly hear everything: public address announcements in airports, sirens approaching through traffic, and so on.

THE CONSUMER'S GUIDE TO CAREFULLY CHOOSING THE BEST HEARING AIDS ■ Who Relies On

FIGURE 12.1: Brochure Sample—page 5

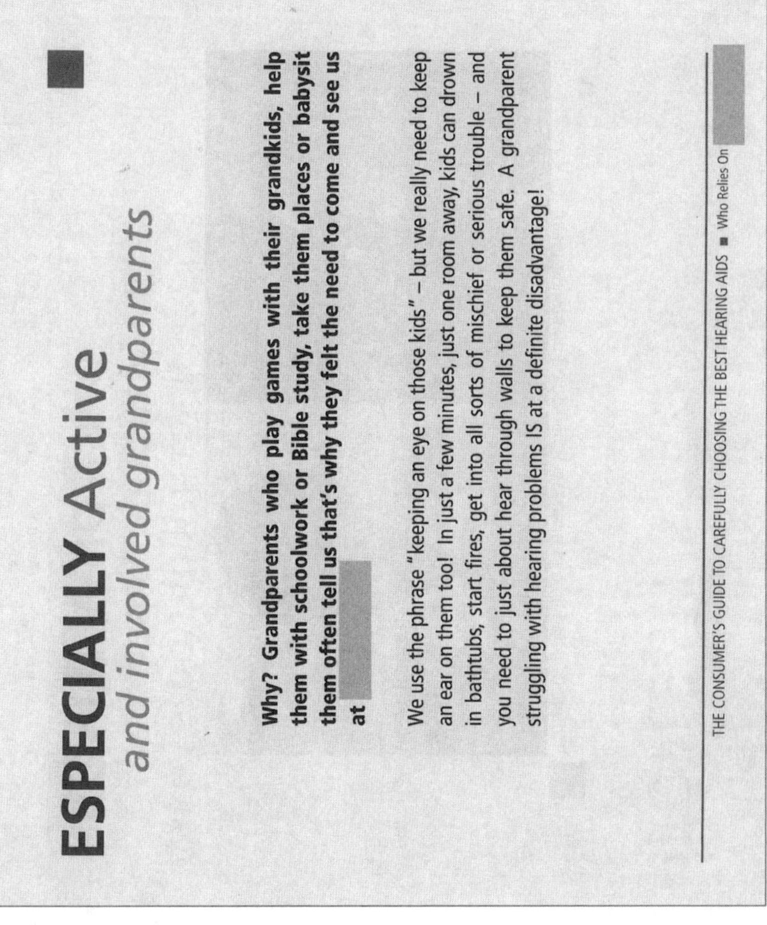

ESPECIALLY Active
and involved grandparents

Why? Grandparents who play games with their grandkids, help them with schoolwork or Bible study, take them places or babysit them often tell us that's why they felt the need to come and see us at

We use the phrase "keeping an eye on those kids" – but we really need to keep an ear on them too! In just a few minutes, just one room away, kids can drown in bathtubs, start fires, get into all sorts of mischief or serious trouble – and you need to just about hear through walls to keep them safe. A grandparent struggling with hearing problems IS at a definite disadvantage!

THE CONSUMER'S GUIDE TO CAREFULLY CHOOSING THE BEST HEARING AIDS ■ Who Relies On

FIGURE 12.1: Brochure Sample—page 6

PEOPLE Who Take
their health seriously and
take responsibility for it

Why? A lot of our clients are very "pro-active" about their health.

That means they read up on foods, vitamins, health topics, try to eat right, take vitamins – and do their best to stay out of the doctor's office and the hospital. The very same motivations to stay out of the doctor's office are the reasons they come to their local Center! They tell us they want to do everything they can to stay healthy, and they know that means staying active – and that means being able to hear everything going on around them!

THE CONSUMER'S GUIDE TO CAREFULLY CHOOSING THE BEST HEARING AIDS ■ Who Relies On

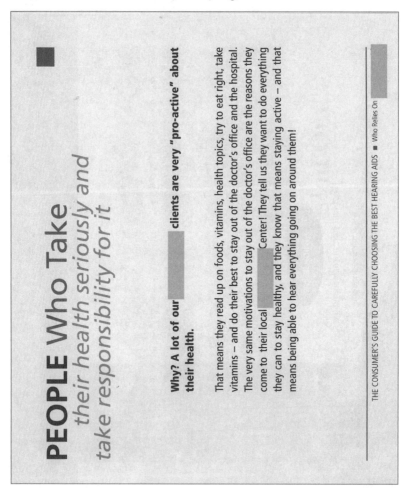

A final example comes from a long-time GKIC Member and outstanding marketer, Everte Farnell, from his "Consumer's Guide to Nuisance Wildlife Remediation," for his company, RJG Environmental. In the "Who Relies On . . ?" piece in that kit, there are:

1. Parents*
2. Homeowners

3. Landlords
4. Pet Owners
5. Retirees
6. Busy Working People
7. Grandparents
8. People Who Take Their Health Seriously

Everte is a highly-skilled direct-response copywriter, so I'll share just a small sample of the opening reason with copy from the page for the first group, parents:

> *Imagine, if you will, your child sleeping safe and sound in his/her bed. All of a sudden you hear an ear-piercing scream from the room. You jump up and run into your child's bedroom. As you flip on the light, you see your child with their hand on the side of their head, blood running through their fingers . . . .*
>
> *Sound far-fetched? I might think so too, if I hadn't gotten the call the next day from the parent this happened to . . . luckily for him and his daughter, it was a rat that bit her, not a raccoon . . . I've been in countless homes where raccoons got into the living space from the attic. And this man's attic did prove to have raccoons in it . . . raccoons carry rabies, canine distemper, encephalitis . . .* *

This is my original, proprietarily developed format, and is often included in comprehensive marketing packages I develop for clients, at fees upward from $100,000.00, plus royalties. It is rare for me to show off and explain such a tool in something like this—a book, or even in a more expensive home-study course. But this is such a powerful and universally applicable tool, I decided to be unusually generous! Matt Zagula and I

*Courtesy of a client of a mine, RJG ENVIRONMENTAL, INC., and is copyright protected by that entity.

presented an entire collection of this kind of tools in a Trust-Based Marketing Workshop that carried a $10,000.00 per person price tag. You may be able to obtain a condensed version of it in a home-study package or online course from GKIC, via www.DanKennedy.com/store, or by calling (800) 871-0147.

This same "Find Yourself Here" format does not have to be limited to a brochure. It could be used within a one-to-one, group, or online sales presentation, or adapted to displayed posters in a showroom, store, or practice's office. It could also be combined with a presentation of testimonials from actual customers, clients, or patients in the different categories.

A Remarkably Simple Tactical Example of the Power of Affinity

Many years back, I had a "standard" lead generation offer for my publishing company that I advertised in a one-third-page column ad in a number of national magazines. It offered an audiocassette tape titled "Expensive Experience" free, just $1.00 shipping and handling. That tape, in turn, sold a home-study course. One of the most productive magazines we advertised in was *Success Unlimited Magazine* (now, *Success Magazine*).

On a whim, I altered the ad ever so slightly just for that magazine, with a few lines like: "Special Offer FOR SUCCESS READERS." Response went up. That spurred me to customize the cassette itself, with some talk establishing myself as an ardent *Success* reader *just like them*, and some reasons why the program was perfectly matched with *Success* readers. Conversions jumped. This took place in the early 1980s, and the experience provided me with a tactic I've used hundreds of times since—always profitably.

The Power Formula: Affinity + Specific Reason Why

How best can someone conclude that a person, product, or service can be trusted to perform as advertised? To meet *his* needs and desires? To prove superior to other options and alternatives? To be a good value worthy of the required price or investment?

Answer: that (many) other people just like him have found it so—for specific, relevant reasons.

CHAPTER 13

Establishing and Asserting Your Authority

Dan Kennedy

My friend Joe Sugarman is a fascinating, odd, and outrageously successful marketer. He will neither confirm nor deny that he was a CIA agent. You might know of him in connection with the BluBlocker® sunglasses he brought to market and made a huge fortune from, via magazine and TV advertising, and sale on home shopping TV for many years. He made his first fortune with a company called JS&A, which, for some years, dominated multiple pages in airline magazines and was a frequent full-page advertiser, bringing new gadgets to market. JS&A was the first to sell hand-size pocket calculators direct to the public via such ads. Joe positioned his company by constant self-proclamation as "America's largest single source of space-age products." Over time, he benefited by JS&A's familiarity to readers of specific media and to its customers (see Chapter 11 regarding the familiarity trust trigger), so that there was eager interest in the next new, revolutionary product Joe would reveal. Joe inspired people like Richard Thalheimer, the founder of the now more familiar Sharper Image, as well as legions of direct-response copywriters like me, all of us romancers of stones.

Joe made sure to do one important thing in his every ad, every commercial, and every catalog. In his outstanding book *Triggers: 30 Sales Tools You Can Use to Control the Mind of Your Prospect*, he puts it this way:

> **Establishing your authority is something that should be done in *each* sales presentation—regardless of how big or little you are.**

I have personally found this critical to nearly every significant success I've ever had. In my first niche-market business, delivering marketing training to chiropractic physicians and dentists, I proclaimed my company "*the* largest practice-building publishing and training organization serving chiropractors and dentists" on day one, a truth based on the fact no one else put chiropractors and dentists in the same seminars, not based on our epic size. GKIC, the organization for marketing-oriented entrepreneurs and sales professionals you can meet on page 273, which began as my own "Inner Circle," then Glazer-Kennedy Insider's Circle, now GKIC, with members worldwide, was labeled with "*THE* Place for Prosperity"™. When I established our chief annual convention, I did not call it *a* Marketing and Moneymaking Conference; I termed it *The* Marketing and Moneymaking *SUPER*-Conference℠. How can you be bigger or grander than "super"? We operate true to title, by the way, showcasing a wildly eclectic array of celebrity-entrepreneur speakers, including Gene Simmons of KISS, Joan Rivers, Jim McCann (founder of 1-800-Flowers), Ivanka Trump, even John

Rich, the country-western superstar and winner of Donald Trump's Celebrity Apprentice competition in 2011. This is all B2B, but the same principle applies to marketing to consumers, as Joe Sugarman did all those years with such great success.

Even Presidential candidates need to establish their own unique authority with an electorate. During the time I was writing this, Mitt Romney, former governor (rejected for re-election) of Massachusetts, former (and once disgraced) Speaker of the House Newt Gingrich, and former Senator Rick Santorum (also fired by his Pennsylvania voters) were duking it out in the Republican primary. That outcome will be history when you read this, but when I was writing this, it was up in the air, and I was watching each struggle for their own unique authority: Romney as (a) the private business experienced, financially knowledgeable, stable and reliable and responsible adult, best qualified to fix America's economy and (b) the most able to beat President Obama; Gingrich as (a) the most articulate, combative fighter best able to frame and persuasively present a starkly contrasted argument for the conservative approach vs. Obama's far-left, radical ideology and (b) as an experienced leader linked to Ronald Reagan, who did successfully balance federal budgets during both Reagan and Clinton years; Santorum as (a) the only truly consistent, reliable, never flip-flopping, true-blue fiscal, foreign policy, *and* social conservative.

All faced hazards. Romney risked being seen as a Wall Street baron, called by Governor Perry a "vulture capitalist" rather than a venture capitalist; an elitist to whom too many voters can't relate or won't trust. Gingrich risked being recognized as a Washington insider at a time Congress and government have the lowest approval rankings in history, or as too combative, darkly Nixonian. Santorum risked being marginalized as too extreme, even as a bigot. Each, through debates and advertising, strove to sharpen the focus of their unique authority, so that voters could easily grasp what they were, as a "product," and to do so, they had to risk coming to a line while trying not to step over it. Unique Authority that has real impact and power is not an easy achievement!

Politicians, of course, have direct opponents—typically, confrontational and ruthless ones. By the time you read this, presumably one of these three—Romney, Gingrich or Santorum—will have become the Republican nominee, and will have been attacked exactly as I've described here, by President Obama's billion-dollar re-election campaign. Fortunately, in business, we tend to face a lot less straight-on confrontation from competitors and can usually assert the Authority Position we select without such forceful and relentless challenge.

Why and How Unique Authority May Be Your Gold Key

Unique Authority is particularly important to anyone selling in a high-trust-required setting, such as financial services professionals, health care professionals, B2B providers dealing with professional purchasing agents, executives and business owners, and service or significant-decision products marketers to homeowners. I am in the third grouping, and I have clients in all these groups who I assist with marketing. Matt Zagula is in the first grouping and primarily assists and coaches peers in his same business, but he also works with me and separately in working with professionals in other fields. What we know for fact from our combined personal success and vast experience with our clients' successes is that a distinction between those at the top of the income and success pyramid and the overwhelming majority who never get close to the peak is that the winners create and present Unique Authority.

As I write this, ordinary auto insurance is being merchandised to the masses by singing pigs, talking lizards, Lucille Ball-esque spokespersons, merrily entertaining in TV commercials, YouTube videos and mobile phone apps—but all of this is extremely uninteresting to somebody like me who requires expertly-crafted insurance for four classic cars worth over $300,000.00. Flu shots and simple diagnostic tests are sold, with increasing success, via closet-sized "clinics" tucked away in drug stores and big-box discount stores, staffed by nurse practitioners in place of doctors. But chances are, you are not the customer for this. For you, your health care is more a matter of trust than convenience or price, as it is for me. That may not preclude you grabbing a flu shot from that nurse at the local CVS, but given any serious health matter, what will you do? By some means, you will try to get to the best-qualified physician or appropriate specialist you can discover. If one already has familiarity with you, he will have profound advantage. That's why physicians like associating with familiar, trusted hospitals and medical institutions such as the Cleveland Clinic, Mayo, etc., and why niche-industry consultants, trainers, and authors seek association and affiliation with me and with GKIC, and why stand-up comics lust and fight for an HBO Special or a few minutes' appearance on Leno, Letterman, or Kimmel. Familiarity by association. People are more willing to take a chance on an evening at their local comedy club if the featured comic has HBO, Leno, etc. association. Businesspeople are more easily trusting of a business expert they have no familiarity with if he or she is connected to me or to GKIC, with which they do have familiarity—as my co-authors of books in this No B.S. series can attest to.

Unique Authority is about a complex stew of things: differentiation vs. competitive clutter and confusion, magnetic attraction for a certain target audience, positioning for certain understanding, reassurance to skittish prospects, support for premium prices or fees, and more. Sugarman's Unique Authority created for his original JS&A enterprise made it about much more than just being a merchant—it made him a finder and friend of early adopters of technology and status symbol products, a provider of fascination, and the source, ahead of all other sources, of the newest, latest, and coolest "space age" products; this led to trusting Joe and JS&A about such things.

Because we are talking about UNIQUE Authority, no one—not even Matt and I—can hand you a ready-made, easy-button one or a catalog of them, for your approval and use. It isn't anywhere near that simple. It's definitely not superficial sloganism. If others can say it too, it's not unique. If it doesn't actually establish authority, it's a waste of time.

How Authority Governs Income

There is a real, honest-to-gum, bona fide *secret* about income I teach in-depth elsewhere, that deserves abbreviated mention here: The higher up the income ladder you climb, the more you find the people there are being paid more for who they are, not for what they do. Conversely, the lower a person's income, the more likely they're being paid for their work. This factors in more than just Authority; also Celebrity, Credibility, Longevity, and other factors. There are, for example, big-name "celebrity" CEOs doing exactly the same work as a little-celebrated CEO, the first getting a gigantic up-front signing bonus to take the job, huge pay, stock options, and a golden parachute; the second earning a small fraction of all that compensation. The same goes for head coaches in professional sports.

Because Authority is such a powerful trust trigger, the more of it you establish and assert, the more you are likely to earn in premium income over and above par in your field. Assume, for example, that there are two M.D.s in Columbus, Ohio who own pain management clinics, where exactly the same treatments are delivered, at both by nurse practitioners under the supervision of these M.D.s. Further assume both M.D.s went to the same medical school, interned at the same hospital, have identical levels of experience and expertise. And make them functional equivalents in any and every other way you can think of but one: the first doctor (a) has written *The Complete Guide to Pain-Free Living,* (b) is affiliated with the Cleveland Clinic, (c) has had his own PBS TV special on pain management aired in the local market and nationally, (d) is a regular contributor to both medical journals and consumer publications, and (e) is the pain management specialist for Ohio State's sports teams. The second doctor keeps to himself and labors in oblivion. The first has created and established authority and actively asserts and promotes it. The second has just gone to his clinic every day and practiced his clinical craft. Which doctor is more able to attract more patients? Which doctor will more patients more easily trust? Which doctor can charge higher fees? If you did not answer "the first doctor" to all three questions, you grossly underestimate the actual marketplace value of manufactured and asserted Authority, and you do not yet understand the secret of income.

For more on this, please read my books *No B.S. Guide to Marketing to the Affluent*, pages 327–330 and *No B.S. Wealth Attraction in The New Economy*, pages 69–75, and *No B.S. Sales Success in The New Economy*, pages 123–135. Oh, and by the way, the more affluent one's clientele, the more beneficial established and asserted Authority can be.

Tactical Advice

In Chapter 5, "How Not to Be Another Salesman," I made the point that there are symbols and clues that telegraph that someone is a salesman. There are ways that consumers can quickly identify a salesman. I then suggested erasing all those things from your appearance, approach, tool kit, and behavior. With regard to Authority, an identical situation exists. There are symbols and clues that telegraph someone is an Authority. There are ways that consumers can quickly identify an Authority. You should think about what those are generically, and what they might be specifically in your field, then do everything you can to make those things part of your appearance, approach, tool kit, and behavior.

How Joe Sugarman Established Authority for BluBlockers®

In this chapter from the book *Advertising Secrets of the Written Word* reprinted on pages 169–171, Joe Sugarman describes how he established Authority for a new brand of sunglasses, and made this product a huge success. The ad that launched this product first appeared in 1986. The product has had a life of more than 24 years, in continuous print advertising, catalogs, TV infomercials, TV home shopping channel advertising, and online advertising.

There are four different keys to Authority that Joe Sugarman employed in this ad:

1. Choosing NOT to present the product as merely another alternative—instead, as something entirely different
2. Including an educational message—the kind that comes from an Authority
3. Scientific explanation for product superiority

4. Proprietary terminology—in this case, a made-up, trademarked name for a "unique" kind of lens. One of the many important things Matt Zagula has done for the financial advisors he and I have coached is to help each one develop proprietary terminology for their advisory process and for the financial products they represent. This not only aids Authority, but also avoids the Google slap Matt describes in Chapter 10.

In addition, Joe's ad relies heavily on "Risk Reversal" (see Chapter 20), as well as on a drama-infused personal story. The use of his own story of curiosity, skepticism, discovery, and conviction is an important trust-based marketing strategy.

These four keys are certainly not the only keys to Authority, but they are four very good ones, and can be applied to product, service, or persons.

FIGURE 13.1: Joe Sugarman Ad

Vision Break-through

When I put on the pair of glasses what I saw I could not believe. Nor will you.

They look like sunglasses.

By Joseph Sugarman

I am about to tell you a true story. If you believe me, you will be well rewarded. If you don't believe me, I will make it worth your while to change your mind. Let me explain.

Len is a friend of mine who has an eye for good products. One day he called excited about a pair of sunglasses he owned. "It's so incredible," he said, "when you first look through a pair, you won't believe it."

"What will I see?" I asked. "What could be so incredible?"

Len continued, "When you put on these glasses, your vision improves. Objects appear sharper, more defined. Everything takes on an enhanced 3-D effect. And it's not my imagination. I just want you to see for yourself."

When I received the sunglasses and put them on I couldn't believe my eyes. I kept taking them off and putting them on to see if indeed what I was seeing through the glasses was indeed actually sharper or if my imagination was playing tricks on me. But my vision improved. It was obvious. I kept putting on my cherished $100 pair of high-tech sunglasses and comparing them. They didn't compare. I was very impressed. Everything appeared sharper, more defined and indeed had a greater three dimensional look to it. But what did this product do that made my vision so much better? I found out.

DEPRESSING COLOR

The Perception sunglasses (called BluBlockers) filter out the ultraviolet and blue spectrum light waves from the sun. You've often heard the color blue used for expressions of bad moods such as "blue Monday" or "I have the blues." Apparently, the color blue, for centuries, has been considered a rather depressing color.

For eyesight, blue is not a good color too. There are several reasons. First, the blue rays have one of the shortest wavelength in the visible spectrum (red is the longest). As a result, the color blue will focus slightly in front of the retina which is the "focussing screen" onto which light waves fall in your eye. By eliminating the blue from the sunglasses through a special filtration process, and only letting those rays through that indeed focus clearly on the retina, objects appear to be sharper and clearer.

The second reason is even more impressive. It is not good to have ultraviolet rays fall on our eyes. Recognized as bad for skin, uv light is worse for eyes and is believed to play a role in many of today's eye diseases. In addition, people with contact lenses are at greater risk because contacts tend to magnify the light at their edges thus increasing the sun's harmful effects.

Finally, by eliminating the blue and uv light during the day, your night vision improves. The purple pigment in your eye called Rhodopsin is affected by blue light and the eyes take hours to recover from the effects.

SUNGLASS DANGER

But what really surprised me was the danger in conventional sunglasses. Our pupils close in bright light to limit the light entering the eye and open wider at night—just like the aperture in an automatic camera. So when we put on sunglasses, although we reduce the amount of light that enters our eyes, our pupils open wider and we are actually allowing more of the blue and ultraviolet portions of the light spectrum into our eyes.

BluBlockers sunglasses are darker at the top to shield out overhead light. The lens used is the CR-39 which most eye doctors will tell you is one of the finest materials you can use for glasses and is manufactured under license.

The frames are some of the most comfortable I have ever worn. The moulded nose rest will fit any nose. The hinge causes the frames to rest comfortably on your face and can be adjusted for almost any size face.

We also have a clip-on pair that weighs less than one ounce. Both come with a padded carrying case and an anti-scratch coating.

I urge you to order a pair and experience the improved vision. Then take your old sunglasses and compare them to the BluBlockers. See how much clearer and sharper objects appear with BluBlockers. And see if your night vision doesn't improve as a direct result. If you don't see a dramatic difference in your vision—one so noticeable that you can tell immediately, then send them back anytime within 30 days and I will send you a prompt and courteous refund.

DRAMATIC DIFFERENCE

But from what I've personally witnessed, once you use a pair, there will be no way you'll want to return it.

Astronomers from many famous universities wear BluBlockers to improve their night vision. Pilots, golfers, skiers, athletes—anyone who spends a great deal of time in the sun have found the BluBlockers indispensable.

Our eyes are very important to us. Protect them and at the same time improve your vision with the most incredible breakthrough in sun glasses since they were first introduced. Order a pair or two at no obligation, today.

To order, credit card holders call toll free and ask for product by number shown below or send a check plus $4 for delivery.

BluBlockers (0020CA 4.00)...$59.95
Clip-On Model (0022CA 4.00)..34.95

BluBlockers is a trademark of JS&A Group, Inc.

One JS&A Plaza, Northbrook, IL 60062
CALL TOLL FREE 800 228-5000

FIGURE 13.2: Joe Sugarman Chapter Excerpt

Chapter 33 Vision Breakthrough

This single ad started an entire business that eventually created a brand name.

The Vision Breakthrough advertisement was among the most successful in my company's history, so it merits a close look.

In this ad I did not want to present the product as another pair of sunglasses, so I presented it as a vision breakthrough that protects you from the harmful rays of the sun. It was one of the first ads that provided a real educational message about the dangers of UV rays on the eyes. Before this ad ran, there was really nothing in the popular press about UV ray damage.

The approach I used was to tell the story of how I discovered the glasses and all the facts I learned about them as well as the sun's light. I did it in a simple yet powerful way.

I also used a tremendous dose of curiosity. You can't experience the pair unless you personally try them on. Thus, you must buy them to satisfy your curiosity.

The BluBlocker advertising campaign was a major success that started with this print ad in 1986 and continued on television for several years. Today BluBlocker is a recognized brand name that is sold in retail stores throughout the country.

Headline: Vision Breakthrough

Subheadline: When I put on the pair of glasses what I saw I could not believe. Nor will you.

Caption: They look like sunglasses.

Byline: By Joseph Sugarman

Copy: I am about to tell you a true story. If you believe me, you will be well rewarded. If you don't believe me, I will make it worth your while to change your mind. Let me explain.

Len is a friend of mine who knows good products. One day he called excited about a pair of sunglasses he owned. "It's so incredible," he said, "when you first look through a pair, you won't believe it."

FIGURE 13.2: Joe Sugarman Chapter Excerpt, *continued*

"What will I see?" I asked. "What could be so incredible?"

Len continued, "When you put on these glasses, your vision improves. Objects appear sharper, more defined. Everything takes on an enhanced 3-D effect. And it's not my imagination. I just want you to see for yourself."

COULDN'T BELIEVE EYES

When I received the sunglasses and put them on I couldn't believe my eyes. I kept taking them off and putting them on to see if what I was seeing was indeed actually sharper or if my imagination was playing tricks on me. But my vision improved. It was obvious. I kept putting on my $100 pair of sunglasses and comparing them. They didn't compare. I was very impressed. Everything appeared sharper, more defined and indeed had a greater three dimensional look to it. But what did this product do that made my vision so much better? I found out.

The sunglasses (called BluBlockers) filter out the ultraviolet and blue spectrum light waves from the sun. Blue rays have one of the shortest wavelengths in the visible spectrum (red is the longest). As a result, the color blue will focus slightly in front of the retina which is the "focusing screen" in our eye. By blocking the blue from the sunlight through a special filtration process and only letting those rays through that indeed focus clearly on the retina, objects appear to be sharper and clearer.

The second reason is even more impressive. It is harmful to have ultraviolet rays fall on our eyes. Recognized as bad for skin, UV light is worse for eyes and is believed to play a role in many of today's eye diseases.

SUNGLASS DANGER

But what really surprised me was the danger in conventional sunglasses. Our pupils close in bright light to limit the light entering the eye and open wider at night like the lens of an automatic camera. So when we put on sunglasses, although we reduce the amount of light that enters our eyes, our pupils open wider and we allow more of the harmful blue and ultraviolet light into our eyes.

DON'T BE CONFUSED

I'm often asked by people who read this, "Do those BluBlockers really work?" They really do and please give me the opportunity to prove it. I guarantee each pair of BluBlockers to perform exactly as I described.

BluBlocker sunglasses use Malenium™ lenses with a hard anti-scratch coating. No shortcuts were taken.

The black, lightweight frame is one of the most comfortable I have ever worn and will comfortably contour to any size face. It compares with many of the $200 pairs you can buy from France or Italy.

FIGURE 13.2: Joe Sugarman Chapter Excerpt, continued

There is a clip-on pair that weighs less than one ounce and fits over prescription lenses. All models include a padded carrying case and a one-year limited warranty.

I urge you to order a pair and experience your improved vision. Then take your old sunglasses and compare them to the BluBlocker sunglasses. See how much clearer and sharper objects appear with the BluBlocker pair. And see if your night vision doesn't improve as a direct result. If you don't see a dramatic difference in your vision—one so noticeable that you can tell immediately—then send them back anytime within 30 days and I will send you a prompt and courteous refund.

DRAMATIC DIFFERENCE

But from what I've personally witnessed, once you wear a pair, there will be no way you'll want to return it.

Our eyes are very important to us. Protect them and at the same time improve your vision with the most incredible breakthrough in sunglasses since they were first introduced. Order a pair or two at no obligation, today.

Credit card holders call toll free and order by product number below or send a check plus $3 for postage and handling.

BluBlocker Sunglasses (1020CD) . . . $59.95
Clip-On Model (1028CD) 59.95

The main feature of this ad is the storytelling approach which wove an educational message—the first of its kind. It brought the awareness of the dangers of sunlight to the attention of the public who were unaware of these dangers.

In addition, it launched the BluBlocker brand name and created a new business which continues to this day. It is a perfect example of the power of the pen—the same power you will have upon completion of this book and with enough practice.

CHAPTER 14

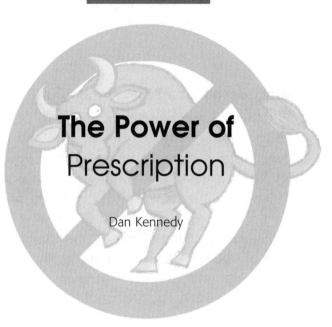

The Power of Prescription

Dan Kennedy

This is a very important chapter. In it, I will reveal a pathway to stress-less selling in a zero resistance zone of your own making—sort of a zero gravity environment for making money. If you are more concerned with marketing than with personal selling, the same breakthrough principles apply.

Imagine having your advice, ideas, information, recommendations, products, services, and prices or fees easily accepted, with little question and no resistance! If that's not your experience, you should know that it *is* the way many "merchants" live.

A person's doctor tells him that his heart trouble is worsening, he needs to see a specialist, and will likely need surgery to implant a pacemaker. His doctor refers him to a cardiologist. He returns home, and the next day calls and makes an appointment with that cardiologist to whom he was referred. When, two weeks later, he gets in to see the cardiologist, surgery and implant of the device is the now unsurprising prescription, and he agrees to it with only a few questions.

Why Doesn't Your Selling Work Like This?

There are, obviously, many factors in play here. There is the established trust relationship with the primary physician and the established habit of obtaining advice and prescriptions from that doctor. There is the fact that a third party—the insurance company—is paying most of these bills, so there's no thought given to the reasonableness of fees and costs or comparison of them with other vendors. There is the worry about the worsening heart condition. And there is the implicit authority of the cardiologist. It would be smart to transfer as many of those factors to your own selling situation as possible. But the biggest overarching factor is that the proposition isn't being *sold* at all; it is being *prescribed*.

Most business owners, marketers, and sales professionals present and sell propositions. Consequently, they are always selling against resistance—because prospects in selling situations *feel compelled* to resist. Even keenly interested, financially capable prospects who have set out on a mission to purchase something specific for which they must deal with a salesman, like a car, home furnishings, a computer—still tend to put up some resistance when the salesman steps in. They are also, often, selling in a competitive environment, thus having to compare and contrast with others, justify and often negotiate price, win some and lose some. They are also often selling against procrastination and delay. Contrast that with the fact that over 70% of all doctor-issued drug prescriptions are filled, i.e. purchased at the pharmacy immediately, on the way home from the doctor's office. In short, selling a proposition for a product or service is selling *against*.

In the above scenario, despite presenting something scary and unwanted (like having your chest cut open for dangerous heart surgery), there's virtually no resistance.

How Matt Zagula and I Position to Prescribe

In Matt's financial advisory practice, he replaces the selling of propositions with prescription as best he can. This starts with source, so as many of his prospective new clients as possible are obtained as referrals from existent clients or referrals from other professionals he has cooperative relationships with, such as estate planning attorneys. In his direct marketing, he "wraps himself" in trusted news media, like the newspaper, the local FOX TV affiliate, and popular hosts' radio programs. He uses mailing lists of trust-based marketers' followers—such as financial newsletter author's subscriber lists—and, with his books and other media establishes authority with the prospects in advance of any meeting or discussion. He attempts to *prepare* the prospective client to accept him as a "financial doctor." Many of these prospects attend Matt's "Evening with the Authors" or workshops, and get to know him as an expert, in a choreographed setting that creates authority. All of this *prefaces* the one-to-one meeting, then structured as diagnosis and prescription. What is being sold here is: first, the person—not the products or proposition, and trust in that person—not in the companies or products he represents; second, the prescriptive plan—not a basket of financial products. The prescriptive plan *is*, of course, a basket of financial products, but they aren't being sold anymore than the cardiac surgeon sells the anesthesia, the anesthesiologist, the hospital, or the brand of surgical instruments being used.

Note the above italicized words: *prepare. Preface.* I teach hard-core closing techniques to salespeople and I do know how to close a sale. In fact, I can get a check out of a rock. But it is far better, for a whole host of reasons, to erase the need for brute force to overcome resistance in advance. This requires careful, thorough preparation of prospects in advance of your selling. This requires preface to the act of selling.

In my professional practice, I provide strategic marketing advice coupled with the actual copywriting and development of advertisements, direct-mail campaigns, radio or TV commercials and infomercials, online media and sales tools. My projects are complex, typically require fees upward from $100,000.00 to $250,000.00 plus royalties tied to results, and the majority of my clients are entrepreneurs building small to mid-sized businesses—not giant corporations with unlimited funds, and not executives spending other peoples' money. Unlike most freelance copywriters or ad agencies, I neither overtly advertise or directly market myself to a cold market, nor do I ever do free pitch meetings. Instead I've painstakingly created a feeder system, where businesspeople get to know and trust me through subscribing to and reading my newsletters, attending my seminars, listening to my recordings, reading my books, so that by the time they step forward and ask if I can and will personally assist them, they are looking for *my* diagnosis and prescription. Even when a client brings forward a referral, I rarely agree to talk or meet with them unless and until they have prepared themselves by reading, listening, and familiarizing themselves with my work—and when I violate that, I always regret it. Finally, as I said, there is no "free lunch." All possible relationships begin with the client buying an initial consulting day (as of this writing, a fee of $18,800.00), and traveling to one of my home cities to spend that day with me, with it framed in advance as a day of diagnosis and prescription. I do not care if they are inconvenienced or grumpy about trekking to me. If that's a problem, I know there will be other problems, so better we never start.

Keep in mind, Matt is a consumer marketer, dealing with Bob and Harriet Boomer, and their personal life's savings. I am a B2B marketer, dealing with the owners of businesses, entrepreneurs growing mid-sized companies, and occasionally the CEOs of much larger firms—up to billions in yearly revenues. It doesn't matter if you are B2C or B2B.

If you go back to the heart patient analogy, assume now, instead of merely accepting his family doctor's referral, he is a more discerning patient, and an affluent patient, and he makes calls to trusted friends and peers, he retains a medical investigator, and he determines who *the* best and most trusted cardiologist in America is. He then works his network of contacts to find somebody who can connect him with somebody to get in to see that doctor, a most difficult task. And he travels across country to see that doctor. Or if you wish a more marketing-oriented version, assume he sees a top-rated cardiologist who has written a book interviewed on a news or talk show and is impressed, obtains that doctor's book and reads it, and decides to get in to see that doctor, come hell or high water. When he gets to this difficult to-get-to-doctor (or seemingly difficult to get to), and he gets his diagnosis done and his prescription delivered, will he then question cost, ask to delay while he comparison shops, resist in any way?

If You Want to Argue That *Your* Business Is Different . . .

All this sounds nifty, you think, but you are quick with some reason it can't work for your business. Yours is more mundane. Or hotly competitive. Or must be mass advertised. Or, for some reason, simply cannot be re-crafted into a process like this. Your conviction is that you must remain in the business of selling, not diagnosing and prescribing, and certainly not having your prescriptions accepted without resistance. That is your choice to make, and given that you have paid less than a foursome's tab at Starbucks for this little book, I'm not going to exert a ton of effort fighting your resistance. I will tell you just a few short stories, though.

The Million-Dollar Dog's Home Away from Home

My wife and I own a Schnoodle dog, which I call "The Million-Dollar Dog," because she is spoiled like a diva heiress. When we needed to board her to travel, there was no way any ordinary kennel would do. We located an upscale doggie hotel near our Ohio home, I believe initially by searching advertisements in this service category. When she called to get information, Carla was politely informed that no new clients were accepted without first having a full informational tour of the facility, and that such tours were conducted only once a day, at 4:00 P.M. Just stop there for a minute. This is, basically, a dog kennel. In a suburb of Cleveland, Ohio, not Beverly Hills or The Hamptons. And they are *dictating* to prospective customers how they may become customers, and the one and only time during the day they may come in. *A dog kennel.* Later, the dog was required to audition and get a psych exam, to determine if participation in group play dates was appropriate. In The Million-Dollar Dog's case, it was not. She is too territorial and aggressive, traits I imagine she picked up from me. Thus, individual playtimes several times per day were part of the prescribed stay plan, at extra fees, naturally. There's more. I won't belabor. Should you wish to see this, visit www.thebarkleypethotel.com.

In Truth, He's Just a Real Estate Salesman, Isn't He?

Story #2. Darin Garman sells heartland-of-America real estate investments, mostly apartment buildings and commercial properties or partnership pieces thereof, mostly in Cedar Rapids, Iowa, to investors, including many first-time real estate investors, from all across the country and even overseas. Over 80% invest without ever meeting him in person, ever visiting Cedar Rapids. They decide and sign documents at a distance, send their tens or hundreds of thousands of dollars by FedEx or wire transfer. Many new investors are now referrals from clients but still, about half originate from his online and offline advertising, so he starts at zero trust and must get to high trust. He has developed his own media platform and feeder system somewhat modeled after mine. He requires investors to pay membership fees just to be permitted to be his client, somewhat akin to concierge medical practices. He has a well-defined intake process for new clients they must conform to, much like The Barkley Pet Hotel does. For most investors, he is providing these investment opportunities within the context of financial security, retirement, income for life, and tax management planning; thus he is engaged in the diagnostic and prescriptive process, somewhat like Matt is. Place helps him creating trust and he develops trust by Personality and Process. You can see this at www.commercial-investments.com.

The Story of the Now-Famous "Carpet Audit"

Last story. Joe Polish was once, long ago, a dead-broke and struggling carpet cleaner, surviving job to job, selling at the cheapest prices to get those jobs. Joe turned his carpet cleaning business around, then went on to become a "marketing guru" to that industry—and, over years, has installed his advertising, marketing, and sales methods and tools in thousands of carpet-cleaning businesses in every city, burg, nook, and cranny in America and more than a dozen foreign countries. Quite a few carpet cleaning business operators pay $10,000.00 to $30,000.00 a year to be in groups coached by Joe and his elite team. Joe has gone far beyond that industry and, in recent years, become a strategic coach and "idea man" for a wide variety of entrepreneurs and celebrities. One of the tactics that began this ascension, back in his original carpet cleaning business, was what we termed a "carpet audit." This is the diagnostic process performed in the home by the expert technician, to determine exactly what is needed in each place, at each spot, to restore the carpet to like-new appearance and condition. The technician even plants little, different-colored flags on the carpet, then walks the homeowner from flag to flag, explaining the varying nature and severity of the soiling or stain at that spot and what must be done to eradicate it. Ultimately, of course, a whole house carpet cleaning, restoration, and on-going maintenance prescription is issued.

It has been a lot of years now, but I believe I suggested the language—*carpet audit*—to Joe. I can tell you definitively where I got the idea. One of my very first clients ever was a company called Brookside Laboratories. Their customers were family-owned farms throughout the agricultural belt in Ohio and neighboring states. The service they sold was scientific soil analysis. Their tech collected soil samples from many, varied spots all over the client's farm. The lab analyzed these collected samples. After diagnosis, the lab presented the farmer with a color-coded map of his fields, prescribing different mixes of seed, fertilizer, nutrients, and other supplements that would maximize the yield of the crop planted there. Every farmer is a small business owner. The farmer is eminently familiar with taxes, his accountant, and the IRS—he knows the term "audit." For Brookside, I coined the term "soil fertility audit." Years later, when Joe and I were scheming to make the process of selling carpet cleaning in a different and more sophisticated way, to escape the tyranny of competitively advertised, how-low-can-you-go pricing, we landed on diagnosis and prescription, I suggested the audit, and I believe he imagined the colored flags.

In any case, with foggy memory, what the heck, I'll claim the credit! And I have been very helpful to Joe and his businesses. At one point, a few years ago, out of the blue, he gifted me a brand new automobile as a thank-you note. (I'm sorry to say not everybody I've helped get rich or much richer has such undying gratitude.)

You can learn more about Joe if you like at www.joepolish.com.

Now, consider the heroes of these stories. The operator of *a dog boarding kennel* near Cleveland, Ohio. A *real estate salesman* in Iowa. The operator of a *carpet-cleaning business* in Phoenix, Arizona: All found ways to switch from a sales model to a diagnosis and prescription model. If they can, and you insist you can't, the obstacle isn't the nature of your business. It's the nature of your thinking.

What Place Do You Want, in Your Prospect's Mind?

Finally, let's loop back to the matter of trust. In Chapter 5, I said that the last thing in the world you want to be identified as is a salesman. I'll broaden that, to somebody engaged in a sales scenario, in the selling of propositions, products, and services. If that's what you are understood to be and to be doing, you automatically, unavoidably place yourself in a low-trust position. You then must fight to overcome that handicap. You can. You can certainly make a good living waging that fight day in, day out, with cleverness and iron-will persistence and dogged effort. But if you will get yourself identified as a "doctor" engaged in diagnosis and prescription, your need for the iron will to wage the endless war against resistance is minimized, because you automatically ascend to a high-trust position.

CHAPTER 15

It's Not What You Say, It's What They Hear

Dan Kennedy

In a Presidential debate, Michael Dukakis destroyed his candidacy with a reasoned, reasonable answer to a "gotcha!" question. When he was asked whether he would stick to his opposition of the death penalty for someone who raped and killed his own wife, he answered:

> *I think you know that I've opposed the death penalty my entire life. I don't see any evidence that it's a deterrent, and I think there are better ways to deal with violent crime.*

In the book *Sold on Language: How Advertisers Talk to You & What This Says About You*, the authors quoted Dave Westen, a communications consultant to politicians' analysis of Dukakis' response: "What the average listener heard was his answer to three very different questions—*Are you a man? Do you have a heart?* and *Are we similar enough* **that I could trust you** *as president to represent my values?* For most Americans, the answer to all three questions was no."

Important tip: it's very useful to determine what are the most important questions about you in the quiet minds of your prospects. These may never be voiced. But they form the prism through which everything you say passes, to be heard.

Dukakis gave a logical policy answer to a personal question. He also misunderstood the American electorate and how we function—for the most part, trying to determine if we can *trust* the candidate far more than whether we agree with him on everything. Reagan famously moved not just independents but Democrats, called "Reagan Democrats," into his corner. Union workers supported him in significant numbers, despite their union leadership's directives not to. These people acknowledged, in surveys, polls, and exit polls, that they disagreed with him on a number of matters, but *felt* they could trust him to do the right thing. In other words, they believed *in him* even if they did not believe in some of his ideas or policies.

As an aside, you may recall the Reagan-Mondale debate, in which Reagan was challenged about his advanced age. He could have given a Dukakis-like answer about the age of other great leaders, the fact that medical science has made 80 the new 60, about his own health. Instead he responded that he was not going to make Mondale's youth and relative inexperience an issue. Even Mondale laughed. And that was that.

In selling, most salespeople strive to give the right answer to every question and objection raised by a prospect, often laden with facts and evidentiary information. This seems like the correct thing to do, but what the prospect hears and is hoping to hear is often different from what is said. There is the famous story of billionaire industrialist Andrew Carnegie's mother going to a store to buy a heater, and after getting pitched by the salesman, raising a question, still, about the heater's power—after all, she lived in a drafty castle, with stone walls and high ceilings. The earnest salesman launched into a detailed technical explanation of BTUs and heating cores and radiant heat technology and what-not until she finally interrupted him, saying, piqued, "I just want to know if it will keep this little old lady warm." She had been looking for reassurance. He gave her facts. What she heard may have been: *He's talking down to me—he thinks I'm an old fool.* Or: *He doesn't understand me or my concerns.* Or: *He's a smart ass, showing off.* What she didn't hear was empathy, concern, and reassurance, which might, by the way, best have been accomplished by the salesman telling a story rather than giving a technical lecture. It is, I suppose, hackneyed, but one of the great sales trainers of old, my friend Cavett Robert, was famous for his admonition that, "They don't care how much you know, until they know how much you care."

Being Heard as You Want to Be Heard, When Speaking from a Distance Away

In a great many cases, as a copywriter, I am creating advertising or marketing materials that must make a sale from a distance, with no opportunity for give and take between the buyer and a salesman. I know in every such instance that my reader, listener, or viewer arrives at the point of being *almost* persuaded. At that point, I have succeeded in getting him interested in the offer and in gaining acceptance for personal, relevant benefit, and ideally, urgency. But. He has lingering trust concerns. If, for example, it's a fitness machine being sold, he may not trust the stranger who has arrived in his mailbox, he may not trust an important claim that 20 minutes a day with this gadget is the same as 2 hours at the gym; he may not trust himself to use the exercise gadget being sold if he gets it; he may not trust the guarantee and fear a major hassle getting a refund. I have to figure out what these trust concerns will be, do all I can in the main sales copy to pre-empt them, and at an appropriate point introduce them and apply reassurance balm to them, in a way that is heard as reassurance. This is not an easy thing to do, but it is a vitally important thing to do.

As I'm finishing this chapter, I'm also engaged in a copywriting assignment for a long sales letter for a tech services company, a B2B marketer, seeking dentists, chiropractors, veterinarians, and other professionals as clients for their management of Google Places, Google's localized search directories—basically, an online replacement for the Yellow Pages. The company *guarantees* keeping the client in first-page position in his category in a Google Places search in his area, and does everything from building the content, maintaining the listing, soliciting patient reviews, to daily monitoring. This can be made a very attractive proposition for these professionals. It requires no work or learning curve on their part or their staffs, costs less than a modest-sized Yellow Pages ad, is necessary defensively to avoid competitors' market dominance, and—given the professionals' transaction sizes, even if minimally productive—it promises return on invested dollars of 10 to 1 or better, and the actual prominent placement is guaranteed. So, a persuasive presentation is no problem. However, I understand that only half of this is selling the Google Places service. More so, I am selling trust, and trust in a stranger at a distance no less. There are many trust hurdles on the list I made for myself, before beginning the writing work. But the chief one is big and broad. At a point of almost persuaded, the doctor will say to himself: *You know, I've invested in a lot of online advertising in the past—in websites, YouTube videos, Facebook—and I've been very disappointed by those results. So, this sounds good, but, really, why will it be any different?* And if I answer that with a re-arranged regurgitation of facts and figures about online search, technical information about how this company's algorithms work, or even by leaning on the guarantee, what he will hear won't be what he wants to hear. He'll hear a salesman talking as salesmen usually do, about features and benefits and facts and warranties. What he wants is reassurance that *this* stove will keep *this* little old lady warm.

If you'd like to see the copy I wrote about this, it's on page 190 —in rough draft form, as the work was just beginning, not ended, when this book's manuscript had to move to the publisher. This copy likely got further massaged, tweaked, and polished. But it gives you the idea of how I have focused on selling reassurance and trust. Keep in mind, this is a B2B selling situation, but I have still made the copy personal, from the seller's CEO to the buyer, in first person. And I have made it about a personal experience. Examine it carefully and thoroughly. You will see that I have bravely raised and acknowledged the distrust. I have worked at establishing empathy, seller for buyer. Shared indignation at disappointment, at over-promising and under-delivering, and an understanding of the emotional letdown and even shame that comes from "being had." I have used a story—this one from the seller's childhood. I have given personal reassurance. *Then*, I have supported it with facts of differentiation.

I think you'll agree, this doesn't sound like the way most salespeople sound, particularly B2B salespeople. That's deliberate and important. When confronted with questions, objections, or hesitation, salespeople revert to regurgitating pieces of the presentation they already gave, more forcefully. In effect, pedaling their bike harder and more furiously. They are heard as: *He doesn't care about me*. This

...pedaling your bike harder and more furiously in the wrong direction only gets you to the dead-end faster.

copy, which could just as easily be verbalized as delivered in print, does not sell the service more forcefully. What it doesn't do is as important as what it does do. What it does is establish a personal, emotional reason to trust that the seller is committed to delivering what's promised. What I'm selling is trust.

Incidentally, the copywriting for this entire project billed at a fee of $150,000.00. You're seeing some pricey work here! Knowing when not to sell the product and when to sell trust is one of the reasons I get the big bucks. If you are keenly interested in this sort of thing, I have a monthly program called "Look Over My Shoulder," which lets you see a lot of my copywriting work for various clients, in different stages of development, with in-depth analysis of the psychology behind it. You can obtain it either as part of a monthly program, with another copywriting resource, *Copy Confidential,* from GKIC at DanKennedy.com/store, or separately from its publisher, PeteThePrinter.com. Yes, that was a crass commercial message. One other: Inquiries about hiring me as a copywriter and marketing strategist can be directed to my assistant Vicky, via fax: (602) 269-3113.

By the way, Dukakis' answer should have been:

> *You've asked a clever "gotcha!" question. A brutally unfair question. But I'll answer it. If someone raped and murdered my wife, I would want to hunt him to the ends of the earth and kill the bastard myself with my bare hands or a tire iron or an axe. If he was arrested, I would want him found guilty the next day, and killed the following day, and I would want to be there to watch him die. But as President, I certainly can't give in to and make my personal desires public policy.* I think you *know that I've opposed the death penalty my entire life. I don't see any evidence that it's a deterrent, and I think there are better ways to deal with violent crime. And I don't believe government should be in the revenge business. The Lord said,*

vengeance is mine. And as much as people might identify with or admire Clint Eastwood's fictional character Dirty Harry *from the movies, I think they want someone more responsible and restrained in the White House. After all, that person has a button that can impose the death penalty on the entire globe. You have to be certain that the man with his finger on that button will NEVER do so out of anger and rage and vengeance—or fear—even if you, frankly, think you might let yourself be ruled by your emotions.*

This would have allowed people to hear: *This guy's tough. Honest. He feels just like I would feel. But he's also consistent. Sensible. I can trust him. Let's move on.* This would have allowed people who vehemently oppose the death penalty to continue feeling Dukakis was with them. It would also have allowed some people who strongly support the death penalty to be willing to vote for him despite disagreement on that one issue, because they felt he exhibited virtues and values they admire; because he came across as a leader they could trust.

It's what they hear that matters.

SAMPLE ROUGH DRAFT

The Story of the Cardboard Submarine: Why and How You Can KNOW That, This Time, You Will NOT Be Disappointed

Doctor, at this point, you probably agree I have made a fine case for your use of Google Places and for my company to handle it all for you. But. You may be thinking, *you know, this sounds great, but I've been disappointed before. I've spent time and money on elaborate websites, on YouTube, on Facebook, I've been to social media seminars, I've paid for social media marketing, and when it's all said and done, I just haven't seen the new patient that I had hoped for and been promised.*

Like you, I really don't want any more disappointment in my life. In 1968, I answered an ad from a comic book for a backyard submarine. It's the first thing I can remember ever getting money from my parents for, and sending away for. I believed a submarine that would take me and my buddies on grand adventures would soon be arriving, probably delivered by a big truck. I envisioned lots of dials.

Clanging metal. Yelling "Up periscope!" What arrived was a small cardboard box, with cardboard parts, to assemble a painfully small, shaky, fragile, sad imitation of a submarine. I have never

Submarine, *continued*

forgotten forcing a brave face, pretending that was exactly what I'd expected, as my father put it together with, as I recall, a lot of masking tape. I have never forgotten my disappointment.

Fast forward to the dawn of internet marketing. I owned several different companies at the time. I hired experts, I bought programs, I spent money and time on all sorts of internet gizmos and strategies, and I was just as disappointed as I was with my submarine. I know what it is like to, again and again, be promised great things only to be disappointed. Maybe even feel a little foolish afterward, like the boy with the tiny cardboard submarine.

My business policy is <u>not</u> to disappoint. There are ___ reasons why YOU will NOT ever be disappointed with this service. Reasons why THIS WILL BE DIFFERENT. And I'll quickly go over them in just a minute. But first, let me simply give you my word of honor on this. As soon as you become a client, you'll be given my direct, personal cell phone number. I'm going to ask and trust you never to use it, unless my team disappoints you. **If, at any time, you honestly feel you bought a cardboard submarine, then I want you to call me personally, directly. And I will personally make it right.** If something's wrong that can be fixed, I will jump in and get it fixed. If, for whatever reason, you can't be satisfied, I will personally order your immediate refund, as described in the Warranty on page __ of this letter. The CEO of Google wouldn't do this. I can't imagine the CEO of any tech company, software company, social media company, ad agency, etc., ever doing this. But I want you to know that, for once, you have no risk

Submarine, *continued*

whatsoever of feeling like you bought a cardboard submarine. For once, what is promised, will be.

Candidly, the field of "internet marketing" is rife with charlatans. They sell a lot of fancy and impressive stuff and promise the moon—and they love talking about visitor counts and numbers of "friends" and clicks, and everything but dollars spent, how many dollars back? Anything but the actual number of new patients brought in this month, by that thing. Consequently, most dentists are loaded up with multiple websites, online videos, Facebook sites, blogs, maybe staff spending time—or worse, the doctor spending time—daily up-dating it all. But "where's the beef?" Well, *in this one case*, the media itself is different although it is online, and it can be counted on to directly deliver patients you know it delivered.

Now, here are the reasons why I can so confidently reassure you that this service will deliver real results . . .

CHAPTER 16

Trust Language

The Book Only You Can Write, That Only You Will Read, That Can Make You Rich

Dan Kennedy

Different people have trust inspired by different language.

It is useful to build your own vocabulary list and language templates for your market or audience. This is done for large companies' sales forces and negotiating teams by industrial psychologists, semanticists, and other experts, drawing from focus groups, surveys, interviews, eavesdropping observations of sales conversations, and other means. I worked at one time with a client, a brilliant sales trainer, Bill Brooks, who is unfortunately no longer with us, whose business included the development of 8- to 24-page booklets of "Words, Phrases, and Language That Sells" for different B2B markets, customized for corporate clients, at six-figure and even seven-figure fees. Over years, I have further refined this as a process of my own, for my clients. I am now often retained to write what I call "Copy Banks" for a particular client, from which their in-house copywriters can draw as needed. Here, I'll give you a peek inside that kind of work, to provide a structural framework for your development of your own, personal reference book.

Here is the template:

1. What Is the Prospect's Primary Desire?
2. What Words and Phrases Can Sync with That Desire?
3. What Makes You/Your Product or Service the Right Means of Fulfilling the Desire?
4. How Can You Move Your Benefits to a Higher Level of Importance?
5. How Can You Best Present Your Price?
6. How Can You Best Reinforce a High-Trust Advisor Position?

Here are a few abbreviated examples—selling to hospital administrators, and to accountants:

Hospital Administrators

1: Primary Desire

- Success and job security
- Strong authority
- Personal visibility and prominence in the health care industry

Why are these the desires? A hospital administrator is subject to conflicting agendas, trying to deliver top-quality care, protect the institution, and operate in a fiscally sound manner, while counterbalancing the demands of physicians, employees working in high-pressure environments, boards of directors, wealthy donors, and patients. His authority is often challenged. He feels his job is in jeopardy every day. Today's administrator is keenly aware of a need to protect his own career—not just protect the hospital—and he is likely to be ambitious for power and advancement.

2: Words and Phrases That Sync with Desires

- The best, most successful, most admired hospitals have strong, tough-minded administrators.
- The President of the United States has, basically, two groups he must manage: Democrats and Republicans. But as a hospital administrator, you have your physicians, your staff, your board, your donors, and the patients. No one can really understand *your* "political hot seat" unless they sit in it.
- These days, hospitals are under unprecedented financial pressure, making every financial decision you make more dangerous and more likely critically scrutinized than ever before.
- The in-industry media and general business media recognition that the CEOs of exceptionally successful and innovative hospitals get these days is obviously very useful in safeguarding their authority and influence.

Why these statements work: The first directly states and reinforces his desire to be strong and to have an admired hospital. The second is an empathy statement, recognizing the unique difficulty of the job. The third acknowledges a reality he would never state on his own: that he worries about his neck every time he approves an investment. The last teases a desirable possibility; it suggests buying your widget may lead to positive media recognition. In all, these kinds of statements transform B2B marketing and make it personal.

3: Connecting Your Products/Services . . .

- Favored by business-minded administrators
- Adaptable to all kinds of challenges

- Sensitive to the need for buy-in and cooperation from all involved parties
- Accountable
- Delivers provable, documented return on investment
- A proven track record with over 20 leading hospitals makes this _______ an investment virtually immune to criticism
- Viewed as bold innovation by media like ______________

4: . . . to a Higher Level of Importance

- Can lead to improvement on a grand scale.
- Breakthrough, not just incremental improvement.
- A way to achieve superior positioning in a competitive environment

. . . more attractive to leading physicians.

5: Price

- Produce favorable economic impact
- Extremely low cost amortized over life of the __________
- If you examine it in the narrow frame of numbers of ________ surgeries required to completely recoup the investment, we are really discussing ___ typical surgeries.
- If considered against increase in revenue, it requires only a __% increase to _____.
- There is more than one return on this investment. There is efficiency, improved surgical outcomes, reduced risk for certain surgeries.

Why these statements work: They provide the administrator different means of justifying the purchase rationally, to himself, and more importantly, to others. If we have succeeded in making the potential purchase *personally* appealing to him, he wants to buy, but he must have a defensible rationale for exercising his want. Three of the four use specific information about the hospital's economics, which (a) makes them more persuasive than general assertions and (b) supports your positioning as a knowledgeable advisor.

6: Trust

- I/we recognize there can be no one-size-fits-all solution, so a thorough diagnostic process and direct input from you . . .
- These detailed case histories from five hospitals similar in size to yours, in other parts of the country, demonstrate how this approach can be pursued with no risk whatsoever .
- CEOs like you trust us for a simple reason. While the hospital is officially our client, we understand that there are institutional and corporate needs to be met but also personal concerns of yours to be honored.

Why these trust statements work: The first subtly assures the administrator that he will retain, not delegate or abdicate control. The second provides peer reassurance with detailed information. The third assures him that his personal security and ambition and political needs are understood.

Understand, I have used generic ideas and statements for this example, as I will for the next one. If actually preparing this for a company or professional selling to hospital administrators, we would want to go much deeper into specifics tied to the product or service being sold, proprietary industry terminology, and timely factors such as pending legislation. That is what you can best do for yourself, drawing on your own knowledge and experience plus trade or industry journals, books or speeches by industry leaders, picking the brain of a particularly friendly, existent client, focus groups, surveys, and other means.

All this works because of the secret, dominant desire of all humans: to be empathetically understood, appreciated, and respected. Evidenced empathy creates trust. Fast.

One more example . . .

Accountants

1: Primary Desire

- Predictability in his work and his client relationships
- Strong authority
- Safety and security

Why are these the desires? Accountants are the easiest professionals to sue successfully, because the "science" of accounting isn't half as scientific as most people think. Further, with each passing year, their liability imposed by federal and state tax authorities grows. The accountant feels "at risk" a lot. Further, by nature, the accountant likes organization; the right numbers in the right columns adding up to the right totals. The father in Disney's *Mary Poppins,* although a banker, not an accountant, eloquently describes in a song early in the movie his determination to have his home, wife, and children run as a predictable, certain, regimented enterprise. This also illustrates the accountant's desire for authority. He is, in many if not most cases, advising and doing work for companies much larger than his practice and for individuals with much higher incomes or greater wealth than he has, yet he must try to impose his will, his rules, and his decisions on these clients.

2: Words and Phrases That Sync

- The best, most successful accountants are well-accepted by their clients as expert authorities.
- The accountant often has unwelcome information and advice, and must tell the clients the truth, protect their best

interests, and also protect his own reputation. No one can really understand *your* "hot seat" unless they sit in it.

- These days, accountants/accounting firms are under unprecedented financial pressure, making it more important than ever for every financial decision you make to deliver certain positive results.
- You need to know how things are going to turn out.

3: Connecting Your Products/Services . . .

- Makes managing a practice more predictable and less stressful
- Replaces seasonal, "roller coaster" income with financial stability
- Delivers provable, documented return on investment
- Thoroughly researched and documented
- Strengthens authority even with difficult clients

4: . . . to a Higher Level of Importance

- Can liberate you from the dollars-for-hours prison
- A way to achieve superior positioning in a competitive environment

5: Price

- About increasing the value of the practice.
- Extremely low cost amortized over life of the ___________.
- If you examine it in the narrow frame of numbers of ________ clients required to completely recoup the investment, we are really discussing ___ typical clients.
- If considered against increase in revenue, it requires only a __% increase to ______.
- There is more than one return on this investment. There is efficiency, easier attraction and retention of desirable clients, and income stability.

- Our formula for pricing hasn't changed over years and has been accepted by more than 2,000 accounting firms.

6: Trust

- A completely customized solution, yet built on a time-tested, reliable platform.
- These detailed case histories from five accounting practices similar in size to yours, in other parts of the country, demonstrate how this approach can be pursued with no risk whatsoever . . .
- Fully guaranteed, in writing.

If you compare the two examples, you'll find some statements are identical in structure and only nominally different in content. There are a few unique to each of the two. Again, if doing this for real, for a specific marketer or seller, the statements would be built with more precision.

The Reason So Few Are at the Top and a Piece of Tactical Advice

In the months I was writing this, the media, driven by Occupy Wall Street, became obsessed with discussion of the 1% vs. the 99%, but neither the Occupy spokespersons nor the media dealt with it from the perspective of behavioral causes. Actually, there is an "Income and Wealth Pyramid" in society as a whole, and in microcosm, inside virtually every industry or profession, every sales organization: 1%, 4%, 15%, 60%, 20%. It has stayed virtually static for many decades despite various government-run wealth re-distribution schemes, despite the advent of the internet and a plethora of technology advancements: 1% reap extraordinarily high rewards, 4% do well, 15% harvest satisfactory incomes, these three groups totaling 20%. A pyramid atop a bigger pyramid. From there, incomes, wealth, prosperity, and security take a precipitous drop. Those at the top of the 80% pyramid may earn less than half what those at the bottom of the 20% pyramid earn. This is really quite remarkable. Thus, 60% of any given group tends to barely get by and never get ahead, and 20% tend to be impoverished. The pyramid could be of hardware store operators in the U.S. or just in the Southwest or Pacific Northwest, or doctors or lawyers or auto sales professionals. Any free-market population. (Schoolteachers, for example, are exempt from free-market forces, so their Income Pyramid is a lot less pyramidal, however, interestingly, they somehow re-arrange themselves in a Wealth Pyramid that still winds up 5%, 15%, 80%.)

There are many reasons for all this, but there is one very significant reason that is never given sufficient credit as cause, and that is directly relevant to what I've presented here. The reason is *behavioral*. Simply, that those at the peak of the income and wealth pyramids do quite a few things everybody else could do but refuses to do. Most such things are difficult or time demanding or involve learning or are complicated to do. Consequently, most avoid them. A comparative few do them. I have just presented you with such a thing here: the painstaking, thoughtful, thorough development of a language, phrase, and sentence book specific to your prospects and to the products or services you sell, for use in developing and learning scripts for your selling conversations, and in developing advertising and marketing. In presenting this, I know full well that few will do it. Most will find excuses for not doing it, or will plan to do it someday when they can "find the time," or will rue that it hasn't been done for them, or otherwise escape this work. I know full well that few will do it. And I could care less about that as a fact, or about whether or not you do it. I tend to write, speak, teach, and develop strategies for the 1% and the 4%, with little regard for the others. I'm *not* an empathetic egalitarian in philosophy or practice. But I will tell you this: If you do this thing that so few will, you will arm yourself and empower yourself as never before in your entire business life to be infinitely more effective and efficient in marketing or selling.

If you are one of the rare ones who are ready and willing to work it, a set of worksheets for this task appears in Figure 15.1, and you're free to copy them for your use.

I would also like to recommend a few general resources that can aid you in choosing language and crafting your statements:

Words That Sell by Richard Bayan
More Words That Sell by Richard Bayan
Roget's *Thesaurus*
Roget's *Super Thesaurus*
Roget's *Descriptive Word Finder*

FIGURE 15.1: Trust Language Worksheets

Your Customer's PRIMARY Desires

1: ______________________________

2: ______________________________

3: ______________________________

4: ______________________________

What Words and Phrases Sync with Desire #1?

____

____

____

What Words and Phrases Sync with Desire #2?

____

____

____

FIGURE 15.1: Trust Language Worksheets, continued

What Words and Phrases Sync with Desire #3?

____

____

____

What Words and Phrases Sync with Desire #4?

____

____

____

What Makes You/Your Product/Your Service THE Right Means of Fulfilling Desire #1?

____

____

____

FIGURE 15.1: Trust Language Worksheets, continued

What Makes You/Your Product/Your Service THE Right Means of Fulfilling Desire #2?

____

____

____

What Makes You/Your Product/Your Service THE Right Means of Fulfilling Desire #3?

____

____

____

What Makes You/Your Product/Your Service THE Right Means of Fulfilling Desire #4?

____

____

____

FIGURE 15.1: Trust Language Worksheets, continued

How Can You Move Your Benefits to a Higher Level of Importance?

Statement #1 ________________________________

Statement #2 ________________________________

Statement #3 ________________________________

Statement #4 ________________________________

How Can You Best Present Your Price?

Statement #1 ________________________________

Statement #2 ________________________________

Statement #3 ________________________________

Statement #4 ________________________________

How Can You Best Reinforce a High-Trust Advisor Position?

Statement #1 ________________________________

Statement #2 ________________________________

Statement #3 ________________________________

Statement #4 ________________________________

CHAPTER 17

Astound and Amaze with THE HOUDINI FACTOR and the Power of Dramatic Demonstration

Dan Kennedy

Hearing something said one thousand times is not **as convincing as seeing it once**. That's an ancient Chinese proverb I saw on a plaque in a Chinese restaurant, so it has to be authentic. It *is* correct. There is nothing more powerful than Demonstration—for good or bad. It can create trust faster and more certainly than anything that can be said or asserted. It can also quickly, savagely sabotage trust.

To the latter effect, consider the contractor you are on the verge of hiring to manage major remodeling of your home or of an investment property. He will be entrusted with overseeing all the work, subcontractors and employees, the budget (thus, your money), and meeting deadlines important to you. He must be able to manage details well and be dependable. And he shows up for two meetings with you in a row 15 to 30 minutes late, lathered, disorganized, on one occasion having left needed documents behind, and while with you, takes cell-phone calls and engages in what sound like crisis management conversations. All the fancy brochures, industry awards, Better Business Bureau accolades, years in business, and even client testimonials probably won't counterweigh this dramatic Demonstration. Nor should they.

Negative and contradictory Demonstration is extremely dangerous. Its damage underestimated. Even the tiniest Demonstration of incompetence, untruthfulness, or other characteristic incongruent with the role the client may be hiring you to fill can be sufficient to erase a mountain of high-powered advertising, ingenious marketing, and persuasive salesmanship.

On the other hand, positive Demonstration is extremely powerful. The same contractor arrives on time, calm, relaxed, organized. He tells you he's turning off his cell phone during your meeting, because, "Everything at all six of our current job sites is well under control. I have a terrific team." He pulls up a prepared, customized "Project Management Diagram" on his laptop, and Demonstrates exactly how your project will be managed—with extensive quality control—for on-time and on-budget completion. He has your documents neatly organized in a presentation binder. He invites you, if you'd like, to take an extra half hour and ride along with him while he makes an unannounced inspection visit to a near-by job site—an invitation to a live Demonstration. Now you actually trust what's in his fancy brochure. You feel reassured.

In Chapter 15, you saw me use Demonstration, on my behalf, as a direct-response copywriter: a demonstration of Demonstration. I have marketed and promoted myself by Demonstration for just about my entire career. In seminar environments, I'll often do a "hot seat" with an attendee, in which he presents an actual business problem or opportunity and—working without a net—I quiz him, then perform as a magician, instantly materializing sound, smart, and specific strategies and tactics for his use, all within a short time frame, typically 20 minutes or less. Either a number in a row or spaced out over two or three days, I provide Demonstration of the range and depth of my knowledge, detective and diagnostic skill, quick-mindedness, and ability to provide profitable and actionable advice. Without ever having to "pitch" consulting, this Demonstration brings forward new clients asking how they can work with me one-on-one. I am not the only one in my field to use this particular type of Demonstration, by the way; a celebrated marketing strategist Jay Abraham, author of *The Sticking Point Solution*, and the late Gary Halbert, a legendary, iconic giant of copywriting, both raised private clients out of audiences like a stage magician levitating a few cards out of a deck in this very same way. Also, as a copywriter, I have gotten clients worth six-figures and up by doing quick but insightful and provocative critiques of their present ads, sales letters, or other media.

The Houdini Effect and the Power of Dramatic Demonstration

It's important to understand that there is demonstration and there is "DEMONSTRATION!"

The best Demonstration has drama of some kind: risk of failure or worse; "Believe It or Not!" physicality, like an example I show in seminars from a direct-response TV commercial for a gel-sole shoe insert: The pitchman puts it over his hand, then smashes down a hammer on his hand, and even has a car driven over his hand—no pain, no injury. I love physical demonstrations like that. One I did, selling in homes in my teens, involved destroying the casual trust people place in brand-name aerosol furniture polish and switching them to my brand. I sprayed their brand into a dish, tossed in a lit match, and—presto—an inferno. I extinguished it with my brand. The one they had all their furniture coated with was shown to be highly flammable and dangerous. Mine demonstrated as safe. (Yes, there's a small trick to it.) Another kind of dramatic Demonstration merely requires a mind-blowing visual aid. A man named Ira Hayes was a star salesman for the National Cash Register Corporation when the cash register was the distrusted new technology replacing the shoebox 'neath the shopkeeper's counter. Ira marched in with a 6-feet-tall high roll of sturdy paper that unfurled to 12-feet wide, covered with snapshots of happy shopkeepers with their shiny new cash registers. In my book *No B.S. Sales Success in The New Economy*, I describe a modern-day all-star auto salesman making only slightly different use of the very same Demonstration.

When you create a truly dramatic Demonstration for yourself, your product, or your service, you employ the powerful "Houdini Effect."

When discussing this in seminars, I show two black-and-white newsreels of Houdini doing his famous straitjacket escape, one of him hanging upside down, suspended several stories in the air by a crane over a huge crowd; another, diving off the boardwalk into the ocean and popping up out of the water, freed. Not to take anything away, but most knowledgeable magicians agree that Houdini was a better showman than magician. Even then, the straitjacket escape was relatively common. Standing on stage doing it was not all that exciting. But doing it hung upside down, high in the air, directly overhead the audience in the street makes it very uncommon.

In an episode of HBO's *Boardwalk Empire*, Houdini's brother, Hardeen, is at a cocktail reception after his performance and, to his annoyance, people ask him about Houdini's performances of the escape in dramatic circumstances like I just described.

Clearly irritated, he growls, "IT'S THE SAME TRICK that I just performed on stage."

And so it was. But the manner in which it was performed made it profoundly more impressive.

To further Hardeen's indignant envy of his brother, the way Houdini did this trick put considerable distance between him and the audience, and distracted them from critical observation, so it was easier for him to do what needed to be done for escape without detection of the method, than for Hardeen standing on an empty stage with the front row of the audience steps away.

I doubt you're ready to hang upside down from a crane to make your points—nor would that necessarily aid you as it did Houdini. But the principle can be applied to everyday selling situations. Consider the matter of standardized power-point presentations. I am opposed to them. If I present a strategy to you with a ready-made power-point presentation on my laptop or pad screen, however glitzy and professional it may be, it does nothing to demonstrate my grasp of the subject and it reveals that you are getting a one-size-fits-all solution, the same for the prospect who came before you yesterday and the same for the prospect who will follow you tomorrow. If instead I draw out my diagrams, do my calculations, and list my ideas on a legal pad from my spontaneous thoughts—drawing on my years of experience—in response to our conversation, I have a dramatic Demonstration of my stored knowledge plus the benefit of appearing to present a customized prescription for you. If I am, in fact, selling the same solution to everybody, then, as Hardeen bemoaned, it is the same trick. But it doesn't feel to you like the same trick.

I have noticed, by the way, that every great salesperson I've had make presentations to me at some point gets a legal pad, sheet of paper, or even a napkin, and "creates" information for me. Dr. Roizen at the Cleveland Clinic does this. Matt Zagula does this. Do you think that either the Cleveland Clinic or Matt's companies are too limited in resources to produce the perfect power-point presentation? Of course not. They choose dramatic Demonstration in place of it.

For many years after white boards and erasable markers came into vogue, the great personal development speaker—and sometimes, recruiter for network marketing companies—Jim Rohn stubbornly continued using a giant chalkboard on stage, scrawling numbers and diagrams and jotting phrases, chalk dust flying, making chalk-to-board clatter. Using different colored markers on a giant whiteboard is cleaner, easier, and more readable for an audience, but doing it with chalk is more dramatic. Many years hence, in 2010, Glenn Beck featured writing on giant chalkboards on his #1-rated FOX TV show, a show that very successfully made one of his books right after another and after another, *New York Times* best-sellers. Mr. Beck has left real TV, but took his giant chalkboards with him onto the internet, with his own GBTV.com.

A Personal Trick of Mine, Revealed Here, for the First Time

Another grounded means of dramatic Demonstration is what I call the ***spontaneous, instantaneous benefit***. So, here, I will officially divulge a trick I've used for years.

Most new clients travel to me for their very first consulting day, out of which will come project work at high fees. We meet in the conference room in my large basement office, in my home. It is not ostentatious at all. It is practical, and an undisguised workplace. My office space features over 900 reference books, from familiar to obscure titles, published in 1700, 1800, 1900, 2000, to present. At the end of a hallway is my Reference Room, where I have told my clients, no one but I am permitted entry. It contains what copywriters call "swipe files"; a treasure trove of samples of my work spanning 35 years—plus collected samples from others—of ads, direct-mail pieces, sales letters, and other materials. Thousands of items. At some point in discussion with each client, I will "remember" or "think of" a specific item or two it would be very useful for him to see, and I will excuse myself to disappear into the closed "mystery room" and—after some noisy travail—emerge victorious with what he needs to see. I have left the cave, braved the wilds, and returned with prey hunted on his behalf. I have escaped from the straitjacket after being dropped into and submerged beneath icy waters. Of course, I know a great deal about the client beforehand so I could pull relevant materials from my files and have them neatly laid out in the conference room ahead of time. I could do that, but it would not be nearly as interesting as spontaneously recalling just the right item's existence and miraculously finding it from within the mysterious vault. That I did, in fact, find these things in advance and have them ready and waiting in the back room, and stand in there counting thousand-one, thousand-five, thousand-ten before emerging is not anything my amazed client needs to know. So keep it to yourself.

The Dramatic Demonstration of Psychic Empathy and Understanding

Trust is greatly accelerated when the person feels understood.

This is why psychics throughout American history have been very effective at bilking even smart, successful people out of money. Houdini became a crusader against the epidemic of psychic fraud in his time. It thrives today, with small-time grifters and big-time con artists, the latter frequently separating rich widows from their fortunes, even separating executives from substantial sums. The power and influence psychics exert often moves a person from small-fee readings to very high-fee, on-going advisory relationships. That power is entirely based on their ability as performers to convince people they know things about them no one but a psychic could, and have deep, empathetic understanding of them and insight into them. It is hard *not* to trust someone who appears to be especially gifted at empathy, who is so knowing about you.

A skill of dramatic Demonstration anyone can learn enough about to use successfully in selling situations is what psychic and mentalist performers call "cold reading." My friend and colleague at GKIC, Dave Dee, a reformed magician turned sales and marketing expert, teaches it for selling purposes in his Psychic Salesperson trainings. (Get more information at www.DanKennedy.com/Dee). A definitive text is Ian Rowland's *Full Facts Book of Cold Reading*. A more elementary introduction is Simon Winthrop's *How to Be a Mentalist: Master the Secrets Behind the Hit TV Show*. With cold reading, you are able to tell people facts, even secrets about themselves. Nothing is more fascinating to most people than themselves. Nothing is more impressive than the ability to divine personal thoughts about your prospect—to know what they are thinking. No human desire exceeds the desire to be understood. Even a little cold reading serves as dramatic demonstration of your perceptiveness, empathy, and insight.

This can be facilitated in one-to-one selling quite easily these days by doing a bit of research on your prospect in advance of your appointment. Google and Facebook offer it on a silver platter, yet in years, meeting with many sales professionals, doctors, financial advisors, etc. trying to sell me something or acquire me as a client, only one ever bothered to type in my name and see what they might discover about me. If you have a guy coming in, age 68, who, 20 years ago, was a high school football coach who won a state championship, or he caught a

King Kong sized marlin on his most recent fishing trip, or flies his own airplane—he's got that at his Facebook site. If he's in business, much may be on Google. This kind of information can be used straightforwardly or as a psychic might use it for dramatic cold reading. Either way, it empowers you to accelerate the establishment of trust.

Why Does the Right Kind of Dramatic Demonstration Create and Support Trust?

In many situations, the prospective customer, client, or patient gets to trust by determining three things about you in his own thoughts:

1. Is this person knowledgeable (about the area in which I am to trust their counsel or service)?
2. Is this person competent (about the area in which I am to trust their counsel or service)?
3. Is this person special—*especially* gifted, talented, capable?

The last item, #3, is one many businesspeople don't really understand. Under ideal circumstances, people want special not ordinary, brilliant not just adequate, the person who is the best at "x" not just one of many doing "x." Because of this desire, they link exceptionally knowledgeable or capable with trustworthiness, despite logical analysis telling us one may very well have nothing to do with the other. The most dangerous thief or con man might shine against these three measurements while the trustworthiest saint might appear dull and uninteresting. I'll keep driving this truth home: People trust for all the wrong reasons.

CHAPTER 18

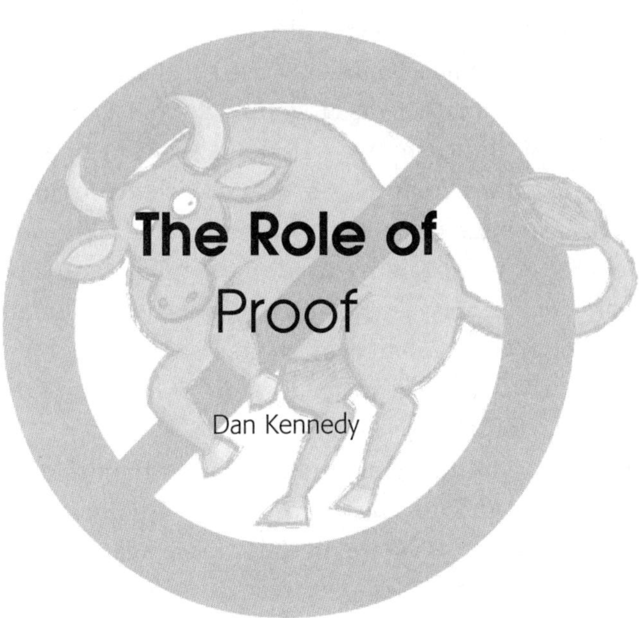

The Role of Proof

Dan Kennedy

Just about everybody reading this book is familiar with customer testimonials. They are ever-present. Many advertisers and marketers use them. As I am writing this, Ford has an excellent series of TV commercials airing, entirely featuring "real customers" talking about their happiness with their Fords, or, in some, just how impressed they are with them as a result of Swap-Your-Ride test drives. I consider customer testimony one of the most powerful trust-based marketing tools of all. Which makes what I'm about to do very unusual—I'm omitting discussion of them from this book. (I refer you to Chapter 8 of the book, *No B.S. Sales Success in The New Economy*.)

In a few fields, like Matt's, the use of customer satisfaction testimonials is actually prohibited by law. In others, recent Federal Trade Commission regulations and expansion of regulatory authority have made the use of testimonials more difficult. (You may want information about this from www.ftc.gov.) Still, in most product and service categories, you will see customer testimonials commonly used—as they should be.

In place of another discussion of the most commonly used sort of proof, the customer testimonial, I want to expand your thinking to a more comprehensive approach to proving your case to your customers or clients. In a legal case, both eyewitnesses and character witnesses are used to the fullest extent possible—the functional equivalent of the customer testimonial—but no prosecutor or defense attorney worth his salt relies only on such "real people" witnesses. Instead, every kind of proof that can be had is used, for much is at stake.

Elsewhere in this book, Matt mentions the use of the expert witness, and I discuss the importance of Demonstration. There is also scientific or faux-scientific evidence available for all sorts of products. As an example of faux-science evidence, there's a legendary marketing premise that has sold freighters full of shark cartilage nutritional supplements: "Sharks Don't Get Cancer!" This is accurate, but it's a very un-scientific leap from that fact to the idea that by eating shark cartilage, humans get immunity from cancer. Nevertheless, millions of people made that leap and considered that single fact as "proof of concept." A similar leap used in B2B is: (a) *INC.* magazine is credible and trustworthy and (b) our company is on the *INC.* "500 List," therefore (c) our company is credible, trustworthy, and worthy of investment.

There is proof by popularity and sheer numbers, illustrated in Figure 18.1. Even celebrity or celebrity endorsement can stand as proof in many consumers' minds. An excellent educational exercise is to become interested in and alert to all the different ways that advertisers and marketers present proof. A good tactical exercise is to apply as many different kinds of proof to your marketing as possible. But here, I'm going to talk about why and how proof is best used, in the context of trust-based marketing . . . .

There are four basic kinds of proof that could be important for you to use:

1. Proof of Concept
2. Proof of Personal Relevance
3. Proof of Promised Benefits and Outcomes
4. Proof of Superiority

Proof of Concept

Too often, we erroneously take for granted acceptance of the underlying concepts that drive our businesses. In Matt's business, for example, the concept of having a single, trusted financial advisor coordinating one's financial plans, investments, and funding of retirement is assumed, as advisors compete with each other. But what if the prospect is merely open to but not yet convinced of the wisdom or necessity of that concept? There was a time when travel by seafaring cruise liner or airplane had to be proven safe as a concept or generic, before you could sell competing providers' benefits, fares, or destinations. In one of my businesses, business coaching, many too quickly leap past acceptance of the concept to selling their particular programs, when, first, the concept of having a business coach or being in a coach-led mastermind group needs to be sold. In Figure 18.1, you'll find a piece first published in a magazine I controlled, then subsequently used by me and many of my clients as Proof of Concept for coaching. Don't miss the use of borrowed trust via Arnold Palmer.

Another way to think about this is as the formula: (a) for you to be trusted, first (b) your concept(s) must be trusted.

Proof of Personal Relevance

Again, to use the above examples, just because I accept financial planning or the use of an advisor or vacationing on a cruise ship as safe, enjoyable, and popular, or business coaching as useful, all as proven concepts, does not mean I accept them as good for *me*. I may accept that thousands love going on cruises, but think that I won't for any number of reasons, including sea sickness, claustrophobia, fear of water, eating at designated times with strangers, etc. I may accept that many need and benefit from having a financial advisor, but may feel I won't, for any number of reasons, perhaps that I have too small a nest egg, or am a control freak and will be uncomfortable delegating authority, or that I'm too old and needed that help sooner. Proof of Concept is foundational, but it needs to be connected to Proof of Personal Relevance.

This can loop back to the tactical tool I have chosen not to discuss: Testimonials from people with precisely the same situation and concerns, in sufficient number, with good believability, can serve as Proof of Personal Relevance. But there are many ways to prove this too, and none should be neglected, all used. If, for example, we are trying to convince a skeptical and recalcitrant senior to begin using Facebook, we can use statistical facts—that the fastest growing segment of new Facebook users is 60 years of age and up; we can focus on features and uses of Facebook most popular with seniors—like a different way to scrapbook, involvement with grandkids, keeping up with old friends who live great distances away; we can create a story or step-by-step diary of a new Facebook user's experiences, that user matched with the senior we're trying to convince; we could even engineer personal Demonstration. We might use free trial of a few functions set up for the person; in selling, this is called "puppy dogging," and it was once used to popularize odd, new-fangled things like cars, phones, and television sets; installed or given to people to use for a few days, a weekend or a week, then removed and taken back if the person didn't come to love them, like putting a puppy dog in someone's home for the weekend then trying to take it back from the kids. If you've never had a puppy dog, and think you wouldn't want one, you might very well find yourself proven wrong in just a few days with a puppy put in your care.

Proof of Promised Benefits and Outcomes

Obviously, to buy, buyers have to feel very confident and reassured, if not rock-solid certain, that the promised and hoped for benefits and outcomes will occur for him.

This is why the GKIC Members, and brilliant marketers selling $4,000.00 to $20,000.00 mattresses created The Dream Room in their store (www.gardnersmattressandmore.com), where a customer checks in and enjoys a nap for up to 4 hours, in a luxury suite, in complete privacy, complete with milk 'n' cookies. You really can't trust a mattress after just stretching out on it for a few minutes, then lying on the next one, and the next. You can only trust it after you've slept on it. Yes, again, a plethora of customer testimonials, especially specific ones about back pain or insomnia resolved, are very helpful. But the only real proof is in the sleeping.

When I was still actively seeking speaking engagements from new clients, I made a point of inviting and working hard-to-get meeting planners who might hire me to sit in on events where I was speaking for a client. If I was going to travel to a distant city to speak for a client's group, I wanted several prospective clients who might book me in that audience, to see living proof of the benefits they would want: my prowess, enthusiastic response of an audience, etc. Sure, client testimonials were a useful tool, as can be "demo" audio CDs and DVDs, credibility and authority tools like books, articles, awards, professional designations. But nothing serves as better proof than actually experiencing the outcomes the prospect desires.

Proof of Superiority

Once somebody has accepted a means of meeting need or desire as a proven, safe concept, and been educated about the existence of a provider, he will quite naturally wonder what other providers and choices may be available. At some point, the issue of choice will always arise. Many tactical tools apply—including those presented in this book—like Leadership Position and Demonstration. Virtually everything in this book is linked to Proof of Superiority, because the ultimate superior position is: *most trusted.*

Preponderance of Proof

In battle, it's best to have *overwhelming* force. The battle for trust in decidedly un-trusting times, to be secured from understandably anxious, skeptical, suspicious, worried, and mistrustful prospects is best waged with overwhelming proof. That means three things: Quantity, Quality, and *Diversity*. The last may be the pathway to greatest advantage: providing as many different forms of proof in each of the above four categories as you possibly can.

FIGURE 18.1: Proof of Concept Example

Example of "Proof of Concept" for Business Coaching—Using Borrowed Trust from Champion Golfer Arnold Palmer, from celebrated success author Napoleon Hill, and from *Newsweek* magazine.

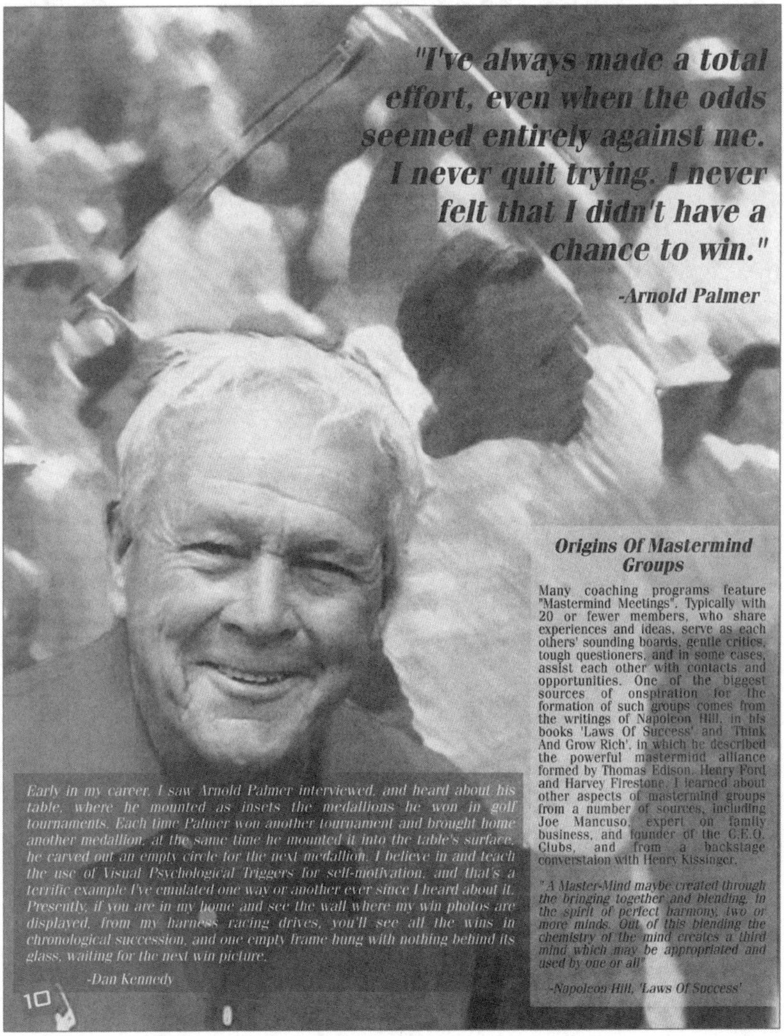

"I've always made a total effort, even when the odds seemed entirely against me. I never quit trying. I never felt that I didn't have a chance to win."

-Arnold Palmer

Early in my career, I saw Arnold Palmer interviewed, and heard about his table, where he mounted as insets the medallions he won in golf tournaments. Each time Palmer won another tournament and brought home another medallion, at the same time he mounted it into the table's surface, he carved out an empty circle for the next medallion. I believe in and teach the use of Visual Psychological Triggers for self-motivation, and that's a terrific example I've emulated one way or another ever since I heard about it. Presently, if you are in my home and see the wall where my win photos are displayed, from my harness racing drives, you'll see all the wins in chronological succession, and one empty frame hung with nothing behind its glass, waiting for the next win picture.

-Dan Kennedy

Origins Of Mastermind Groups

Many coaching programs feature "Mastermind Meetings". Typically with 20 or fewer members, who share experiences and ideas, serve as each others' sounding boards, gentle critics, tough questioners, and in some cases, assist each other with contacts and opportunities. One of the biggest sources of onspiration for the formation of such groups comes from the writings of Napoleon Hill, in his books 'Laws Of Success' and 'Think And Grow Rich', in which he described the powerful mastermind alliance formed by Thomas Edison, Henry Ford and Harvey Firestone. I learned about other aspects of mastermind groups from a number of sources, including Joe Mancuso, expert on family business, and founder of the C.E.O. Clubs, and from a backstage converstaion with Henry Kissinger.

" A Master-Mind maybe created through the bringing together and blending, in the spirit of perfect harmony, two or more minds. Out of this blending the chemistry of the mind creates a third mind which may be appropriated and used by one or all"

-Napoleon Hill, 'Laws Of Success'

10

Reprinted from *Renegade Millionaire* magazine, Spring 2006.

FIGURE 18.1: Proof of Concept Example, *continued*

Why Do Top Performers Use Coaches?

- by Dan S. Kennedy

When Arnold Palmer needed to "tune-up" his game, to compensate for his age, he sought out a 26yr old 'swing coach'. Everybody who follows golf knows about the troubles Tiger had with his game after parting with his coach, Butch Harmon. We know most athletes in every sport use coaches, personal trainers and sports pyschologists. But do sales professionals and entrepreneurs need coaches too?

Having personally had over 200 high-flying entrepreneurs, small business owners, salespeople and self-employed professional participate in my coaching groups and telecoaching programs over the past 8 years - some for all 8 years, and been the coach and advisor to nearly 100 business coaches in different fields, I think I have a pretty good understanding of why coaching seems to work so well for entrepreneurs, and why you might want a coach of your own. There are six reasons:

Being Held Accountable
Being Questioned And Challenged
Being Listened To
Being Recognized For Your Achievements
Being Accepted
Being Motivated

Different people have different needs at different times in their lives, but I find most entrepreneurs share all six of these to varying degrees.

Accountability

On many occasions, as a speaker, I was on programs with, and had private "green room" time with legendary athletes like Joe Montana, Troy Aikman, Olympian Mary Lou Retton, George Foreman, and coaches like Tom Landry, Lou Holtz, and Jimmy Johnson. The athletes all agreed that high perfomers personally hold themselves to gruelingly high standards, but even so, were it not for feeling accountable to teammates, fans and coaches, and being held accountable by their coach or coaches, who monitored their statistics, replayed film of mis-judgements and mistakes, analyzed and assessed their performance, they would never have reached the levels of success they did. The joke of entrepreneurship is: good news and bad news. You're your own boss! Having a coach guide you in committing to doing, changing, testing certain things between now and the next call or meeting, then having you report on those things is guaranteed to improve your follow-through on your own best ideas! In short, accountability automatically improves performance and results.

Questioned and Challenged

The more successful you are, the less likely the people who work for you or are around all the time are to challenge your ideas. It's easy to wind up surrounded by "yes men". The outside coach with no axe to grind can be both objective and frank. He can ask the provocative questions that force you to defend your idea. If you can, that's valuable. If you can't, that's valuable too.

Listened To

A Newsweek magazine article about professional business/life coaches described us as "part therapist, part consultant". A lot of entrepreneurs have no one to talk to about business OR personal matters who dare "let their hair down with"... who will listen without any agenda. I often find that a client will talk his way to his own terrific answer, solution or plan of action if I'll just listen. Having a coach with life and business experience relevant to your own, who is personally successful, who can relate to you and who you can relate to is extremely beneficial.

Being Recognized For Your Achievements

Everybody needs recognition and celebration - but to whom can the entrepreneur brag? Certainly not to his employees, his competitors, his vendors. Since most of the people I and the coaches I advise work with are "Renegades", using unorthodox marketing strategies, most of the people around them actually dissapprove of a lot of what's working, even if they grudgingly acknowledge the results. And often, if the owner of the business takes the garish black on neon green oversize postcard he spent days slaving over, that just pulled a 14 to 1 ROI, home to show his wife and kids, he gets a very disinterested response. A "that's nice, dear" - not a "holy crap! 14 - 1! You're a genius! Can I get a copy of that?" Having a knowledgeable coach or, better yet, being part of a coaching/mastermind group gives everyone of us an appreciative audience who "gets it", who understands our accomplishments, and is able and willing to celebrate our achievements because they are secure in their own success.

Being Accepted

I call my most successful clients (and myself) 'Renegade Millionaires' because we violate just about every norm of our industries and professions... we are actually quite dysfunctual in one way or another ... we think and talk differently than almost everyone around us in our day to day lives. Because of this, a lot of successful entrepreneurs actually suffer silent frustration and loneliness. In many instances, we can't even explain what we do to 'civilians'! Feeling like "the fish out of water" most of one's waking hours is not all that pleasant. That's why being part of a coaching/mastermind group with like-minded 'Renegades' is so invigorating. One of the core human needs is to be accepted for who you are, without need of mask or cautious editing of expressed thought.

Being Motivated

Surely a top pro athlete being paid millions of dollars to play a game doesn't need "motivated --" but, actually the fact that they are paid millions, win, lose or draw, means they do need a great deal of other motivation to do all the behind-the-scenes hard work required for peak performance on the field. In almost every locker room after every game, grown men who are paid millions to play their games are awarded game balls. Coaches cry, hug, atta boy! , nudge. Ultimately, all motivation is self-motivation, but there's definitely contributions made by the people and ideas you associate with, the involvements you're in, the successes of others you're exposed to.

What Exactly Is Business/Life Coaching?

Most of the industry-specific advisors I work with deliver coaching much the same as I do; with different "levels" appropriate for different people. The most common options begin with simple group tele-semminars or classes often with open question/answer for the participants, sometimes support with website resources or communities. Next, plus some 1-on-1 tele-coaching. Next, all that plus periodic mastermind group meetings. At the highest levels, people travel from all over the country to attend the meetings. New in 2006, I'm also organizing local Dan Kennedy "Study Groups" combining education, mastermind meetings and coaching facilitated by someone in each city. Information about Kennedy and Glazer/Kennedy programs can be found at www.renegademillionairemarketing.com.

Why Should You 'Plug-In' To One Or More Coaches And Coaching Programs?

If any or all of the six needs I described apply to you, then the best investment you'll ever make is finding and joining one or even several appropriate coaching programs!

11

CHAPTER 19

The Cache Client as Its Own Form of Proof

Dan Kennedy

David Ogilvy, the former fry cook and door-to-door salesman who became one of the most iconic leaders of the golden age of advertising, early on, secured Rolls Royce as a client. They weren't a particularly good or profitable client, and few other ad agencies wanted them. They were small, boutique in nature, not likely to spend huge sums on advertising, and difficult to do effective advertising for. But they were *Rolls Royce.* Ogilvy saw the leverage of having such a cache client. It didn't matter if they were a profitable client *per se*. The attention he got from other potential clients because he had Rolls Royce was compensation. Immediately upon getting them, he leased a Rolls Royce, got a custom plate for it—OM2, standing for Ogilvy & Mather, and suggesting it was the second Rolls Royce in the fleet—and paid to park it and have it guarded in front of his offices in Manhattan. If you have the kind of interest in advertising you should, and/or you've watched the *Mad Men* television show, you'd enjoy the definitive biography of Ogilvy, *King of Madison Avenue.*

> **Having a cache client can instantly elevate you in the eyes of others. It can also provide a certain amount of automatic trust from others. It is its own unique form of proof.**

For a number of years, the Guthy-Renker Corporation was a cache client of mine. After over 20 years, they still are a client, although now sporadically rather than continuously. If you don't know them, everybody involved with direct marketing, a world I live in and conduct a lot of business in, does. They have grown from zero to be a $1.5-billion+ company, best known for hit TV infomercials featuring celebrities, as launch vehicles for successful brands in skin care, cosmetics, nutrition, and other product categories.

For a number of clients, the fact that I was a trusted advisor to Guthy-Renker meant they could trust me as well—and wanted to secure my assistance, if they could possibly get it. *This one fact,* that Guthy-Renker was an on-going client of mine, was persuasive in getting companies like International Correspondence Schools, Weight Watchers International, Amway Corporation, Miracle Ear®, and others as clients, as well as many, many more smaller, less well-known but excellent clients. It even directly brought clients to me, pursuing me because of it.

In every industry, every field, every city or community, there are cache clients to be had. Years back, an owner of a Columbus, Ohio area landscaping company, Marty Grunder, got the former Ohio State University football coach Earl Bruce as a client. In Ohio State territory, this coach was famous and beloved. I do not know if Marty specifically, proactively targeted the coach or wound up taking care of his lawn by serendipity, but he was smart enough to capitalize on it. The coach appeared at the top of published client lists, and he even got the good-natured coach to record a testimonial for him (just as he gets other clients to do), then played it as the "on hold" recording to callers to Grunder Landscaping's office. Marty did very deliberately pursue commercial clients with landmark properties in his area—like hospitals, universities, country clubs—all cache clients. Charlie Jones says to himself: If *they* trust Grunder, that's good enough for me.

A simple thing like a client list can create trust or persuade others. In marketing GKIC's seminars, I often put out a piece like the one reproduced in Figure 19.1, that features a partial list of the GKIC Members already registered, noting their type of business or something about them. The Member who gets this, who isn't yet registered, is drawn in by the list. He looks to see if he knows people on the list, personally or by reputation within our fraternity. He looks to see if others in his kind of business have registered (see Chapter 12, on Affinity). He sees that people he thinks of as smart and accomplished, and people in his own field, trust me and trust that this event will be valuable, and is reassured and encouraged by that. Some of the names on this list are cache clients, in that they are known to our entire membership as exceptionally successful, accomplished entrepreneurs—so if *they are* going, that tells you that you should go, too.

When Ogilvy started out in advertising, he made a list of, I believe, 50 cache clients and much-desired accounts he wanted for his agency. Rolls Royce wasn't one of them. They fell into his lap, but he was astute enough to grab them and capitalize on them. Over time, though, he captured nearly all on the list. When I started marketing into my very first niche market, in 1977, the membership of the National Speakers Association, a small fraternity of a few thousand professional speakers, I made a "hit list" of 20 with considerable influence and cache with all the other members, who I wanted to do business with, and I implemented customized campaigns to put myself in front of these twenty. Within months, I had created relationships with a few; over a couple of years, all but two. I recommend such list making. Who would be your ideal cache clients that, just the fact of having them as clients, would create the trust and interest of many others? Then you need to thoroughly research those on your list, which today is easier than ever to do thanks to the internet. Next, develop customized schemes for being visible to, for being interesting to, for marketing to each of the targets on the list. To get to one, you may need to become active in support of a charity the client actively supports, so that it brings you together. To get to another, you may need to create information—white papers, reports, articles, even a book—tailor-made to that client's interests. Each "target" may require a customized approach. The right ones are worth all the effort.

FIGURE 19.1: GKIC Seminar Marketing Example

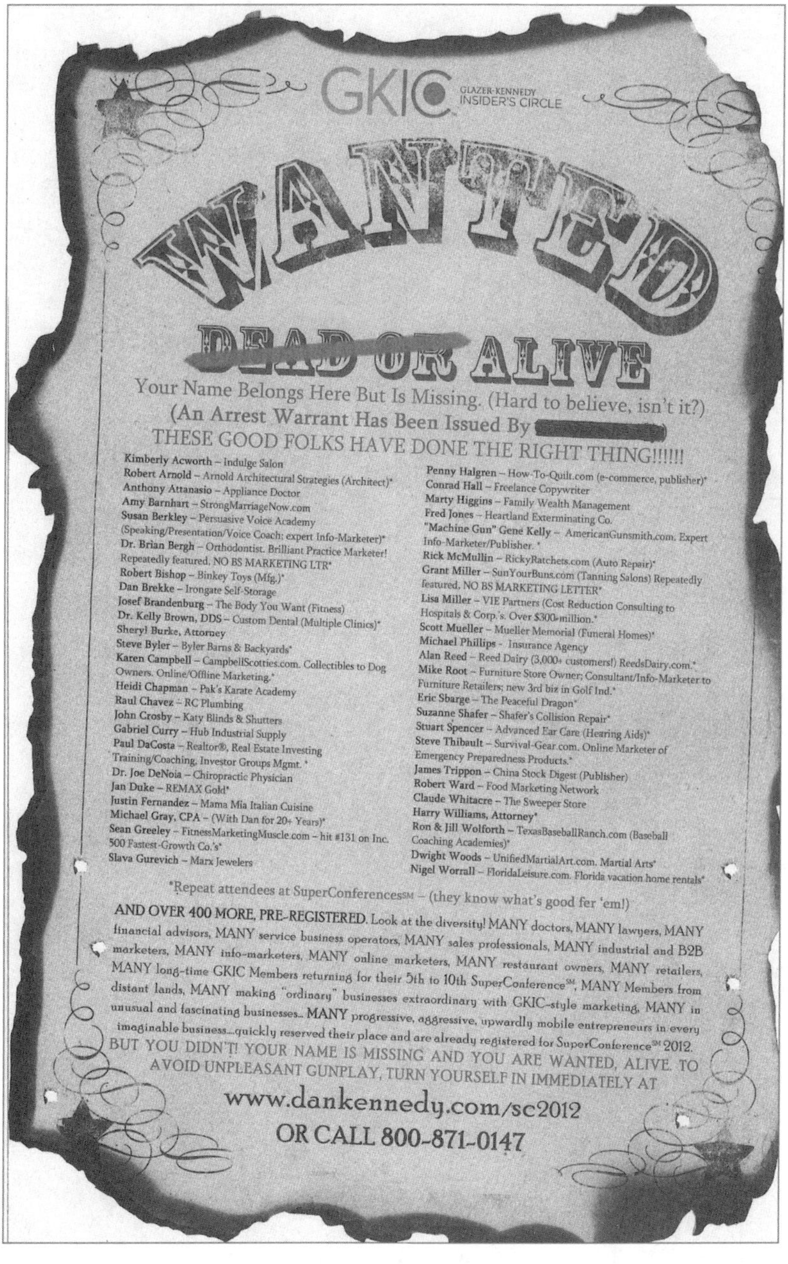

GKIC GLAZER-KENNEDY INSIDER'S CIRCLE

WANTED

~~DEAD OR~~ ALIVE

Your Name Belongs Here But Is Missing. (Hard to believe, isn't it?)

(An Arrest Warrant Has Been Issued By [redacted])

THESE GOOD FOLKS HAVE DONE THE RIGHT THING!!!!!!

Kimberly Acworth – Indulge Salon
Robert Arnold – Arnold Architectural Strategies (Architect)*
Anthony Attanasio – Appliance Doctor
Amy Barnhart – StrongMarriageNow.com
Susan Berkley – Persuasive Voice Academy (Speaking/Presentation/Voice Coach: expert Info-Marketer)*
Dr. Brian Bergh – Orthodontist. Brilliant Practice Marketer! Repeatedly featured, NO BS MARKETING LTR*
Robert Bishop – Binkey Toys (Mfg.)*
Dan Brekke – Irongate Self-Storage
Josef Brandenburg – The Body You Want (Fitness)
Dr. Kelly Brown, DDS – Custom Dental (Multiple Clinics)*
Sheryl Burke, Attorney
Steve Byler – Byler Barns & Backyards*
Karen Campbell – CampbellScotties.com. Collectibles to Dog Owners. Online/Offline Marketing.*
Heidi Chapman – Pak's Karate Academy
Raul Chavez – RC Plumbing
John Crosby – Katy Blinds & Shutters
Gabriel Curry – Hub Industrial Supply
Paul DaCosta – Realtor®, Real Estate Investing Training/Coaching, Investor Groups Mgmt.*
Dr. Joe DeNoia – Chiropractic Physician
Jan Duke – REMAX Gold*
Justin Fernandez – Mama Mia Italian Cuisine
Michael Gray, CPA – (With Dan for 20+ Years)*
Sean Greeley – FitnessMarketingMuscle.com – hit #131 on Inc. 500 Fastest-Growth Co.'s*
Slava Gurevich – Marx Jewelers
Penny Halgren – How-To-Quilt.com (e-commerce, publisher)*
Conrad Hall – Freelance Copywriter
Marty Higgins – Family Wealth Management
Fred Jones – Heartland Exterminating Co.
"Machine Gun" Gene Kelly – AmericanGunsmith.com. Expert Info-Marketer/Publisher.*
Rick McMullin – RickyRatchets.com (Auto Repair)*
Grant Miller – SunYourBuns.com (Tanning Salons) Repeatedly featured, NO BS MARKETING LETTER*
Lisa Miller – VIE Partners (Cost Reduction Consulting to Hospitals & Corp.'s. Over $300-million.*
Scott Mueller – Mueller Memorial (Funeral Homes)*
Michael Phillips – Insurance Agency
Alan Reed – Reed Dairy (3,000+ customers!) ReedsDairy.com.*
Mike Root – Furniture Store Owner; Consultant/Info-Marketer to Furniture Retailers; new 3rd biz in Golf Ind.*
Eric Sbarge – The Peaceful Dragon*
Suzanne Shafer – Shafer's Collision Repair*
Stuart Spencer – Advanced Ear Care (Hearing Aids)*
Steve Thibault – Survival-Gear.com. Online Marketer of Emergency Preparedness Products.*
James Trippon – China Stock Digest (Publisher)
Robert Ward – Food Marketing Network
Claude Whitacre – The Sweeper Store
Harry Williams, Attorney*
Ron & Jill Wolforth – TexasBaseballRanch.com (Baseball Coaching Academies)*
Dwight Woods – UnifiedMartialArt.com. Martial Arts*
Nigel Worrall – FloridaLeisure.com. Florida vacation home rentals*

*Repeat attendees at SuperConferences℠ – (they know what's good fer 'em!)

AND OVER 400 MORE, PRE-REGISTERED. Look at the diversity! MANY doctors, MANY lawyers, MANY financial advisors, MANY service business operators, MANY sales professionals, MANY industrial and B2B marketers, MANY info-marketers, MANY online marketers, MANY restaurant owners, MANY retailers, MANY long-time GKIC Members returning for their 5th to 10th SuperConference℠, MANY Members from distant lands, MANY making "ordinary" businesses extraordinary with GKIC-style marketing, MANY in unusual and fascinating businesses... MANY progressive, aggressive, upwardly mobile entrepreneurs in every imaginable business...quickly reserved their place and are already registered for SuperConference℠ 2012.

BUT YOU DIDN'T! YOUR NAME IS MISSING AND YOU ARE WANTED, ALIVE. TO AVOID UNPLEASANT GUNPLAY, TURN YOURSELF IN IMMEDIATELY AT

www.dankennedy.com/sc2012

OR CALL 800-871-0147

CHAPTER 20

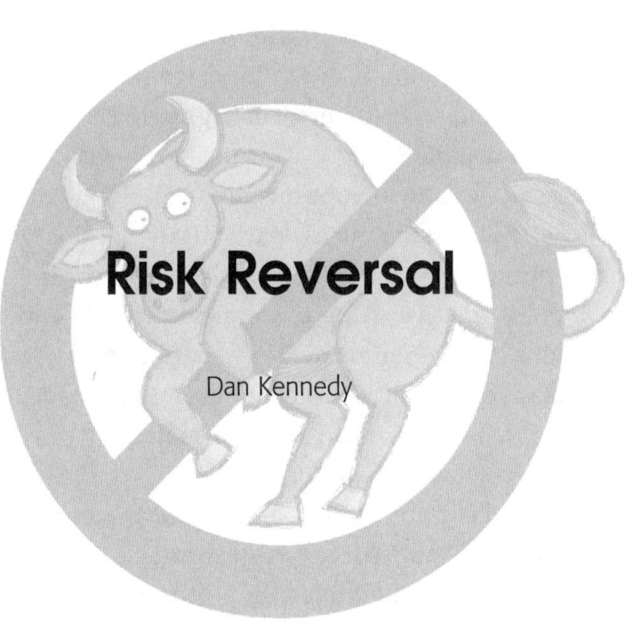

Risk Reversal

Dan Kennedy

Yeah, right.

How many times have you been burned by promises not kept?

We used a company called 3 Day Blinds to replace window blinds in one of our homes, immediately before the holidays. I was attracted by the three-day promise, and cared little about price, and had no interest in price shopping—*if* that three-day thing was real. I had my doubts, but the salesperson was convincing. To my surprise, they actually did deliver and install the blinds within three days, exactly as promised. So I'm happy to recommend them (www.3dayblinds.com). This seemingly mundane event is exciting and memorable because it is so damned rare. "We'll be there between 9:00 and 10:00 A.M." usually means: "We're bullshitting you, telling you what it takes to get the sale, then we'll make excuses, take your grief, and do the best we can."

Talk is cheap, unless it is with a lawyer. Promises are the cheapest talk of all. "Put it in writing," would growl the cynical customer, but most customers don't growl. They keep this to themselves and smile politely at you, a mask over cynicism. But why not put *something* in your business in writing?

Talk is cheap. Guarantees, particularly specific guarantees put in writing, and carrying penalties, are not. In situations where there is low trust due to frequent prior disappointment, such as with completion or delivery dates and times, or where very aggressive, credulity-stretching claims are made, or where price is stiff, risk reversal can serve as something of a substitute for trust or a trust accelerator or booster.

Consider the four-minutes-a-day ROM exercise machine, widely advertised and successfully sold at a very high price. You can go and see the advertising at www.fastexercise.com. They offer to put this thing in your home for 30 days, and if you are unhappy, come and remove it at no cost to you. The Sleep Number® bed is sold the same way. Of course, you will instantly want to tell me that there is nothing in your business that can be guaranteed, that it's illegal in your profession to do guarantees. Phooey. Matt Zagula and I figured out how financial advisors could legally provide guarantees. There are chiropractic physicians and dentists offering guarantees. At least some of the consumer's risk can be moved to the provider via written guarantee in place of hyperbole, in every business.

With my seminars, I routinely invite attendees to exit at the end of the first day if disappointed, with a full fee refund plus reimbursement for their air travel and lodging costs in hand. Sometimes, I extend it all the way to the end, so someone could take the entire three days of training and still decide they're disappointed, and still get their refund. When you have, say, 200 people at $5,000.00 each, there's technically $1 million at risk, but as a practical matter, in 25 years or so, and I'd guess at least 75 such training events, I may have issued as many as a dozen refunds, and a couple of those people didn't exit voluntarily; I threw 'em out. In my early years of consulting, I offered full refund of the day's fee at day's end. I no longer do so; it's no longer necessary. But I was happy to do it when it was, and it cost me little.

In B2B, you are often asking a client to switch from a vendor performing satisfactorily, if not superbly, to you, an unproven and therefore dangerous replacement. One of the best and boldest risk reversals I ever saw in this environment was done by an industrial parts repair company, in the power plant industry: In addition to full warranties for speed, meeting deadlines, and performance of the part, they offered first-time accounts the option of firing them within 90 days of the installation, getting a refund, and having them pay any competitor to replace the part. Years back, I had a client selling employee and deliveryman theft control training to supermarket, convenience store, and other retail chains, and we began offering qualified entities the option of paying zero up-front and paying only after a calendar quarter to measure results—but they then had to pay double the pre-pay fee. Another very bold B2B risk reversal is sometimes done by two of my clients, both providing turn-key direct-mail campaigns to certain kinds of businesses: Dean Killingbeck's www.GetCustomersNow.com to restaurants; Jerry Jones's www.jerryjonesdirect.com to dentists. They'll warranty the first mailing by refund of their fee, the printing, and even the postage!

Simply, with risk removed, trust can be earned by results, rather than required in advance. If you think about this as a visual: A series of high hurdles between you and the sale and ensuing relationship with the customer, any and every hurdle lowered or removed makes success easier and more likely.

Certainly, making it possible for the customer to give you trust you earn by performance rather than have to trust you in advance lowers or removes one of those hurdles.

At the retail level, the spectacular growth of Zappos.com—selling shoes that most people prefer trying on and walking around in before buying from its web store—has been fueled by a very liberal return policy and speedy shipments. They *had to* remove the risk inherent in each purchase. But many businesses, global or local, who don't have to, would be well advised to mimic Zappos, and are likely to find the costs of refunds from wide-open, aggressive risk reversal small in comparison to the heightened responsiveness, thus lowered acquisition cost per customer, and accelerated speed of growth. Were I launching a new local restaurant, in-home service business like carpet cleaning, other services like auto detailing, even chiropractic care—pretty much anything—I'd find a way to do "If You Aren't Thrilled, You Don't Pay" for new customers (carefully targeted).

Short-Term vs. Long-Term Risk Reversal

Guaranteeing ten minutes or less waiting time when you arrive for your doctor's appointment on time may be persuasive, but it is obviously very short-term. While I was working on this book, guaranteeing specific wait times at emergency rooms was a growing trend in hospital marketing—a potentially good idea used stupidly by most hospitals doing it—advertising on billboards of all things, rather than soliciting consumers ahead of need and making them "members" of the E.R., with member privileges, to create certain preference rather than random chance at the time of need. In any case, all this is about immediate and short-term risk reversal, and is more aimed at making a sale, not at building trust. Well-executed, trust-based marketing may use these kinds of guarantees, but will focus more on long-term relationship warranty.

Long-term warranties, built into your fees or prices, are a twist on risk reversal, and can foster trust. For example, one of the very upscale cosmetic and implant dental practices that advertise in national media (like airline magazines, *Robb Report*, etc.) to draw patients from all over the country rather than just in their local area, makes this warranty:

Last Time You Pay

The extensive experience of Dr. Schiro and Dr. Kline has allowed them to implement a most unique Last Time You Pay policy. This written policy provides for the repair or replacement of any porcelain that they place for any reason, even accidental trauma, at no fee.

This is presented in the context of a two-page ad, largely devoted to trust-building, including facts and credentials like: over 15,000 all-porcelain restorations completed; over 700 hours of continuing education; graduate of all courses in Advanced Aesthetics. The ad also calls out to its intended patient, with: "Big Cases Deserve Big Experience and Big Security." You can see their marketing at www.SmileTexas.com.

By the way, if you think the idea of getting a patient who lives in Michigan to go to a dentist in Texas is far-fetched, you know little about the affluent consumer—and I urge reading my book, *No B.S. Guide to Marketing to the Affluent*. Increasingly, we can market without boundaries, whether a cupcake bakery shipping baked goods across the country, essentially a shoe store doing the same, or a dental practice, financial advisor, or even a kitchen cabinet maker getting clients to board airplanes and travel to them. A friend of ours who lives in Virginia traveled to Amish country in Pennsylvania, to spend a day at an Amish-owned factory, planning and buying her kitchen remodeling. Patients travel considerable distances, from out of city area, and out of state, to be patients of my own dentist, Dr. Charles Martin. (www.MartinSmiles.com). I bought my restored 1986 Jeep Wagoneer from the Orvis catalog, and flew my "car guy" (trusted advisor and service provider) to Texas to inspect it.

Key words above, not to go unnoticed, *are built into your fees or prices*. More often than not, the actual costs associated with risk reversal prove much smaller than fearfully imagined by the business owner adding this strategy. As a simple example, assume you sell something for $1,000.00 and strong risk reversal increases your current refund rate from, say, 4% to 6%—a 2% bump. You need only then add $20.00 to the price and/or shipping and handling to be back where you began, but with a powerful sales message advantage. If that advantage boosts sales by 10%, then the cost of the risk reversal is negated with no price increase at all. You've increased the sale from $1,000.00 to $1,100.00, incurred a $20.00 cost—you're $80.00 per sale ahead.

The Relationship of Risk Reversal and Price/Fee Elasticity

The last thing to consider about risk reversal is that it can be a way to buy price elasticity. If risk of some kind—be it financial, inconvenience and frustration, or emotional—is high enough, and, generally, the products, services and providers competing are all felt as untrustworthy, bold risk reversal can be such a competitive advantage it erases comparative price issues and allows selling at prices stretched substantially higher than all others. For more about this, refer to the book I co-authored with Jason Marrs, *No B.S. Price Strategy*.

Carla and I swam for a month or so in the price competitive ocean of furniture retailers. We set out to replace our long owned, sturdy and comfortable but unfortunately stained in various spots, leather couch. While preferring leather, we were both concerned about winding up with the same problem of unsightly stains. In one store, a salesman presented a stain protection warranty I'd never heard of and no other retailer's salespeople presented to us, in any of the *many* stores we visited: Five years, any stain; if we can't make it disappear, we'll replace the couch, with any of same or lesser price. The highest hurdle to the sale was removed, and a happy fellow had my credit card in his hand. Does such a warranty give them price elasticity they would otherwise not have? Absolutely. I don't think they know it, I don't think they use it intelligently to gain that advantage. But they certainly could. It writes its own ad.

I'll give you one other, more dramatic risk-reversal-to-price-relationship example, this one B2B. In the early 1980s, a company I advised sold over 3,000 doctors a three-year practice improvement coaching program, at a then princely price of $30,000.00 per year, $90,000.00 total. In 1980, $30,000.00 was a lot of money. $90,000.00 was a whale of a lot of money. It was five- to six-times higher than numerous consultants and coaches were charging at the time. *That's* price elasticity! This was accomplished with a switch from a much higher price, *initially presented in context of complete risk reversal.* In consulting, it's called POB; Percentage Above Base. To these doctors, it was presented like this: "We take your average revenues from the past three years, we add on your own growth rate, we add on inflation—that's your base. We then take 30% of the increases above base. You take zero risk and pay nothing unless we perform." With math, this might look like this: Average yearly revenue of $300,000.00; year to year growth rate average of last three years, 10%, and inflation at 8%, so we add 18% to $300,000.00, which equals the first-year base of $354,000.00; we add 18% to $354,000.00 yielding a second-year base of $417,720.00; and we add 18% to $417,720.00 giving a third-year base of $492,909.60. Now, if we can convince this doctor that the program can double his practice the first year and bump it by 50% each of the subsequent years (which we could), he'll pay in fees—*with zero risk*:

$600,000.00–$354,000.00 = $246,000.00 x 30% =	$73,800.00
$900,000.00–$417,720.00 = $482,280.00 x 30% =	$144,684.00
$1,350,000.00–$492,909.60 = $857,090.40 x 30% =	$257,127.12
	$475,611.12

OR, he can pre-pay at $30,000.00 plus a $60,000.00 balance divided over the first 24 of the 36-month contract, i.e., just $2,500.00 a month OR get bank financing or, from a financing company in place with the consulting firm, a 60-month finance plan with a monthly payment below $1,700.00. In any case, the doctor saves $385,611.12—more than his current gross for an entire year! IMPORTANT: when the doctor opted to switch from the POB contract to the pre-pay contract, the risk reversal went away, and the service was sold with no guarantee whatsoever. But the fact that the consulting firm was cheerfully willing to take all the risk remained, like the scent of rare perfume still subtly but persuasively in the air even after the beautiful woman's departure.

This is a complicated sale done by highly-skilled professionals under controlled conditions, so I would not recommend doing this at home without further assistance! I give it to you as an example of how powerful risk reversal can be in alleviating fear and skepticism, and accelerating trust even when the entire process is engineered to offer risk reversal but have clients decline it! In this case, nearly one-third of all doctors presented with this program bought it, and three-fourths of them opted for pre-pay (with no warranty) vs. POB with risk reversal. In all, this facilitated selling at fees five times higher than almost all competitors, thus providing a power advantage in a crowded, cluttered marketplace: more money to invest in making the sale, and in effectively delivering the services, and still more profit. While they tried to buy clients with cheap fees—thus having to market and deliver on the cheap—this firm presented its clients with the highest fee and enjoyed dramatic growth, from 0 to 3,000 clients in 36 months.

Two Pieces of Tactical Advice

There are two actionable takeaways from this chapter, one broad, one narrow. First, broadly, a useful exercise is the making of the list of all the hurdles lined up between the starting line, i.e. first notice of you by a prospective client, and the finish line, i.e. consummation of the first sale in what is intended to continue as a long, fruitful relationship. Also, set their comparative height. Then brainstorm how each hurdle's height can be lowered, or a hurdle removed altogether. Second, narrowly brainstorm risk reversal possibilities for different hurdles or for the entire line-up of them.

CHAPTER 21

The Power and Hazard of Leadership Position

Dan Kennedy

As a big sweeping generalization, the older your customer, the more likely they care about Leadership Position; the younger the customer, the less likely it is persuasive. However, I said this is a sweeping generalization. Apple has very successfully marketed and monetized its Leadership Position of "cooler than all others" to a young clientele. Leadership Position takes on added significance in settings where most of the consumers require trust or high trust. A lot of people derive comfort and reassurance from dealing with the biggest, the best known and most familiar, the oldest, the most recommended, the provider with some sort of leadership bragging right.

The hazards should be obvious—but shouldn't be ignored. One is fragility: if you use a Leadership Position as an integral part of your sales message, you'd better feel confident you can sustain it and defend it. Hertz has long been #1, and nobody can say otherwise—Avis battled them for a time with "We're #2 But We Try Harder" and National and Enterprise circumvent the argument with different unique selling propositions of their own (pick any car you want on the lot; we'll pick you up—respectively), but still, for those who instantly think of and take comfort in doing business with the number-one company, Hertz owns them. Few other companies are able to maintain #1 in their industry over a long term. Even Walmart chose to abandon its "THE Low Price Leader" claim as too costly to defend, moving to low prices everyday, to even vaguer positions. Of course, there is more than one #1 in most categories, so the creative marketer may find one to carve out that is so narrowly constructed it is unassailable. Being "THE Chimney Sweep Trusted by More Homeowners in Grand Rapids, for More Years Than Any Other" may well be yours forever, if you had a good head start as the only chimney sweep there. And such a statement would bring a trust-based competitive advantage.

The second main hazard is going all in, betting everything on, and being fixed in the public's mind to a Leadership Position you must walk away from. Dominos® Pizza leapfrogged past a number of established national chains to top-dog status at breakneck speed with its original Leadership Position based on guaranteed 30-minute delivery. This was its Unique Selling Proposition, foregoing any other claims to taste, quality, ingredients, special sauce—just "Fresh, Hot Pizza Delivered in 30 Minutes or Less, Guaranteed." This was the Leadership Position it became universally known for—and trusted on. It never had it taken away by anybody doing "29.5 Minutes or Less, Guaranteed." It was never diluted by everybody else matching it. Dominos® itself had to abandon it because, rolled out nationally, it proved undoable. There were areas where consistent quick delivery wasn't possible. There were increasing incidents of desperate Dominos® delivery drivers' auto accidents. There were skyrocketing insurance costs. You can argue it may have been the only launching pad available to Tom Monaghan for Dominos®, and I would probably agree. But having to walk away from that Leadership Position presented a very difficult business problem.

The third, last main hazard is lazily over-relying on Leadership Position, because complacency, or worse, arrogance, is a parent of poverty. Countless companies that achieved Leadership Position, then lazily, or complacently, or arrogantly lived on them as if they could never change, have either disappeared from the landscape they once dominated, or are skinny shadows of their former selves. Holiday Inn and Howard Johnson's in the hospitality field, Kmart in discount retail, Borders and Barnes & Noble in bookselling, American automakers vs. the first Japanese invaders—who believed they were forever safeguarded by a "Buy American" mentality and their size—and IBM all come to mind. The booksellers are of particular interest to me as an author, an advisor to various publishers and info-marketers, and a lover of the physical bookstore experience. I was mournful over the demise of Borders and I worry for Barnes & Noble, but at risk of annoying the latter, thus biting a hand that feeds me, they both had good swift kicks in the privates coming. They reacted arrogantly, dismissively, and very slowly to the threat Jeff Bezos' Amazon represented, somewhat akin to the old Big Four American Automakers' reaction to the Japanese car companies. They let an upstart bypass their Leadership Positions with impunity. Further, they both acted sluggishly and uncreatively (Borders worse than B&N) at protecting their turf and engaging, involving, and iron-caging their core customer with preference for the brick 'n' mortar bookstore and utterly neglected creating new customers with that preference. As a retailer, B&N is pretty good; as a marketer, asleep at many wheels, I'm very sorry to say. I suspect this third hazard is the most dangerous of the three. Too many entrepreneurs who achieve bona fide Leadership Position take it as permission to relax, like a diabetic put on insulin takes it as permission to eat badly.

Arguably, the lion has The Leadership Position in the jungle. Still, simply being king is not enough. From a source unknown: "Every morning in Africa, a gazelle wakes up. It knows it must run faster than the fastest lion or it will be killed. Every morning a lion wakes up. It knows it must outrun the slowest gazelle or it will starve to death. It doesn't matter whether you are lion or gazelle—when the sun comes up, you'd better be running."

I would never advise against pursuing and achieving or otherwise crafting Leadership Position, and I would rarely advise having it and not trumpeting it—but I do caution against over-valuing it or being overly reliant on it. With that caution in place, let's look at the best opportunities to get and use Leadership Position in connection with Trust-Based Marketing.

"Most Recommended" Leadership Position

Osteo-Bi-Flex® claims to be "the #1 doctor and pharmacist recommended" joint pain remedy. Crest®, for decades, was the toothpaste "more dentists recommend." Subway® is the "training diet" of famous Olympic and pro athletes. A particular motor oil is the "official" motor oil of NASCAR. How much do these recommendations and connections matter?

They can get ridiculous. The NFL has, I think, an "official" soup, even pizza, and soda pop. Really? But when the connection is rational, the recommendation relevant, the safety-in-numbers position meaningful, facts like these can be reassuring, if not attractive. Even if they don't cause someone to seek out the product or provider, they may help carry the prospect through to consummating a purchase or beginning a relationship. This kind of Leadership Position, i.e., leading by type and nature, or quantity of recommendations and endorsements, or by unique, official association, matter to some people and not at all to others. Pretty much only NASCAR fans are moved by the official NASCAR link of a given brand of oil. Arguably, a lot of seniors might be responsive to a product being recommended by more doctors and pharmacists than any other—due to the respect for medical authority in their age group, and their desire for authoritative reassurance. You have to really understand whom you are selling to, and how they relate to the source of the recommendations to evaluate how strong and significant or weak and insignificant the recommended-by card you hold actually is.

By the way, I'm sure you know that most of these ribbons 'n' medals are bought and paid for, one way or another, often outright. "Most Recommended by Doctors" can be achieved by flooding doctors with free samples of a product to give to patients. NASCAR likely sells its blessing to the highest bidder. A number of years back, a client of mine in the business of publishing customized, private label magazines for corporations, associations, and universities became "the official journal publisher of" a collection of prestigious alumni organizations by publishing their magazines free for a year in exchange for their endorsements, a most useful tool in gaining the trust and the business of over 100 academic institutions and groups as clients almost overnight.

How to "Borrow" Leadership Position

There's nothing wrong with—*carefully*—trading on borrowed Leadership Position. Often, the further your claims stretch credulity or the further outside the mainstream norm your product or service is, the more useful links to another's Leadership Position can be, if you lack your own. And they need not be specific to you or your product, but only to validate the concept behind what you offer.

An investment counselor who has his seemingly unorthodox and mysterious money management system *based on* the five rules espoused by Warrant Buffett is obviously not as compelling as one recommended by, certified by, personally trained by, or affiliated with Buffett, but the positioning still borrows trust—given the prospect's knowledge of Buffett as the world's most successful conservative investor. If I'm writing ad copy for Icelandic Salmon Oil gel capsules, I'm going to talk about the extra long life spans of Icelanders, and the absence of arthritis in aged Icelanders who live on a diet of salmon caught in the pure waters there, even though I can't say any of the arthritis-free, 80-year-old Icelanders merrily dancing the mamba every night are taking these pills. In both cases, I'm transferring one or more factual Leadership Positions from their true owners to borrowers; there is foundation of fact, stretched like Silly Putty®.

Just about anybody can find a way to build this kind of case. For example, I've used the Forbes 500 list a number of different ways, to substantiate different propositions. This is the list of the 500 richest people, published yearly by *Forbes* magazine. *Forbes* is a trusted publication. The 500 on the list obviously have a Leadership Position appealing to ambitious, wealth-oriented entrepreneurs and investors. In writing ad copy for a client teaching aggressive real estate investing, I make the point that nearly everybody on the Forbes 500 has much of their wealth in/from real estate. In truth, some have actively invested, others own companies that own the land their stores or warehouses occupy, and virtually all have stock in their portfolios or family trusts, in companies that, one way or another, own real estate. I imagine a similar statement could be made about these 500 using annuities as a wealth preservation and legacy tool. What are the odds that anybody with enough money to make this list doesn't own *some* annuities? They probably own *some* of *every* financial instrument that exists. In writing ad copy for my own seminar about using direct mail to fuel businesses and create wealth, I make the point that virtually every one on the Forbes 500 owes a significant portion of their wealth to direct-mail marketing. Get the *Forbes* 500 list, review it and you'll see—it's an obvious truth. What fast-food empire doesn't distribute coupons by direct mail, solo or in merge mail, like Valpak? What retailer—Walmart, even Amazon.com—doesn't mail fliers, catalogs, offers, or insert stuffers in credit card statements? Direct mail does, still, play a major role in just about every business as it always has, thus, yes, the rich heirs of Walmart's founder Sam Walton, Warren Buffett, and even Bill Gates does, in fact, have direct-mail marketing as a common ingredient in their fortunes. So, if I say:

Put The Marketing Secret
Behind Virtually Every Fortune
Of Those On The Forbes 500 List of Richest People
To Work For Your Business

. . . I create intrigue, mystique, curiosity, and appeal, with borrowed Leadership Position. Regrettably, I can't lay claim to *personally* helping anybody on the *Forbes* 500 List with *my* direct-mail strategies. If any of you on the list are reading this, I specialize in helping the rich get richer, and I can be rented. My fax number is (602) 269-3113. But whether or not I've personally worked with the 500 does not limit my ability to reference them as "proof of concept."

How to Buy Leadership Position

Increasingly, Leadership Position is being bought. To those in the know, this devalues it. But to the public, not privy to behind-the-scenes machinations, purchased Leadership Position can have the same effect as earned Leadership Position.

Most people do not read the entertainment industry trade journal, so they do not see the different amounts spent by different studios, production companies, and networks advertising films and programs to influence voting in various awards ceremonies. Nor is the public cognizant of how much is spent on junkets, wining, dining, gifting, and other influence of movie critics and entertainment "reporters." In the book publishing business, the internet unleashed a Pandora's Box of opportunities to manipulate the best-seller lists and create well-organized sprints for books, featuring giant bribe offers, conspiratorial assistance of affiliates, and orchestrated bulk purchases disguised as individual buyers' activity. Today, in the non-fiction category, I'd stake a big wager that more than half the books that reach and briefly hold spots on the major best-seller lists get there by this kind of manipulation. In some cases, the author or his company or a consortium of friendly interests buy a large quantity of books through ghost customers, quite literally buying their spot on the scoreboard.

There are more egregious examples, some arguably bordering on fraud. Example: A famous "guru" of making money on eBay® skyrocketed to prominence with the documented feat of selling $100,00.00 of various goods in just 10 days, from a standing start. Undisclosed, the fact that he spent over $300,000.00 on those goods, and sold them at irresistibly deep discounts, at a giant loss, and still, also used an army of faux buyers he funded. He outright bought his claim to fame, then leveraged it into millions selling business coaching to fledgling eBay® merchants. Example: In the network marketing industry, a new company often creates a lot of in-industry buzz and attracts huge numbers of distributors in a hurry by being chosen by a big-name superstar distributor who leaves the company he's with and moves to the new one. Hordes leave their companies to follow the well-known leader. Unseen, that leader is paid a large, up-front signing bonus, given an off-the-books, confidential master override on the entire company's volume, and other secret compensation. The upstart company outright buys its leader. Example: in a popular magazine, you notice an ad for "Most Celebrated Gourmet Steakhouses of America," with a list and description of, say, the top ten award winners. Did you know that the ten restaurant owners all share the cost of the ad?

There are so many ways Leadership Position is purchased in the marketplace. One candidate may pay off a rival's campaign debts in order to get him to exit the race, and proffer endorsement. Unfortunately, politics is all about money. No matter a candidate's ideas' merits, it is very hard to overcome a 3-1, 5-1, 7-1 spending advantage held by an opponent. Leadership Position bought this way can morph into unstoppable momentum. Premium shelf and display space in airport bookstores, supermarkets, and other types of retailers is bought with special payments, so when you see a book displayed on the "Best New Books" table or on the end-cap, i.e. side of an aisle's shelving, cover out, or a food item displayed atop the meat counter with "Chef's Pick of the Week," it's a safe bet that a fee was paid for that position.

Regardless of how you feel about the ethic of these kinds of shenanigans and capital investments in purchasing Leadership Position, it all stands as evidence that Leadership Position can be an incredibly valuable, to asset leverage.

How to Best Use Owned Leadership Position

My client, Proactiv®, has a genuine Leadership Position. It *actually is* the #1 acne remedy brand in the world. Its years with this Leadership Position exceed any other brand's. Its roster of celebrity users and endorsers, greater than any other brand, includes Jennifer Love-Hewitt, Justin Bieber, and Katy Perry. Its number of repeat customers dwarfs all other brands. But it's not as simple and easy to productively use this Leadership Position as you might imagine. Pre-teens and teens who make up the majority of the product's users don't care about anything but the celebrities, and, while their attention can be attracted with the stars, they aren't actually convinced to buy by those stars. In fact, the teens are cynical about celebrities, and overall, very distrustful of everything: product claims, guarantees, testimonials, the works. Getting the trust of a teen via advertising is at least as difficult as coaxing a squirrel from the edge of the woods to your backyard deck, to eat mixed nuts from your hand. It can be done. I did with squirrels as a kid, at my backyard swing set. But it's a tough way to make a living. Fortunately for Proactiv®, both parents paying for the product, and adult acne sufferers do care about and can be persuaded by Leadership Position.

In short, Leadership Position has to be used according to situation: maybe with some target audiences, but not others; maybe in front-end advertising, maybe only after a lead is generated and actual selling begins; maybe as the most important point, maybe as a minor point. Good, smart trust-based marketing finds the right use for Leadership Position, without relying on it.

CHAPTER 22

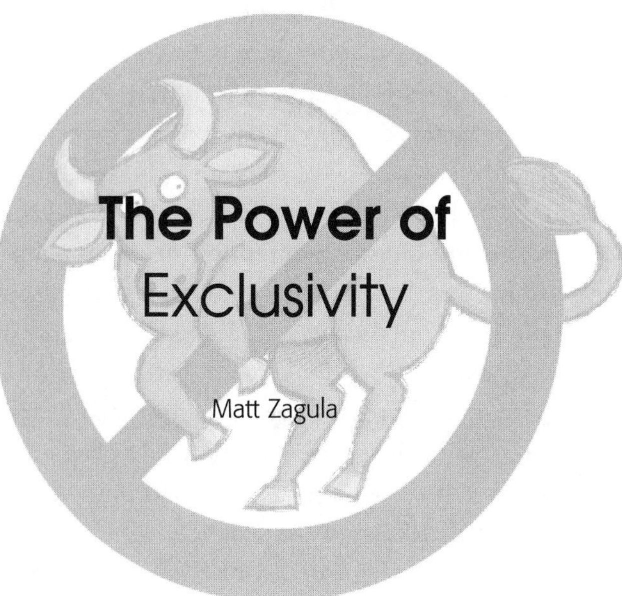

The Power of Exclusivity

Matt Zagula

People, like cats, want into the other room, the one with the *closed* door. Universities that are famously difficult to get into, condo buildings or communities you can't purchase a home in without submitting yourself for approval (or rejection) by a board of existent residents, clubs or societies requiring sponsorship by a present member, the popular night club with the long velvet rope line and few selected for admission—these are all made more seductive and appealing than if their entrances were wide open, democratic, and easy. "Limited edition" automatically adds value and raises desire for ownership, as does all the language of exclusivity: rare, one of a kind, etc. Art, collectibles, automobiles, antiques, and other items often bring higher prices at auction than via advertisement and direct, private sale because of the visible competition ending with exclusivity: only one can own this thing, all others disappointed. When people apply to universities, condo boards, or clubs, what do they eagerly wait for? *The letter of acceptance*. When the person approaches the guardian at the door of the nightclub, telling their story, seeking admission even as a hundred others wait behind the velvet rope, what do they hope for? *Acceptance*. Exclusivity plus Acceptance equals one of the most powerful motivators of all. But it is more than that. It can also be a powerful trust trigger. If many people are bidding something up at an auction, others trust its rising value, based on exclusivity. If many are striving to get into a place but only a few are accepted, the value of being in that place is trusted. If many vie for the attention and assistance of a particular service provider but only a select few are accepted, that service provider is easily, automatically granted high trust. I'll tell you how I use the Exclusivity + Acceptance Trust Trigger formula in my financial services practice.

As you can see in Figure 22.1 of the scanned images of the thank-you card we received from our new client Suzanne, she is thrilled we **ACCEPTED** her as a new client. Now, I am guessing that term, *accepted*, is quite foreign to most business owners.

What Suzanne knew was that her friend Bob trusted us. When he recommended us as her best option for safety and yield, he also warned her that we don't always accept new clients. This is powerful positioning because it is 100% true and accurate—we don't take on everyone who comes to us with money, and that makes us much more magnetically attractive to our target prospective client.

Five years ago, our firm adopted a new business philosophy after an intense study of how Dan Kennedy had coached cosmetic dentists and surgeons to position themselves. The best of these doctors in the country are ultra-exclusive and anyone "lucky" enough to be walking through their door never asks,"How much is this going to cost?" The "lucky ones" are just thrilled to get IN.

FIGURE 22.1: Thank-You Note from a New Client

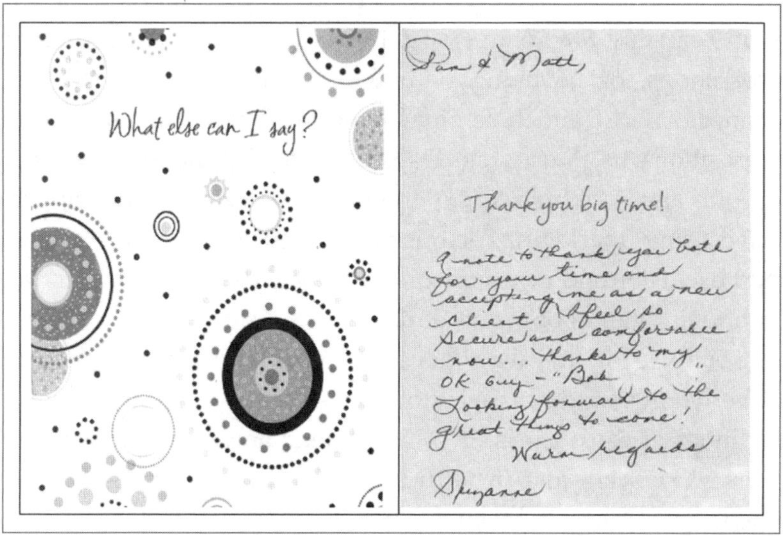

What else can I say?

Dan & Matt,

Thank you big time!

A note to thank you both for your time and accepting me as a new client. I feel so secure and comfortable now... thanks to "my OK Guy - "Bob"

Looking forward to the great things to come!

Warm regards

Suzanne

I immediately contrasted that business positioning to the typical insurance-based financial advisory practice; many advisors get into their cars and drive to a prospective client's home on a Saturday morning, leaving their own family to <u>accommodate</u> their prospect's schedule, with the typical result of driving back home that beautiful Saturday morning to their kids waiting for their dad to go out to the park for the family picnic—while those time vampires he wasted his Saturday morning on are supposedly "thinking over" what he offered.

I wanted no part of this "typical." So I set out to develop a practice where new clients were thrilled just to get IN. And that is exactly what I've done for myself, and assisted many other advisors to achieve as well.

So, let's dissect how we successfully <u>manufactured</u> this level of exclusivity and how today, frankly, we *are* that exclusive.

First, we run a real business. We work very hard to put into our market an attractive marketing message that draws the prospects most likely to benefit, and therefore, invest in our offers. How? We NEVER rely on bribes common in our field—notably Free Dinners—to attract clients to our seminars, workshops, or "Evening with the Authors" events. A FREE dinner or FREE lunch seminar is not an option for us because it positions us poorly, as desperate looking and certainly not as our area's definitive expert. (Tactical advice: Identify any advertising, marketing, or business practice that marks you as non-exclusive and common, or overly eager and needy, and find a different means of promotion.)

Think of it this way: does that ultra-exclusive surgeon in Beverly Hills we discussed above have to buy prospective clients a dinner at Ruth Chris to fill his calendar with super wealthy clients? Hell no, and if he did, it would freak out his existing clients and hurt his business. It would destroy his position of authority and leadership within his respective profession. The position of leadership in your field, your business, is a decision that *you* make. In most fields, being the dominant force is a decision to be the "big dog" and then to manufacture all the required collateral to prove that point. Unlike the business of professional sports where your actual rank is defined by the number of victories you've amassed compared to the number of defeats you suffered, the highest-paid and most profitable dentistry practice in a market isn't necessarily going to the dentist with the greatest dentistry skill, but the money and market notoriety goes to the best positioned, best marketed, and most trusted professional.

This is an extremely important point. A sports franchise has a clear win-loss record, visible to all. College athletes being considered by coaches for draft to pro teams also have their own win-loss record, revealing statistics, and can be auditioned in measurable ways—how fast they run a quarter of a mile, how long a field goal they can kick six times in a row. Few consumers or clients have or go to the trouble to get comparable factual data about the different providers they might buy a product or service from. How many car buyers actually investigate and then compare the numbers of complaints and unsatisfactorily resolved complaints different dealers' service departments have, before choosing the dealer to buy their car from? How many people invest similar investigation into the hospitals they go to, doctors they let prescribe to them or operate on them, plumbers invited into their homes? Few. A small percentage. Instead, you can guide them to decision-making in a vacuum, based only on the information you provide. *Your* decisions can govern theirs.

An Example of Acceptance at Work

Let's talk about how you can become your area's exclusive source and how to be viewed as an extremely important and influential person allowing you to switch from selling to clients to accepting clients. Being well-positioned at the top of your market is counterintuitive to what most sales training programs teach folks: to "strike when the iron is hot." I'd tell you that in today's marketplace, specifically on high-dollar transactions, you'll sell more and get more referrals by NOT making it too easy for folks to get to you.

Here's an example. To get on our schedule you must do one of three things:

1. Come through a public workshop, agree to divulge your financial information, in advance, through our "triage" process and, depending on your situation, accept waiting two to six weeks for an appointment. If a prospect is unwilling to divulge financial information in advance, they are respectfully told that they cannot come in because this is a part of our procedure and there's no flexibility.
2. Be referred into our firm by one of the four "Blue Chip"

Estate and/or Elder Law Practicing Law Firms. These firms are not here in my small town. In fact, a significant percentage of my business comes from Chicago, Illinois from the premier Elder Law Firm in that city. My lawyer referral source and friend, Rick Law, describes his firm best: "We are our area's number one source for elder law services and our closest competitor is number four." It's true they are so dominant that there's no number two or three to speak of, they own their market. The same is true of my referral source from Overland Park, Kansas, Attorney Bill Hammond, and the firm I work with in North Carolina—they are the entrenched leaders. So, we only work with the best.

3. Have an existing client refer you IN. Getting the thank-you card shown in Figure 22.1 from Suzanne was awesome because she is as sweet of a client (of a person) as anyone of us could dream for, BUT I may not have had that opportunity if it wasn't for Bob fully appreciating the value we bring and understanding that we welcome personal referrals from an A+ client like Bob, but do not necessarily accept any and every client who responds to our advertising/marketing presence in the community or even to clients referred by any of our clients. We need Bob to understand that we accept *his* referrals without question and give them priority. We need him to convey the exclusivity to anyone he refers, and we go to considerable lengths to make sure we stay positioned that way with Bob.

The Ultimate Marketing Media Available to You via Exclusivity and Acceptance

The ultimate media that most business owners fail to see as media, and do a poor job of investing in and managing, is not an ad media you can simply buy space in. It is referrals from your good clients—making the clients the media.

Bob has this trust and confidence in us because we have always delivered on the promises we made to him and he has been with us for several years; so we have built significant goodwill and trust. Suzanne respects Bob because he is accomplished in business and is a powerful, known success story in our community. **(Referrals are always strongest when they come from a person of power or influence.)** Bob is a well-known entrepreneur, a real-life rags-to-riches story and a family man with a generous heart, so people listen to him. Bob is a special "who" in our community—so our firm benefits from Bob because Bob benefits from being one of a very small group of clients to which we offer a golden key, to refer into our practice. If Bob refers, the client is IN. This gets us more clients like Bob, which is great because he is a perfect client, and Bob gets the recognition from being able to gain Acceptance for his friends—so everyone involved benefits.

CHAPTER 23

How Do You Know If You Are Succeeding at Trust-Based Marketing?

Dan Kennedy

Converting prospects to clients, customers, or patients, with less resistance and less fee resistance, should occur. You should see this improvement in your statistics, and you and/or your salespeople should *feel it* in your direct work with clients. But the most dramatic and measurable indicator of success is…

Clients brought to you.

Not just told about you. Not just referred to you. *Brought to you.*

How do you know if you are really trusted? How can we best objectively measure your success at creating trust with your clients? I am sometimes dubbed "The Professor of Harsh Reality." In this case, the harsh reality is revealed by your referrals.

How Many Endless Chains Do You Own?

I first heard about "The Endless Chain of Referrals" from Paul J. Meyer, a famously successful insurance company developer, who went on to create the Success Motivation Institute (SMI), a leading force in sales and success training and publishing for decades. Paul and SMI also spawned many successful businesses and their leaders, including: David Sandler, founder of the Sandler Selling System, which is taught today in hundreds of cities; and Don Dwyer, a client of mine who created a collection of home services franchises, today under the Dwyer Group umbrella, with Don's daughter, Dina Dwyer-Owens at the helm, generating over $800 million a year. She is a truly phenomenal CEO. I'm certain Dina is still teaching her 1,500+ franchise owners about the endless chain of referrals. We had her as a speaker at one of the GKIC annual conferences (in 2012), and she challenged our Members in many ways. Here, I want to put a challenge on you.

Paul's premise was that you never needed to be without a good prospect as soon as you had just one client, <u>unless you were inept at trust.</u> *Every* client should beget another. I grasped it, and made this challenging concept a major part of my own business approach. In my own professional practice as a business advisor and direct-response copywriter, I have over an 85% repeat/reoccurring patronage factor and nearly that high a referral factor—unheard of in my industry, unimaginable to my peers. Clients as valuable as $2 million (in fees and royalties) have been brought to me by other clients—not just told about me—brought to me; in my entire career, a big multiple of that. This reveals how effective I am at creating and managing trust. When a client brings a business peer of theirs to me, they know that person will be risking $100,000.00 or more on my advice and work-product, and if that person has an unsatisfactory experience, the client who brought him *will* hear about it.

Endlessly. This is a critical fact few marketers grasp: There is risk in referring, more risk in hand-delivering clients to you—greater risk than there was and is in doing business with you. The trust hurdle for buying is lower than the trust hurdle for good word of mouth, and is lower than the trust hurdle for actually bringing clients to you.

Dare to Compare—Do You Measure Up?

You may not like the comparison, but one of the most successful salespeople at having customers bring in other customers to him is an automobile salesman. You can read the whole story in my *No B.S. Sales Success in The New Economy* book, starting on page 65. The pay-off is that this guy stayed #1 in an entire state because he had large numbers of his customers *insisting* that their spouses, family members, friends. and co-workers go to Bill when ready to buy a car, often actually calling to make the appointment for their friend, even accompanying, thus bringing them, to the dealership. I did this myself with wife, parents, brothers, and two business associates. Because Bill's new customer is brought to him in this way, his quoted prices are rarely challenged, let alone negotiated—in a business where it is universal knowledge you're supposed to haggle. Also, these customers have been trained by their experience so they, in turn, bring Bill their family members and friends. This gives him a pretty cushy existence as a car salesman.

I challenged Matt Zagula with the concept of endless chain, just as Paul Meyer challenged me about 40 years ago. I challenged Matt with Bill's story. I dared him to actually look at his true statistics: how many clients brought clients to him, how many endless chains he had. I told him that a trusted financial advisor managing clients' life savings should be in a better trust position than *a car salesman*. I basically insulted him on this point. Matt is a proud and competitive guy accustomed to leading his field. When he examined this aspect of his business at my prodding, he was not proud of what he discovered. He dug in, went to work. He created a simple but highly effective process for starting an endless chain with each new client. And in the 18 months or so that I've been working with him intimately, he has more than doubled his total number of client referrals, accelerated the speed of the first referral, improved the quality of those referrals, and significantly increased the number actually *being brought to him* by clients *insisting* their friends or family members get in to meet with Matt.

If you do not have clients bringing you good clients, a number repeatedly bringing you new clients, and endless chains of referrals emanating from clients, you won't like this, but: *you are failing.* There's something wrong. You are creating only enough trust to get customers but you are NOT creating enough trust to multiply those customers. Don't BS yourself or me about how beloved you are. These statistics are reality. If they are harsh reality, do something about them.

Master Checklist of Trust Triggers

Affinity

Authority

Believability

Celebrity

Comfort

Consistency

Credibility

Customized Solutions

Demonstration

Diagnosis + Prescription

Endorsements

Exclusivity

Familiarity

Feasibility of Relationship

Frequency

Language

Leadership Position

Longevity

NOT-A-Salesman Status

Place

Proof

Risk Reversal

Safety

Second-Party Transfer

Superiority

Value

About the Authors

DAN S. KENNEDY is a *strategic advisor, consultant*, business coach, and editor of six business newsletters, and he directly influences more than one million small business owners, private practice professionals, and sales professionals annually. He is one of the highest compensated direct-response copywriters in America, commanding six-figure and seven-figure project fees plus royalties, with 85% of all clients returning repeatedly or in on-going relationships. Dan is a multi-millionaire, seven-figure-income serial entrepreneur with diverse business interests. He has also had long tenure as one of the most sought-after professional speakers, frequently and repeatedly sharing the platform with celebrity entrepreneurs and CEOs, including Donald Trump, Ivanka Trump, Jim McCann (1-800-Flowers), Joan Rivers, George Foreman, and Gene Simmons (KISS). He may be contacted directly for speaking, consulting, or copywriting engagements via fax: (602) 269-3113. Information about his books can be found at www.NoBSBooks.com. Information about GKIC newsletters, seminars, and services at www.DanKennedy.com.

Other Books by the Author, Published by Entrepreneur Press

No B.S. Grassroots Marketing for Local Businesses (with Jeff Slutsky)

No B.S. Price Strategy (with Jason Marrs)

No B.S. Business Success in The New Economy

No B.S. Sales Success in The New Economy

No B.S. Wealth Attraction (for Entrepreneurs) in The New Economy

No B.S. Time Management for Entrepreneurs

No B.S. Direct Marketing for Non-Direct Marketing Businesses

No B.S. Marketing to the Affluent

No B.S. Ruthless Management of People and Profits

Uncensored Sales Strategies (with Sydney Barrows)

MATT ZAGULA leads exceptionally successful financial advisory practices based in Wierton, West Virginia, and Pittsburgh, Pennsylvania, generating millions of dollars of revenue annually. He is the author of the book *Invasion of the Money Snatchers,* host of his own radio program, and a dominant presence in his markets in all media. Matt also publishes *The Millionaire Advisor Letter* and consults with and coaches many top financial advisors throughout the United States. In his field, he is best known for his Total Market Domination® System. Matt is available for speaking engagements and consulting assignments. Contact him by fax at (304) 740-5003 or visit www.MattZagula.com.

Index

U

V

W

Z

Special Free Offer from Trust-Based Marketing Expert Matt Zagula

For more information about Matt Zagula
specific to one-on-one marketing consultation go to:
www.mattzmarketing.com
and provide details of your project or question there.

For financial advisors and insurance agents only, you can obtain the soldout *Creating Trust Book in an Undestandably UN-Trusting World* to gain a more sophisticated insight into the specific details of client and prospective client trust building in our industry by going to www.themillionaireadvisor.com/nobs.

As a companion to this book and you'll gain a number of industry specific concepts that may prove beneficial to your marketing and client retention efforts.

WARNING: the financial advisor companion book will not prove beneficial for business owners outside of the financial and/or insurance industry. For business owners not in the financial advising or insurance selling business the book you are holding is far more beneficial as a stand alone guide.

If you are a coach or consultant to your industry and would like to learn how to teach trust concepts to those who entrust you for valuable information and a competitive edge please FAX me a bio about who you are, the industry you serve and your contact information to **1-304-740-5003**.